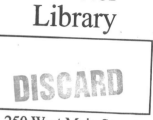
8 Degrees of Ingredi

by Melisa K. Priem

A must-have, comprehensive cookbook
including over 250 everyday recipes,
all free of the eight most common food allergens

WHEAT-FREE	SOY-FREE
EGG-FREE	MILK-FREE
PEANUT-FREE	TREE NUT-FREE
FISH-FREE	SHELLFISH-FREE

For those suffering from food allergies, sensitivities,
and intolerances,
and the people who cook for them

Beaver's Pond Press, Inc.

8 Degrees of Ingredients © copyright 2008 by
Melisa K. Priem. All rights reserved. No part of this
book may be reproduced in any form whatsoever, by
photography or xerography, or by any other means, by
broadcast or transmission, by translation into any kind
of language, nor by recording electronically or otherwise,
without permission in writing from the author, except
by a reviewer, who may quote brief passages in critical
articles or reviews.

ISBN 10: 1-59298-214-X

ISBN 13: 978-1-59298-214-1

Library of Congress Control Number: 2007941376

Book design and production: Mighty Media

Cover: Colleen Dolphin • Interior pages: Chris Long

Printed in the United States of America

First Printing: January 2008

12 11 10 09 08   5 4 3 2 1

7104 Ohms Lane, Suite 101
Edina, Minnesota 55439 USA
(952) 829-8818
www.BeaversPondPress.com

To order, visit www.BookHouseFulfillment.com or call
1-800-901-3480. Reseller and special sales discounts
available.

The recipes in this book are intended for use by persons
with food allergies. However, the recipes are not
intended to serve as therapies, remedies or treatments
for any allergy or other condition. In addition, since
allergies and allergic reactions can vary from person
to person, it is the reader's responsibility to check the
ingredients for each recipe to determine if any ingredient
may cause any allergic or other adverse reaction.
This book is not intended as a substitute for medical
advice. Readers who have questions about a particular
condition, possible treatments for that condition or
possible reactions resulting from that condition should
consult with a physician or other qualified health care
professional.

Contents

Acknowledgements

I cannot begin to thank all the people who continually encouraged and supported me during the completion of this cookbook. But I must mention the sacrifices my husband, Troy, my daughter, Piper Mallen, and two sons, Theodore Ludwig and Chester Anthony, have made, in allowing me to take time away from them so that I could help others. Thank you for never complaining about dinner, but instead thanking me for dinner every single night, even when you faced the same meal three times in a row so I could get the recipe "just right."

Thank you to my mother, Mallen Komlyn, for keeping me in tune with individual dietary needs, and my father, Anthony Komlyn, who taught me that hard work and perseverance have many rewards, and that maintaining a perspective in life can get you through most situations.

Thank you to Renee Ketchmark and Judith Palmateer of Beavers Pond Group, my editor Jennifer Manion, and my designers Pam Scheunemann, Chris Long, and Colleen Dolphin. Additionally, I would like to thank Michele Bassett, Benham Lattimer, and Catherine Fahy. Your professional expertise and encouragement in completing this book not only provided the motivation I needed, but also made the process extremely rewarding.

And finally, my eternal gratitude to Milt Adams. Your passion in life is an honorable trait that not only helps those in need, but warms the heart and lifts the soul in the process. Thank you for your desire to help those with food sensitivities, and thank you for making my dream come true.

To my husband, Troy

Your everlasting love and support, along with your lively enthusiasm for every single meal I prepare, have not only allowed me to write this cookbook, but have made me happier than I ever imagined I could be ...

Introduction

The proverbial "six degrees of separation" theory suggests that each person on earth is connected to any other person on the planet by a chain made up of no more than six people. The theory was first proposed in 1929 by the Hungarian writer Frigyes Karinthy in a short story called "Chains." By extension, we often use the same phrase when describing the connections between individual entities grouped together in a large set.

Since my daughter was diagnosed with severe and multiple food allergies in 2003, I have often found myself wondering about the degrees separating, or rather connecting, us all, especially with respect to the food we eat. Whenever I speak of my daughter's food allergies, the conversation always includes a discussion about another person's allergy, intolerance, or sensititivity (or *food sensitivities*, for short) to one or more of eight common ingredients. I quickly concluded that if the six degrees of separation theory was indeed true, it was certainly possible to link every one of us to one another through our hypersensitivities to eight common ingredients. *8 Degrees of Ingredients* hypothesizes that we can all be linked to one another through food sensitivities to wheat, soy, eggs, milk, peanuts, tree nuts, fish, and shellfish.

Further research on my part confirmed that my hypothesis is likely true. The number of Americans diagnosed with food allergies has grown to over twelve million people, with 90 percent of reactions attributed to the eight most common allergens: wheat, soy, eggs, milk, peanuts, tree nuts, fish, and shellfish. It is estimated that approximately three million people have celiac disease, a lifelong condition caused by the ingestion of gluten, a substance found in wheat, rye, and barley. Individuals with celiac disease must avoid gluten for the rest of their lives. The number of individuals suffering from other gluten intolerances has never been quantified, but numerous studies indicate it is definitely a dietary issue many people deal with on a daily basis. It is also estimated that between thirty and fifty million Americans suffer from lactose intolerance. These individuals are not able to tolerate the lactose found in dairy (milk) products. And what's most staggering is that these numbers continue to grow.

If you suffer from food allergies, intolerances, or sensitivities, you may often feel very isolated. *But did you know that one out of every three people believes he or she has a food allergy, or modifies the family diet to accommodate someone with a perceived food allergy, intolerance, or sensitivity?* Contrary to how you may feel at times, you are not alone.

Food allergies, intolerances, and sensitivities exist for different reasons and can result in a diverse range of short-term or long-term reactions. Whether you are allergic, intolerant, or sensitive to a food, people with food sensitivities have one important aspect connecting them all together: *there is no cure for any type of sensitivity*. The only means of prevention is to avoid the offending food. So whether you are allergic to eggs, intolerant to dairy, or sensitive to wheat – in essence, regardless of your diagnosis – the approach to your health and well-being is the same. Avoid one or in some cases all of these ingredients.

Discovering that you have a food sensitivity to one or more of these ingredients can bring relief, but for most people, having this knowledge is only the beginning. Doctors can diagnose you and they can tell you what not to eat. But inevitably your stomach starts rumbling and you begin to feel more lost than ever before. You know what not to eat, but what can you eat? What do you do? Perhaps you have heard of alternative ingredients like tapioca starch and rice flour, but how do you use them? Where do you buy them? Will you ever be able to eat your favorite foods again? Will you now be forced to follow a tasteless diet for the rest of your life? Whether you need to avoid one ingredient or many, the list of forbidden foods can seem endless while the list of safe foods can seem diminutive and consist of barely tolerable, not-so-appetizing options. Facing this can make you more stressed than you were before your diagnosis, especially when hunger pangs beseech you to have one final hamburger, one ultimate order of onion rings, one last scoop of ice cream.

Well, there doesn't have to be a last time when you cook with *8 Degrees of Ingredients*. *8 Degrees of Ingredients* is a cookbook full of over 250 delectable recipes aimed at helping those with food sensitivities regain some normalcy in their lives. Each recipe in this cookbook faithfully excludes the eight ingredients that plague so many people. But this cookbook is not just for those suffering from food allergies or for those who have been clinically diagnosed with intolerances or sensitivities; it is for everyone who experiences adverse reactions to wheat, soy, eggs, milk, peanuts, tree nuts, fish, or shellfish, and who is trying to avoid one or all of these ingredients. As a bonus, since gluten and lactose intolerance appear to be growing concerns, every recipe is conveniently gluten-free and dairy-free as well. This cookbook does not seek to diagnose diseases, analyze symptoms, or prescribe a particular lifestyle. But it does provide numerous recipes and know-how power, allowing you to make your meals free of one or all eight ingredients.

This cookbook is also unique in the way it lays down the foundation for hypoallergenic cooking while simultaneously allowing you to start cooking immediately. Unlike the majority of hypoallergenic cookbooks on the market, it does not assume you already have a working knowledge of alternative ingredients. Nor does it assume you know all about cross-contamination risks and the time-consuming task of label reading. In contrast to many other hypoallergenic cookbooks, this cookbook has no prerequisites. Whether you are newly diagnosed or an old pro, I guarantee you will be able to cook with this cookbook immediately. Using it involves no overwhelming commitment on your part: you won't need to spend precious time and money researching and hunting down exotic ingredients. What you will find in this cookbook are original and innovative recipes combining common, easy-to-find ingredients in ways you've never seen before. By maximizing the properties of allowable ingredients and working with their potential, I have created fabulous, mouth-watering, hypoallergenic recipes that no other cookbook can offer you.

While you can get started with the recipes in Chapter 1 right away, you'll find that the remaining chapters provide fundamental information about the properties, tastes, and textures of alternative products. The pertinent information I have provided on alternative ingredients will assist you in adapting your own conventional favorites into safe, hypoallergenic masterpieces as well.

Although eight common ingredients may connect us all together, we shouldn't have to adopt the same preferences and lifestyles as one another in order to accommodate dietary changes. In fact, we shouldn't have to change what we love to do just because we have food sensitivities. Rather than have food sensitivities dictate my family's lifestyle, I have made it my philosophy to have my family's food allergies and issues *adapt* to our desired lifestyle. The ingredients I use to keep my family safe and healthy do not define us. This philosophy has allowed me to create over 250 recipes that will allow you to do the same, regardless of your personal lifestyle.

Ironically, the number of people suffering from food sensitivities continues to grow at a time when Americans cook less and less. But those of you who suffer from food allergies, intolerances, or sensitivities have to cook. With so few pre-made choices on the shelves in the supermarkets, you are probably in the kitchen more than you like, whether you enjoy cooking or not.

Personally, I don't like to cook, I love it! As a self-taught cook, I was inspired to learn how to cook as a means to survival, so to speak. Unlike the stories of those individuals in the culinary world who inherited their passion from their families' love of cooking, mine is unique: I learned how to cook at a very young age from a mother who hated to cook and a father who hated to eat out. Raised amongst these two extremes, I was faced with either living on pasta with red sauce and the occasional over-cooked, bland chicken, or cooking for myself. I chose the latter and learned very quickly how a nourishing, home-cooked meal can provide true comfort.

Going out to restaurants was a rare occurrence for my family. On those infrequent restaurant visits I savored every bite. I memorized the taste, texture, and flavor of each dish with the intention of recreating the meal at home. I strove to discern the ingredients through taste alone, since I was always too shy to inquire about them. To my delight, I recreated fabulous meals at home using my palate and memory as my recipe.

Although unaware of my talent at the time, my self-taught kitchen skills, combined with my ability to refine tastes via memory, became a tremendous asset years later when I was forced to cook for a daughter with multiple food allergies and when I lacked a resource to guide me through the basics of hypoallergenic cooking. When you have been trained in particular culinary methods and developed specific skills, it is often difficult if not impossible to stray from certain "rules" of the kitchen. Fortunately being a self-taught cook has allowed me to be more open-minded and adventurous in the hypoallergenic kitchen, helping me to think outside the box when using different and somewhat limiting ingredients.

I've found, for example, that when you don't have the world's longest shopping list to work with, obtaining specific tastes and textures can be difficult. This becomes especially true in traditional cooking, in which at least one of the eight common ingredients is routinely used to obtain particular results. For example, eggs, with their terrific binding and rising capabilities, are habitual ingredients in any conventional recipe for meatloaf or cake. Accordingly, most allergen-free recipes automatically substitute egg-replacement products in these dishes. However egg-replacement products don't always work well in all recipes calling for eggs. They do not pair well with meats, for example, nor do they work consistently well with gluten-free flours. But interestingly, other ingredients do. Ignoring conventional kitchen wisdom has enabled me to create unique ingredient combinations that result in outcomes that are amazingly similar to their conventional counterparts.

This cookbook provides you with cooking techniques, kitchen strategies, and shortcuts so you may enjoy a variety of cuisines without tremendous hassle. By gaining the necessary foundation that this book offers, you will be able to transfer techniques and your knowledge of the properties of ingredients to make some of your own recipes hypoallergenic. By combining simple and safe ingredients in creative ways and maximizing inherent properties and flavors of natural ingredients, you will quickly enjoy a flavorful, plentiful cuisine with ingredients that are familiar and easy to locate.

8 Degrees of Ingredients lets you be you, all the while helping you maintain a diet that is safe for your health. In fact, *8 Degrees of Ingredients* takes the issue out of food issues, leaving you with simply delicious food. It allows you to be different without seeming different. It enables you to follow a personally satisfying diet without changing who you are. I have researched and experimented with numerous ingredient variations to create your mouth-watering favorites. You just have to follow the recipes and cook!

To ease the transition to entirely hypoallergenic cooking, the Recipe Notes sections provide helpful information categorized according to the following abbreviations

☐ cooking tips and ingredient information

♡ viable ingredient substitutions

🍲 recipe variations

◉ leftover suggestions

🧊 freezing guidelines

"There is little correlation between the circumstances of people's lives and how happy they are."

DENNIS PRAGER

The Spark That Lit the Fire

Eight degrees below zero. That was the air temperature on the day we brought our baby girl, Piper Mallen, home from the hospital for the very first time. As a new mother, I was so ready for this moment. The nursery was complete right down to the adorable mobile hanging over the crib. The changing table was stocked with an abundant supply of newborn diapers, wipes, and the essential wipe warmer for those frigid Minnesota mornings. Our car seat had been properly installed by the fire department. The baby clothes were all washed, twice, in baby-sensitive detergent, and the house was sterilized. I had read and re-read *The Girlfriends' Guide to Pregnancy*, and persistently referenced the bible for pregnant women, *What to Expect When You Are Expecting*. In addition to having completed a birthing class with my husband, I had taken not one, but two classes on breastfeeding. After learning the benefits, I intended to nurse my baby for the recommended twelve months. I was ready. But that very first night in our townhouse with our new baby, I did a horrible thing. I committed the ultimate sin. Looking back, it was probably my biggest parenting blunder of all. That night I ordered takeout Chinese food!

The combination of my Kung Pao chicken and vegetable lo mein sent my daughter spiraling into a fourteen-month bout of "colic." In addition to suffering from unexplainable fussiness, she threw up every single day her first six months of life. I was told babies are fussy, babies spit up. Besides giving us all the other stresses and surprises a parent encounters that first year, Piper contracted croup four times, twice requiring hospitalization. We were led to believe that Piper was experiencing typical baby problems, and that parenting young babies was just going to be hell. We didn't know that she was, in fact, suffering from food allergies, since her symptoms were atypical.

When Piper turned one year old, I did what all the other moms in my baby class were doing. I offered her peanut butter. Fortunately, Piper did not eat the peanut butter but broke out in hives upon merely fingering the cracker. Finally, we could not ignore the possibility that our daughter might have food allergies.

The rest of our wake-up call occurred in the doctor's office when Piper's test results revealed she was indeed allergic to peanuts as well as wheat, soy, eggs, tree nuts, peas, rye, oats, barley, strawberries, raspberries, chick peas, apples, pears, cantaloupe, and white beans. Due to her hypersensitivity to so many foods, we were advised to avoid fish, shellfish, and all other legumes as well. I was stunned.

With my always-irritable daughter on my hip, a baggie of Cheerios in one hand, and her diagnostic results in the other, I was somewhat relieved, I have to admit. Finally everything made sense. I wasn't a bad mother after all! At last there was an explanation for all those mysteries. As I habitually reached into the plastic baggie to offer Piper a snack, I froze. Cheerios. What was in Cheerios? Could she still have Cheerios? Could these tiny little Os that have become staples in every toddler's diet really be causing Piper so much distress?

My relief turned into reality as I ventured off to the grocery store for the first time post-diagnosis. It was a nightmare. After two hours, cross-eyed from reading labels and bleary eyed from my tears, I left the store with three bags of potato chips in my cart wondering if my one-year-old would have to survive on the Atkins Diet. As my own stomach rumbled from hunger pains, my mind screamed: "What on earth am I going to feed my child?"

The next few months were extremely difficult. I was motivated to maintain a new diet for our daughter when, after maintaining a diet of "safe" foods, we witnessed a complete change in her personality as well as exponential advancement in her development. While she was racing ahead, I, however, was falling behind. Our new "safe" diet consisted of chicken, white rice, and frozen green beans. Researching about food sensitivity consumed me as the list of forbidden foods and products seemed to grow endlessly. And we all learned by trial and error: Piper threw up a lot that year as I learned the hard way about the dangers and risks associated with cross-contamination. My stress level escalated daily. We knew the problem but I couldn't figure out how to fix it fast enough. I struggled for months and would not let go of my determination to maintain a sense of calm in the midst of a raging storm. I knew that most storms eventually pass, but this one seemed to be getting worse by the hour. The fear that an accidental exposure to peanuts could result in my daughter lapsing into potentially fatal anaphylactic shock kept me up almost every night. I finally realized that the safest food for our daughter was food prepared from scratch, by me, with the foods I knew were safe. So I started cooking.

And soon I began to inch forward as I remembered my past love of cooking. I immediately renewed my subscriptions to *Martha Stewart Living* and *Gourmet*. I anxiously awaited my Amazon.com shipment of several food allergy cookbooks. I went to my two favorite kitchen stores, salivating over new gadgets and remembering a time when I was a frequent attendee at their many cooking classes. I habitually grabbed the cooking class schedule and started to scan the selections while chasing after Piper in one of the stores. The list of possibilities always excited me. But as I looked at the classes offered, I felt like I had been slapped in the face. What was I thinking? "Japanese Vegetarian Cooking," "Authentic Indian Home Cooking," "Advanced Cake Decorating," "Crash Course in Sushi," "Hands-On Pasta"; these were courses that would have excited me in the past. Now they induced fear, dread, and despair. Instead of becoming excited, I thought of all the offending ingredients that would be involved: soy and fish in "Japanese Vegetarian Cooking"; tree nuts and peanuts in "Authentic Indian Home Cooking"; wheat and eggs in "Advanced Cake Decorating"; fish and shellfish in "Crash Course in Sushi"; and all that gluten in "Hands-On Pasta." Moreover I thought of all the culture my daughter would have to forego by not being able to indulge in these cuisines.

I became even more despondent when my books arrived on my doorstep. I anxiously scanned the recipes hoping to find something to make for dinner that night. But to my discouragement, many of these cookbooks were full of recipes with common allergens that were off-limits for my daughter. The few recipes that fit her dietary needs did not fit my personal needs. "Sunflower Millet Loaf?" What was millet? And was I actually supposed to convince my family that this would be a tasty alternative to meat loaf?

And so I took a different approach. Instead of letting food choices change who we were, I decided I would cook our favorite meals, but change the ingredients. I began a bottom-up approach and created familiar, favorite meals from scratch using safe ingredients. Instead of focusing on what we couldn't have, I focused on the safe foods that we could have. With limited time and a ravenous toddler, I'll admit my creations were not always perfect the first time. But as I cooked my creations over and over again, I continued to refine the taste from memory, as I have always done when cooking. I continued to make notes and suggestions for the subsequent versions and, before I knew it, I had a three-ring binder full of allergen-free recipes that my family was now thriving on.

Using my self-taught kitchen skills and my developing hypoallergenic approach, I began to realize I had a knack for making turkey tetrazzini without gluten or dairy. However as I continued to satisfy the needs of my children, my husband, and me, I craved something more. Not a day passed when I wasn't discussing food allergies with other people. No matter where we went, Piper's allergy situation was, and remains, a hot conversation topic. The severity of her food allergies always initiated a lengthy conversation but Piper's allergies never remained the focus of the conversation. We always ended up talking about the other person's suspected or diagnosed food allergies, intolerances to, or sensitivities with one of the top eight allergens. I quickly realized not only that many people suffer from food allergies, intolerances, and sensitivities, but that so many seem to be perpetually stuck in that dreadful transition between phasing out of eating problem foods and fully embracing problem-free foods. I found myself distressed after these conversations, as I had so much knowledge and experience but lacked the tangible means to help other sufferers. Although our family had settled into a balanced groove, I was feeling out of balance again. My passion for cooking and providing for my family was charging down the highway while my passion and ability to help others was stuck in the mud.

My true inspiration for this cookbook came to me one day while I was shopping at a natural food store alone, a rare occurrence. I had ten minutes to shop, check out, and be back in the car. I brushed past a woman with her little girl as I reached for a package of gluten-free cookies that I had never tried before. As soon as I saw the word "nuts," I quickly returned the product to the shelf as the woman asked me, "Are those good?" I informed her that I had not tried the cookies and hastily returned to my shopping. But something about that woman seemed so familiar to me. I couldn't place her face although I felt as though I knew her; I just couldn't remember where I knew her from.

Eight minutes later I was checking out. The friendly cashier noticed all the gluten-free products I was purchasing and asked if I was on a gluten-free diet. I easily slipped into my daily food allergy conversation mode when the clerk interrupted me. She informed me that she always felt better avoiding wheat. I recommended a few products to her as she helped me pack my groceries. Her next words hit me like a rock as she said, "Did you see the woman who just checked out? Her little girl has autism and she just learned that she needs to be on a gluten-free diet."

Suddenly, I knew how I knew this woman. I couldn't get out of the store fast enough to search the parking lot to track her down. That face. How could I have been so foolish? I knew that face, that mixed face of agony, fear, frustration, confusion, and love for her child. I knew that woman because that woman was me, two years ago in the very same grocery store.

Why didn't I stop to help her? I will never forgive myself knowing some of the anguish I could have saved her had I just stopped for one moment. But how would I have helped her? If I had my binder of my recipes with me, I would have given it to her. The satisfaction of knowing I helped her would far surpass the hours of labor I had spent creating safe, tasty recipes for my family. But I also knew there were millions of people just like her. If I gave the binder to her, how could I help everyone else? At that moment, the answer became obvious: by creating a cookbook for everyone with food allergies, intolerances, and sensitivities.

I have never seen that woman or her daughter since that day when, unbeknownst to her, she became the spark that ignited the flame for *8 Degrees of Ingredients*. Perhaps she is reading this now and perhaps she is realizing that no matter how isolated you can feel at times, you are not alone. At the very least, I hope this cookbook can make everyone's life a little bit easier.

"As a first-time mother, figuring out that my son had food allergies was exceptionally difficult as I did not know what was normal and what symptoms were being caused by reactions to food. But once he was diagnosed with allergies to milk, soy, peanuts, corn, and eggs, and we eliminated those allergens from his diet, he became a different baby and is now thriving!"

ANDREA WILDERMAN (MOTHER TO CAELEB), ELEMENTARY SCHOOL TUTOR, NEW CANAAN, CT

Chapter ❶

Let's Eat!

Have you been dealing with food allergies your whole life or are you cooking for someone who has been recently diagnosed? Maybe you are contemplating an elimination diet to determine why you feel sick all the time. Perhaps you are breastfeeding and have been advised to eliminate the top eight allergens from your diet to alleviate your infant's colic. Maybe you are hosting a party for an individual with a sensitivity to monosodium glutamate (MSG) and want to provide safe and healthy options. Maybe you suspect you have a gluten intolerance and crave a meal that will not put you into a "food coma." Perhaps your child has ADHD and the removal of dairy reduces or eliminates the symptoms. Maybe you are just tired of reading labels. Whoever you are and whatever your symptoms, you have something in common with each other. You don't want to think about food; you just want to eat! This chapter is dedicated to you.

Here you will find over thirty-five delicious recipes with convenient ingredients that can be readily purchased at your favorite grocery store. You don't need to seek out alternative ingredients to make these dishes or make multiple trips to specialty markets. Additionally, these recipes don't require reading labels with long lists of ingredients. The ingredients for every recipe in this chapter consist solely of fresh produce, fresh meats and poultry, rice, olive oil, canola oil, and spices. Does this sound too good to be true? It is not. In fact, all of the ingredients for every single recipe in this chapter are conveniently listed on the following page. If you can find these ingredients, you can make any recipe in this chapter.

The only packaged ingredients in this chapter, and thus the only ingredients with labels, are the rice, olive oil, canola oil, and spices. Since these ingredients generally have been minimally processed and have labels consisting of very few words, using them will provide an easy introduction into the practice of label reading. Furthermore, the ingredients are easy to find: imagine preparing meals for a month without visiting three different stores to accumulate the ingredients for just one dish. And you are probably familiar with them all. You won't have to worry about where to locate acceptable pasta and bread alternatives. You won't have to waste time searching endlessly through cookbooks hoping to find a recipe that meets your personal and dietary needs. All these recipes are conveniently located in one chapter!

This chapter even has recipes for homemade stocks, andouille sausage, and marinara sauce. Consequently, you won't have to pester manufacturers about the makeup of "natural flavorings," as there aren't any in these homemade versions. When you are ready to venture past Chapter 1, you can use these homemade staples in subsequent recipes if you haven't already found ready-made varieties. However, proceed with caution. The recipes in this chapter and those that that follow yield extremely tasty results and you actually might prefer them over the store-bought versions.

The transitional phase from conventional to hypoallergenic cooking placed a huge amount of stress and hardship on my family. It took time to find products that were safe for my daughter to consume. It took even longer to find products that were *desirable* for my family to consume. And for everyone, this transitional phase can become very stressful, since you still need to eat as you discover what's safe! With this chapter I hope to ease this transition for some and provide immediate relief for others. Bon Appétit!

FRESH MEATS

beef: stew meat, tenderloin tips, rump roast, shanks, strips
pork: loin roast, loin filet, ground
chicken: breast, thighs, ground
turkey: breast, cutlets
lamb: leg, ground
veal: breast

FRESH PRODUCE

apples, asparagus, bell peppers, broccoli, carrots, celery, eggplant, garlic, ginger root, green beans, leeks, lemons, mushrooms, onions, oranges, parsnips, peas, potatoes, shallots, snow peas, spinach, squashes, tomatoes, turnips, zucchini

FRESH HERBS

basil, dill, lemon grass, mint leaves, oregano, parsley, sage, thyme

DRIED HERBS AND SPICES

bay leaves, cayenne pepper, chili powder, coriander, cumin, dill, fennel, garlic powder, ginger, marjoram, nutmeg, oregano, paprika, parsley, pepper, red pepper flakes, saffron, sage, salt, thyme

PACKAGED PRODUCTS

dried cranberries, dried mushrooms, raisins, red wine, canola oil, olive oil, *rice:* white basmati rice, white long-grain rice, brown rice, arborio rice, wild rice

Easy Beef Vegetable Soup

Food historians tell us the history of soup is probably as old as the history of cooking. Over the years, countless soup varieties have evolved based on local ingredients in diverse cultures. However, these variations are all based on the same theme: creating a nutritious, filling, easily digested, and simple-to-make meal.

The first colonial cookbook in America (published circa 1740) included several recipes for soups and a later cookbook (published circa 1770) contained an entire chapter on soups. Over 250 years later, soup remains one of Americans' favorite foods. Unfortunately, while popular canned soups may appear safe for those suffering from food allergies, intolerances, and sensitivities, I've discovered that most canned varieties contain unsuspecting ingredients such as wheat, soy, or eggs.

Deciding on the recipe to begin this cookbook was easy. What better way for some to begin a new way of cooking, and others an improved life, than with a simple recipe for a historic entrée: soup. No one should feel deprived of his or her heritage and I assure you, this soup is mmmm, mmmm, good.

⏏◎ǀↂ

INGREDIENTS

1/2 cup olive oil

2 cloves garlic, minced

1 large white onion, chopped

3 large carrots, diced

2 pounds cubed beef stew meat

4 teaspoons salt, divided

12 cups water

2 pounds vine-ripe tomatoes, seeded and coarsely chopped

1-1/2 pounds red potatoes, peeled and chopped

1 cup green beans

1 cup peas

4 tablespoons fresh chopped parsley

INSTRUCTIONS

1. In a large soup pot, heat oil over medium-high heat. Add garlic and onion and sauté for 2 minutes. Add carrots and sauté until carrots are softened, about 3 minutes.

2. Add cubed beef and 1 teaspoon of salt directly to vegetables and sauté until all sides of beef are browned, about 5 minutes.

3. Add water, chopped tomatoes, and remaining 3 teaspoons of salt. Bring to a boil, reduce heat, and simmer for 10 minutes.

4. Add remaining vegetables. Bring to a boil, reduce heat, and simmer, uncovered for approximately 30 minutes, or until potatoes are cooked and tender are soft.

5. Remove from heat, stir in parsley, and allow soup to cool for at least 20 minutes before serving.

RECIPE NOTES

Freeze in individual servings for up to 3 months.

Serves: 6. Preparation Time is 5 minutes. Cooking Time is 1 hour.

Citrus Chicken and Vegetable Stir-Fry

¡○¡†

INGREDIENTS

2/3 cup water

2 tablespoons minced lemon grass

2 tablespoons minced ginger root

1 tablespoon lemon juice

1/4 cup freshly squeezed orange juice

1 teaspoon salt, divided

1/4 cup canola oil

16 ounces boneless, skinless chicken breast

1 cup shredded carrots

1 cup broccoli floret

1 medium red bell pepper, julienned

1 medium orange bell pepper, julienned

1 medium yellow bell pepper, julienned

1 cup snow peas

4 ounces shiitake mushrooms

2 cups cooked white basmati rice

INSTRUCTIONS

❶ Combine the water, lemon grass, ginger root, lemon juice, orange juice, and 1/2 teaspoon of salt in a small saucepan. Bring to a boil. Continue to simmer until liquid reduces by about half, approximately 10 minutes.

❷ Meanwhile, heat canola oil in a large sauté pan. Slice chicken into 1-inch pieces, season with remaining 1/2 teaspoon of salt, and add to the pan. Sauté chicken until cooked through, about 3 to 5 minutes per side. Remove chicken from pan and set aside.

❸ Add carrots and cook for about 2 minutes, until carrots soften. Add broccoli and peppers and sauté for another 5 minutes.

❹ Add snow peas, mushrooms, and citrus sauce. Return chicken to pan and stir until chicken and vegetables are well coated. Serve warm over rice.

Serves: 4. Preparation Time is 5 minutes. Cooking Time is 25 minutes.

Chicken Cacciatore

¡◎¡¡

INGREDIENTS

3 pounds roma tomatoes

3 teaspoons salt, divided

1 teaspoon pepper, divided

3-1/2 pounds chicken parts

4 tablespoons olive oil

1 medium white onion, chopped

2 medium red peppers, chopped

1/2 cup shredded carrots

3 cloves garlic, chopped

1 cup dry red wine

8 ounces button mushrooms, sliced

2 tablespoons fresh chopped sage leaves

2 tablespoons fresh chopped thyme

INSTRUCTIONS

❶ Chop and seed the tomatoes and place in a large mixing bowl. Add 1 teaspoon of salt and, using hands, mash and squeeze the tomatoes. Set bowl aside.

❷ Season the chicken with 1 teaspoon of salt and 1/2 teaspoon of pepper. In a large skillet or Dutch oven, heat olive oil over medium-high heat. Working in batches, add the chicken to the pan and fry until golden brown, about 5 minutes per side. Remove browned chicken from pan and set aside.

❸ Reduce heat to medium and add the chopped onion, red pepper, shredded carrots, garlic, and another 1/2 teaspoon of salt to the pan. Sauté until vegetables soften, about 5 to 7 minutes.

❹ Add red wine to the pan, scraping up any brown bits on the bottom of the pan. Simmer until liquid is reduced by about half, about 5 minutes.

❺ Return the chicken to the pan and add the mushrooms and tomatoes with their juice. Bring the sauce to a simmer, cover the pan, and continue to simmer over low-medium heat until the chicken is cooked through, about 30 to 40 minutes.

❻ Uncover, add the fresh herbs and remaining 1/2 teaspoon of salt and 1/2 teaspoon of pepper.

❼ To serve, transfer the chicken pieces to a platter. If you desire a thicker sauce, bring sauce to a quick boil for 3 to 5 minutes, then spoon over the chicken pieces. While traditionally accompanied by polenta, this dish also goes well with white or brown rice.

RECIPE NOTES

Generally all wine is allergen-free and gluten-free, but always check with the manufacturer to make sure that there are no glutinous additives incorporated into the wine and to also ensure that they were stored in gluten-free storage tanks. Some wines are aged in barrels that once contained another substance that could have held an allergenic or glutinous product. Although rare, it can happen.

Freeze in airtight containers for up to 3 months.

Serves: 4. Preparation Time is 5 minutes. Cooking Time is 55 minutes.

Arroz con Pollo

¶◎↓↑

INGREDIENTS

2 pounds chicken parts

2-1/2 teaspoons salt, divided

1/2 teaspoon pepper

2 tablespoons olive oil

1 large white onion, chopped

2 large carrots, diced

1 medium red pepper, chopped

2 cloves garlic, minced

1 tablespoon paprika

2 cups long-grain white rice

5 cups water

1/4 teaspoon saffron

1 medium bay leaf

1 cup peas

INSTRUCTIONS

❶ Pat chicken dry and season with 1/2 teaspoon of salt and pepper. Heat oil in a medium Dutch oven over medium-high heat. Brown chicken on all sides, about 10 minutes total. Transfer chicken to a platter and cover with aluminum foil to keep warm.

❷ Reduce heat to medium and add the onion, carrots, red pepper, and 1 teaspoon of salt to pan. Cook until vegetables soften, about 5 minutes.

❸ Add garlic, paprika, and rice. Stir to evenly heat and coat the rice for about 1 minute.

❹ Add the water, saffron, bay leaf, and remaining 1 teaspoon of salt. Return chicken to pan, nestling it into the rice. Be sure to add any juices from plate. Reduce heat to low and cook, covered, until chicken is cooked through, rice is tender, and all the liquid is absorbed, about 20 minutes.

❺ Remove from heat and stir in peas. Cover pan and let stand 10 minutes to heat the peas through. Discard bay leaf and serve.

Serves: 4. Preparation Time is 5 minutes. Cooking Time is 45 minutes.

Turkey Stir-Fry

¶⊙¶

INGREDIENTS

16 ounces turkey cutlet(s)

2 tablespoons olive oil

2 cloves garlic, minced

1 tablespoon fresh minced ginger

1 large red bell pepper, julienned

1 large green bell pepper, julienned

1 large white onion, thinly sliced

1/4 cup water

2 tablespoons freshly squeezed orange juice

1 teaspoon orange zest

1 teaspoon salt

1/2 teaspoon pepper

2 cups cooked white or brown rice

INSTRUCTIONS

❶ Slice the turkey cutlets into 1-inch strips. Heat olive oil in a large sauté pan over medium-high heat. Add garlic, ginger, and turkey and sauté over medium heat until turkey is no longer pink, about 4 to 5 minutes.

❷ Add peppers and onion to the turkey pan and continue to sauté until vegetables soften, about 5 minutes.

❸ Meanwhile, combine the water, orange juice, orange zest, salt, and pepper, and add to the sauté pan. Bring to a low simmer and continue to cook for another 1 to 2 minutes. Serve warm over rice.

RECIPE NOTES

Freeze stir-fry without rice in airtight containers up to 3 months.

Serves: 4. Preparation Time is 5 minutes. Cooking Time is 15 minutes.

Tuscan Turkey Cutlets

The Tuscan cuisine is ancient and sophisticated, consisting of tasty ingredients and fabulous dishes that are never excessively elaborate. Accordingly, many Tuscan dishes are naturally free of most common allergens. While easy to prepare, this recipe is reminiscent of the simplicity of traditional Tuscan dishes, allowing each ingredient to bring something to the table.

🍴◎🍴

INGREDIENTS
16 ounces turkey cutlet(s)
1 teaspoon salt, divided
1/2 teaspoon pepper
2 tablespoons olive oil
4 cloves garlic, minced
1 large white onion, chopped
1 cup shredded carrot
10 ounces fresh spinach
24 ounces plum tomatoes, seeded and chopped
1/2 teaspoon dried oregano
1/2 teaspoon dried thyme

INSTRUCTIONS
❶ Place cutlets on cutting board and sprinkle with 1/2 teaspoon of salt and 1/4 teaspoon of pepper.
❷ Heat oil in a large nonstick skillet over medium-high heat. Sauté turkey cutlets for 2 to 3 minutes per side, or until cooked through. Remove cutlets, cover with aluminum foil, and keep warm.
❸ In the same pan, sauté garlic, onion, and carrots until tender, about 5 minutes. Add spinach and sauté for an additional 2 minutes or until spinach is wilted. Add tomatoes, oregano, thyme, and remaining 1/2 teaspoon of salt and 1/4 teaspoon of pepper. Reduce heat to low and simmer for 5 minutes.
❹ To serve, place one or two cutlets on a plate. Top with spinach-tomato mixture and serve alongside white rice, rice noodles, or roasted potatoes.

RECIPE NOTES
Individually wrap leftover cutlets in aluminum foil. Place in a resealable freezer bag and freeze up to 3 months.

Serves: 4. Preparation Time is 5 minutes. Cooking Time is 20 minutes.

Turkey Harvest Salad

†◎†¡

INGREDIENTS

1-1/2 cups wild rice

1/4 cup dried cranberries

1/4 cup raisins

1 cup hot water

2 tablespoons extra light tasting olive oil

2 tablespoons lemon juice

1/2 small red onion, diced

1 celery stalk, diced

1/2 cup red seedless grapes, quartered

12 ounces cooked turkey breast, diced

INSTRUCTIONS

❶ Cook wild rice according to package; drain and set aside to cool.

❷ Meanwhile, place the cranberries and raisins in the hot water and allow to sit for 30 minutes. Drain the fruit and reserve about 1/4 cup of the liquid. Add the rehydrated fruit to a small food processor. Add the reserved liquid, extra light tasting olive oil, and lemon juice. Pulse together a few times to create a base.

❸ Combine the fruit with the cooked wild rice and remaining ingredients. Toss ingredients together and serve at room temperature or refrigerate for up to 2 days and serve chilled.

RECIPE NOTES

This recipe calls for extra light tasting olive oil as opposed to extra virgin olive oil. Extra light tasting olive oil is basically a flavorless oil. Accordingly, the oil will not overpower the sweet flavors of the rehydrated fruit. Canola oil is an acceptable substitute.

Serves: 6. Preparation Time is 10 minutes. Cooking Time is 45 minutes.

Grilled Lamb Kabobs

These lamb kabobs are a great alternative to steaks or burgers when you want to spice up your grilling options. I make this dish just to experience the amazing aroma of the marinade which compliments the flavor of the lamb fabulously. These lamb kabobs are so refreshing as an ideal summer-time meal or as a way to combat wintertime blues.

🍴◎🍴

INGREDIENTS

2 pounds leg of lamb

1/3 cup fresh mint leaves, loosely packed

2 tablespoons dried oregano

2 cloves garlic, chopped

1/3 cup lemon juice

1/2 cup olive oil

1 large white onion

2 large bell peppers

1 pint cherry tomatoes, diced

8 ounces button mushrooms

INSTRUCTIONS

❶ Trim the fat off lamb and cut into 2-inch cubes.

❷ Combine the mint leaves, oregano, garlic, lemon juice, and olive oil in a blender. Blend to a fine pulp. Place marinade in a large resealable bag.

❸ Add lamb to bag and marinate for at least 12 hours, preferably overnight. Remove bag from refrigerator 30 minutes prior to grilling, allowing lamb to come to room temperature.

❹ Chop onion and peppers into 2-inch pieces.

❺ Assemble ingredients on skewers, alternating lamb, onion, peppers, tomatoes, and mushrooms, as desired.

❻ Grill skewers, rotating every 4 to 5 minutes, until meat is charred on all sides, but pink on the inside. Be careful not to overcook. Remove from grill and serve over a bed of steaming white rice.

RECIPE NOTES

The kabobs can also be cooked in the oven, on a high broil, using the same turning methods.

Serves: 6. Preparation Time is 15 minutes. Inactive Preparation Time is 12 hours. Cooking Time is 15 minutes.

Roasted Leg of Lamb

This is a simple yet robust roast that can be enjoyed for Easter or any day, for that matter.

¶◎¶

INGREDIENTS

1/2 cup olive oil

1 large lemon, juiced

1-1/2 teaspoons oregano

2 teaspoons coarse sea salt

16-pound leg of lamb, bone-in

INSTRUCTIONS

Preheat oven to 475°F.

❶ Whisk olive oil, lemon juice, and oregano together in bowl. Using your hands, rub the lamb with the marinade, working it into the meat and its crevices. Let lamb stand at room temperature for 30 minutes.

❷ Season lamb all over with coarse sea salt just prior to putting in oven.

❸ Roast lamb in middle of oven for 15 minutes at 475°F. Turn lamb over and return to oven. Reduce oven temperature to 325°F and continue to roast lamb for 1 hour and 10 minutes or until a meat thermometer registers an internal temperature of 145°F (or 135°F for rare).

❹ Remove lamb from oven and cover with foil for 15 to 20 minutes before carving. Serve with roasted new potatoes and steamed artichokes.

RECIPE NOTES

◉ Slice leftovers into slices for sandwiches and spread with tapenade for a succulent lunch.

Serves: 6. Inactive Preparation Time is 30 minutes. Cooking Time is 1 hour 25 minutes.

Beef and Broccoli Stir-Fry

While Chinese restaurants are no longer feasible options for my family, I still need to sat-isfy my Asian cravings weekly. This recipe for beef and broccoli stir-fry is reminiscent of my takeout days with its pronounced Asian flair that the whole family will enjoy.

🍽️

INGREDIENTS

1/4 cup olive oil

6 cloves garlic, chopped

16 ounces beef tenderloin tips

3 cups chopped broccoli florets

1/2 medium red onion, chopped

1/2 teaspoon red pepper flakes

1/2 teaspoon salt

INSTRUCTIONS

❶ Heat olive oil in a large sauté pan over medium heat. Add garlic and sauté for about 2 minutes. Add beef tips and sauté until all sides are browned, about 5 minutes.

❷ Add chopped broccoli and onion. Continue to sauté until the onions soften and the broccoli turns a vibrant green, about 2 to 3 minutes.

❸ Remove from heat, add red pepper flakes and salt, stir, and cover. Let the stir-fry stand for about 20 minutes, covered. The juices and steam will fin-ish cooking the broccoli and beef while they absorb the flavors of the garlic and red pepper. Serve over a plate of steaming white rice.

RECIPE NOTES

Serves: 4. Preparation Time is 5 minutes. Cooking Time is 30 minutes.

Salt the Strip Steak

For many people, even a single food allergy, intolerance, or sensitivity to one ingredient can be troublesome, making many seemingly safe foods actually off-limits, especially our beloved condiments. Many steak sauces contain soy, and most soy sauces contain wheat. Traditional Worcestershire contains anchovies while store-bought marinades are flooded with natural and artificial flavorings as listed on the ingredient label.

This is a recipe you really must try to believe. A mere sprinkling of salt will get your grilled steaks rave reviews and have people wondering about your secret marinade. Sprinkling coarse sea salt on the steaks disperses the crystals in isolated areas of the meat. This allows the juices to circulate without drying out the steak as fine, granulated salt crystals would. The coarse crystals will also add a punch of flavor without making the steak too salty. Letting the steak rest for 5 to 10 minutes after grilling will enhance the juiciness of each bite.

🍽️

INGREDIENTS
4 medium New York strip steaks (about 16 ounces each)
2 teaspoons coarse sea salt

INSTRUCTIONS
❶ Preheat grill and allow steaks to come to room temperature.
❷ Salt the strips by sprinkling approximately 1/2 teaspoon of coarse sea salt per pound of steak. Allow steak to sit with salt for exactly 5 minutes.
❸ Grill strips to desired doneness, about 6 to 8 minutes per side at a grill temperature of 400°F for medium rare. Remove steaks from grill and allow to rest for 5 to 10 minutes before serving.

RECIPE NOTES

Serves: 6. Preparation Time is 5 minutes. Inactive Preparation Time is 20 minutes. Cooking Time is 15 minutes.

Roasts

The following three recipes for roasts are wonderful introductions to working with natural ingredients that maximize the dishes' potential as well as flavor. The recipe for stuffed pork roast shows how ingredients can work together to produce gratifying results, while that for stuffed veal breast introduces tips for maximizing flavor from individual ingredients. Finally, the recipe for Yankee pot roast demonstrates how various ingredients can possess wonderful, inherent cooking properties, alleviating the need to add extra ingredients.

Stuffed Pork Loin Roast with Sweet Potatoes

†◎†

INGREDIENTS

2 cups water

1/2 cup wild rice

6 ounces fresh spinach

8 ounces baby portabello mushrooms, sliced (about 2 cups)

2 cloves garlic, chopped

2 teaspoons salt, divided

1/2 teaspoon pepper

13-pound pork loin roast, center cut

8 medium sweet potatoes with skins, chopped into 1-inch chunks

2 tablespoons olive oil

INSTRUCTIONS

Preheat oven to 325°F.

❶ Bring two cups of water to a boil. Add rice, reduce heat, and simmer on low, covered, for 55 minutes or until rice is cooked. Remove from heat and let stand an additional 5 minutes.

❷ Meanwhile, cook fresh spinach in about 1/4 cup boiling water and drain. Add sliced mushrooms, garlic, and 1 teaspoon of salt to the spinach and set aside. When rice is cooked, add rice to spinach mixture.

❸ Place roast on a clean surface. To create the cavity for the rice stuffing, use a long sharp knife (like a boning knife), and score the roast lengthwise by making an X on the flat surface at the end of the meat; follow through with the knife to the center of the roast, without slicing through to the edges. Leave about a 1-inch circumference around the edges. Turn the roast around and score the other end so that the center is hollow. Insert a wooden spoon into the cavity to make sure the hole is even and goes all the way through lengthwise, creating a tunnel. Season the inside and outside of the roast with remaining 1 teaspoon of salt and 1/2 teaspoon of pepper, as you gently massage the meat and stretch the cavity.

❹ To stuff the roast, hold the roast upright and begin to spoon rice mixture into the cavity. Use your fingers make sure the stuffing goes all the way through. Pack the stuffing in firmly.

❺ Toss together sweet potato chunks and olive oil in a roasting pan. Spread potatoes out evenly over bottom of pan. Place stuffed roast, fat side up, on top of the potatoes in the roasting pan.

❻ Roast in oven, uncovered, for 60 minutes or until instant-read thermometer inserted into the pork registers 150 to 155°F. Remove from oven and cover with aluminum foil. Let the pork rest for 20 minutes. The temperature of the pork should rise to 160°F to ensure it has cooked through.

❼ Slice the roast into 1-1/2 inch slices. Serve warm with sweet potatoes on the side.

RECIPE NOTES

🔲 This stuffed roast demonstrates how natural ingredients can work together to develop robust flavors without any seasonings other than salt and pepper. Here, the salty pork drippings from the roast slowly marinate the sweet potatoes throughout the cooking, while the wild rice stuffing within keeps the pork nice and tender.

🔲 The most time-consuming segment of this recipe is cooking the wild rice. To minimize this time-consuming task, cook the entire bag at once. Freeze unused rice in 1-cup portions using resealable freezer bags. When ready for use, thaw the frozen wild rice in a bowl of hot water. Alternatively, cut a small slit in the resealable bag and microwave on high for 2 to 4 minutes.

◉ Slice leftover roast into 1-1/2 inch slices and wrap slices individually in aluminum foil. Place wrapped roast slices in a plastic freezer bag and store in the freezer for up to three months. By pre-slicing the roast, you will decrease the thawing time dramatically. Thaw pre-cooked slices in the fridge and reheat in the oven still wrapped in foil, or remove foil and reheat in microwave.

Serves: 6. Preparation Time is 1 hour 15 minutes. Cooking Time is 1 hour.

Stuffed Veal Breast with Stewed Tomatoes

¶◎¶

INGREDIENTS

1 pound Yukon gold potatoes, or other yellow-fleshed potato

4 tablespoons olive oil, divided

1 large white onion, chopped

2 cloves garlic, minced

1 tablespoon fresh chopped dill, or 1 teaspoon dried dill

2 teaspoons salt, divided

1 teaspoon pepper, divided

4 pounds vine-ripe tomatoes, seeded and coarsely chopped

4 pounds bone-in, back portion veal breast, at least 3 inches thick

1 cup water

2 tablespoons lemon juice

2 medium bay leaves

2 tablespoons fresh chopped parsley

INSTRUCTIONS

Preheat oven to 325°F.

❶ Place unpeeled, whole potatoes directly in a large pot and cover with water. Bring to a boil and then reduce heat to a low simmer. Continue to simmer, uncovered, until potatoes are tender but not completely cooked, about 20 minutes. The potatoes will finish cooking in the oven. Drain potatoes and allow to cool.

❷ Heat 2 tablespoons of olive oil in a small skillet over medium heat. Add onion and garlic and sauté just until they begin to sweat and soften and release juices. Remove from heat.

❸ Peel potatoes and add flesh to a large mixing bowl. Using a fork, break up the potatoes, slightly mashing them. It is best to leave them fairly chunky. Add the cooked onions and garlic along with the fresh dill, 1/2 teaspoon of salt, and 1/4 teaspoon of pepper. Mix together to incorporate and set aside.

❹ Toss tomatoes together with 1/2 teaspoon of salt and 1/4 teaspoon pepper in a bowl and set aside.

❺ Season the veal with remaining 1 teaspoon of salt and 1/2 teaspoon of pepper. Cut a large pocket in the center of the veal, parallel to the bone. Leave at least 1/2-inch border of meat around the outside. Stuff the breast with the potato mixture, pushing the bulk of the potatoes toward the center of the veal. Secure the ends of the veal together with toothpicks or kitchen string.

❻ Heat remaining 2 tablespoons of oil in a large Dutch oven or large heatproof casserole over medium-high heat. Place veal in, meat side down, and sear until well browned. Remove from heat; add water and lemon juice. Scrape up any brown bits of flavor off bottom of pan.

7 Scatter tomatoes, along with any juices, around the veal, along with the bay leaves. Cover tightly and place on middle rack of preheated oven. Bake until meat is cooked and tender, about 2-1/2 hours.

8 Remove from oven, and allow breast to rest while still covered in the pot with tomatoes, for 20 to 30 minutes before slicing. Slice the breast between the bones and plate. Ladle stewed tomatoes over the top and garnish with fresh parsley.

RECIPE NOTES

This recipe combines a few creative techniques for maximizing flavor without adding fancy seasonings or preservatives. First, boiling potatoes with the skins on preserves the flavor of the delicious gold potatoes rather than boiling it away. Second, leaving the bone in while roasting is a great way to add even more flavor, as the juices are released during cooking and season the stuffing naturally. Finally the acidity from the tomatoes not only assists in the braising process, but provides a wonderful contrast to the tenderness of the veal.

Place leftover tomatoes in a food processor, add a little broth, and puree into a tasty tomato sauce for another day.

Serves: 4. Preparation Time is 35 minutes. Cooking Time is 2 hours 30 minutes.

Yankee Pot Roast
with Vegetable Gravy

🍴◎🍴

INGREDIENTS

1/4 cup canola oil

6 cloves garlic, chopped

3 pounds bottom round or rump roast

3 cups water

1 large white onion, quartered

2 medium turnips, coarsely chopped

3 medium bay leaves

2 teaspoons salt, divided

1 teaspoon pepper

4 medium carrots, peeled and halved

3 celery stalks, halved

2 pounds boiling potatoes, skin on,
      chopped into 1-inch chunks

1 ounce dried porcini mushrooms
      (optional)

1 cup hot water

INSTRUCTIONS

❶ In Dutch oven or heavy kettle, heat canola oil over medium-high heat. Sauté garlic until it begins to soften, approximately 3 minutes. Add roast and brown roast on all sides, about 2 to 3 minutes per side.

❷ Add water, onions, turnips, and bay leaves. Cover and simmer for 1 hour.

❸ Remove bay leaves and discard. Add 1 teaspoon of salt and pepper and stir to dissolve.

❹ Add carrots, celery, and potatoes. If necessary, add more water so all vegetables are covered. Cover and simmer for another hour until beef is cooked and tender and vegetables are well cooked. Remove beef from pot and cover with aluminum foil to keep warm.

❺ Meanwhile, place dried mushrooms in a bowl and add hot water. Let steep for 30 minutes. After 30 minutes, drain the mushrooms and reserve all the stock. Strain the stock through a paper towel to remove any dirt or particles and set aside.

❻ Using a slotted spoon, remove carrots, celery, and onions from the pot and add to a blender. Add the rehydrated mushrooms to the blender and puree the vegetable mixture. Add remaining 1 teaspoon salt and 1/4 cup of the reserved mushroom stock. Liquefy the gravy. Continue to add 1/4 cup of mushroom stock until gravy reaches desired consistency. If necessary, thin gravy with additional liquid from the beef pot, or thicken with one or two potato pieces.

❼ To serve, slice roast into individual servings. Scoop potatoes and desired vegetables onto plate. Pour gravy over top.

RECIPE NOTES

The gravy derived from this recipe is a perfect example of how well-cooked carrots and onions work fabulously as thickening agents. No one will believe that this gravy consists solely of natural ingredients.

Omit the mushrooms and substitute extra cooking broth to thin the gravy. Using only carrots and onions will produce a vibrant orange color, perfect for a unique rendition of a traditional dish.

Serves: 6. Preparation Time is 10 minutes. Cooking Time is 2 hours.

Herb-Crusted Pork Loin

¡◎¡¡

INGREDIENTS

1 tablespoon olive oil

2 cloves garlic, minced

1 teaspoon coarse sea salt

1/2 teaspoon pepper

1 teaspoon dried parsley

1 teaspoon dried sage

1 teaspoon dried thyme

2 pounds boneless pork loin filet

INSTRUCTIONS

Preheat oven to 350°F.

❶ Combine the olive oil, minced garlic, sea salt, pepper, parsley, sage, and thyme together in a small bowl. Using a mortar or fork, grind the salt and garlic while mixing the spices until you develop a nice paste. Rub the paste all over the pork, massaging the meat as you work.

❷ Roast the pork in the oven, uncovered, for 1 hour or until the pork reaches an internal temperature of 155°F. Allow the pork to rest for 20 minutes before carving. Serve with roasted potatoes or a side of applesauce.

RECIPE NOTES

Slice leftover pork into individual slices, wrap in aluminum foil, place in a resealable freezer bag, and freeze up to 3 months.

Serves: 4. Preparation Time is 5 minutes. Cooking Time is 1 hour.

Andouille Sausage and Potato Casserole

ⲓ◎ⲓ

INGREDIENTS

3 tablespoons olive oil, plus more for drizzling

1-1/2 pounds boiling potatoes, skin on, chopped into 1-inch chunks

1 large green bell pepper, chopped

1 large white onion, chopped

1 teaspoon chopped fresh thyme

1 teaspoon chopped fresh sage

1/2 teaspoon salt

1/4 teaspoon pepper

2 pounds Andouille sausage, see recipe on page 36

1/2 cup water

3 medium tomatoes (about 1 pound), seeded and chopped

2 tablespoons chopped fresh parsley

1/2 teaspoon coarse sea salt (optional)

INSTRUCTIONS

Preheat oven to 375°F.

❶ Lightly grease a deep casserole with 1 tablespoon of olive oil. Layer the potatoes, green pepper, onion, fresh herbs, salt, and pepper in the prepared dish and pour in water. Drizzle with 2 tablespoons of olive oil. Cover with aluminum foil and bake for 40 minutes.

❷ Meanwhile, prepare Andouille sausage (recipe follows).

❸ Remove potatoes from oven and stir. Using a fork, lightly press down on potatoes to mash them slightly, adding up to 1/2 cup of water if necessary.

❹ Layer the andouille sausage on top of the potatoes. Sprinkle chopped tomatoes and parsley on top of sausage. Drizzle with extra olive oil and sprinkle with coarse sea salt (optional). Return casserole to oven, uncovered, for 20 minutes, or until the sausage begins to crisp on top. Serve warm.

Serves: 6. Preparation Time is 10 minutes. Cooking Time is 1 hour.

Andouille Sausage

¡◎¡↑

INGREDIENTS

2 teaspoons salt

1 teaspoon pepper

1/4 teaspoon red pepper flakes

1/2 teaspoon ground thyme

1/8 teaspoon cayenne pepper

1 teaspoon paprika

1/2 teaspoon garlic powder

1-1/2 teaspoons fennel seeds

2 tablespoons water

2 tablespoons extra light tasting olive oil

2 pounds ground pork

INSTRUCTIONS

❶ Combine all the spices together in a small bowl. Add water and stir until the spices are evenly distributed. Set aside.

❷ Heat olive oil in a large sauté pan over low to medium heat. Add ground pork and begin breaking up the meat. Cook for about 2 minutes and add the spice liquid. Continue to break up the pork as it finishes cooking, about 10 minutes.

❸ When sausage is finished cooking and no longer pink, remove from heat. Serve warm or refrigerate up to 3 days.

RECIPE NOTES

Freeze in a resealable freezer bag up to 3 months.

Serves: 4. Preparation Time is 5 minutes. Cooking Time is 15 minutes.

Baked Stuffed Peppers

¶◎¶

INGREDIENTS

3 tablespoons olive oil, divided

4 large green bell peppers

16 ounces ground lamb

2 cups cooked long-grain rice

1 cup chopped tomatoes

1 tablespoon oregano

1 tablespoon fresh lemon juice

1 teaspoon lemon zest

1 teaspoon salt

1/4 teaspoon pepper

INSTRUCTIONS

❶ Lightly oil a baking dish large enough to hold the peppers with 1 tablespoon of olive oil. Using a sharp knife, carefully cut the tops off the peppers. Remove the seeds and membrane from inside.

❷ Optional: Using a steamer or colander, steam the peppers over boiling water until slightly softened, about 10 minutes. Although this step is optional, it is highly recommended to achieve a desired texture of the peppers that enhances the flavoring of the stuffing. For a firmer pepper, skip this step.

❸ Meanwhile, sauté ground lamb over medium heat until cooked through.

❹ In a large bowl, combine the cooked lamb with the remaining ingredients. Fill the peppers with the lamb mixture and set them upright in the baking dish. Drizzle the peppers with the remaining olive oil.

❺ Cover with aluminum foil and bake until heated through, about 35 minutes. Serve warm or chilled.

RECIPE NOTES

Serves: 4. Preparation Time is 10 minutes. Cooking Time is 45 minutes.

Indian Summer Hotdish

This dish makes an amazing vegetarian meal for those warm fall days when you fancy something light but yearn for the fresh flavors of the season.

¡◎¡¡

INGREDIENTS

2 cups peeled and chopped turnips

2 cups peeled and chopped butternut squash

1/3 cup olive oil, plus 2 tablespoons for drizzling

1 large white onion, chopped

3 cloves garlic, minced

1 medium eggplant, peeled and chopped

2 medium zucchini, chopped

2 medium summer squash, chopped

1 large yellow bell pepper, julienned

1 large orange bell pepper, julienned

4 medium roma tomatoes, chopped

1 teaspoon salt

1/2 teaspoon pepper

2-1/2 cups cooked brown rice

1 tablespoon chopped fresh basil

1 tablespoon chopped fresh parsley

1 tablespoon chopped fresh oregano

INSTRUCTIONS

Preheat oven to 350°F.

❶ Spread turnips and squash on a non-stick baking pan. Roast in oven for 20 minutes, or until edges are browned.

❷ Meanwhile, heat 1/3 cup of olive oil in an extra-large skillet over medium-high heat. Add onion and cook until onions become translucent, about 5 minutes. Add garlic, eggplant, zucchini, summer squash, peppers, and tomatoes. Cook until vegetables begin to soften, about 5 minutes.

❸ Remove the vegetables from the oven and increase the oven temperature to 425°F. Add the turnips and squash to the sauté pan, along with the salt and pepper. Stir and cook for another 5 minutes. Remove from heat.

❹ Lightly grease a 9×12-inch glass casserole dish with olive oil. Spread 2 cups of the cooked brown rice over the bottom. Spread vegetable mixture over the rice. Top with remaining 1/2 cup of rice and fresh herbs. Drizzle with remaining 2 tablespoons of olive oil.

❺ Finish cooking on the top rack of the oven for 15 minutes, or until the rice begins to brown. Serve warm.

Serves: 8. Preparation Time is 10 minutes. Cooking Time is 40 minutes.

Ratatouille

*A wonderful option during the steamy, summer months, this dish is light, yet satisfying.
Serve as a colorful accompaniment to chicken or even as a main course.*

†◎⏐†

INGREDIENTS

1 large eggplant

2 teaspoons salt, divided

1/2 cup olive oil

2 cloves minced garlic

2 large white onions, chopped

1 medium orange bell pepper, chopped

1 medium red bell pepper, chopped

6 large tomatoes, chopped and seeded

1 medium zucchini, chopped

1 tablespoon fresh basil

1/2 tablespoon marjoram, dried

INSTRUCTIONS

❶ Slice the eggplant lengthwise into 1/2-inch thick slices. Begin layering the slices by sprinkling a slice with salt and covering the slice with a paper towel. Add the next slice on top of the paper towel. Continue to layer. You should use about 1 teaspoon of salt for this step. Cover the top slice with a paper towel and place a weight on top. Let stand for 30 minutes. When the eggplant has drained, chop into 1-inch cubes.

❷ Heat olive oil in a large sauté pan over medium heat. Add garlic, onions, and bell peppers. Cook until the onion and peppers soften, about 5 minutes.

❸ Add tomatoes, zucchini, and eggplant. Bring to a boil and quickly reduce the heat to a low simmer. Add remaining 1 teaspoon of salt. Continue to simmer, slowly, for approximately 45 minutes.

❹ Remove from heat; stir in basil and marjoram. Serve hot or cold.

Serves: 6. Preparation Time is 45 minutes. Cooking Time is 1 hour.

Morning Breakfast Sausage Patties

¡◎!¡

INGREDIENTS

2 pounds ground pork

1-1/2 teaspoons dried sage

1/2 teaspoon dried marjoram

1/8 teaspoon ground ginger

1/8 teaspoon crushed red pepper

2 teaspoons salt

1-1/2 teaspoons pepper

1/4 cup cold water

2 tablespoons canola oil

INSTRUCTIONS

❶ Place ground pork in a large mixing bowl. Whisk together all spices with the water and add to the ground pork. Using your hands, knead and squeeze the meat mixture until well blended.

❷ Form the mixture into thin patties measuring approximately 2-1/2 inches across, yielding about 16 to 20 patties.

❸ Heat oil in a large non-stick skillet over medium-high heat. Working in batches, cook patties until evenly browned and centers are cooked through, about 3 to 4 minutes per side. Serve warm.

RECIPE NOTES

Uncooked sausage patties will keep refrigerated for 3 days or frozen up to 3 months. Cooked patties can be frozen up to 2 months.

Serves: 6. Preparation Time is 10 minutes. Cooking Time is 15 minutes.

Country Chicken and Apple Sausage Patties

¶◎¶

INGREDIENTS

1 large green apple

1 medium white onion

4 tablespoons extra light tasting olive oil, divided

1-1/2 teaspoons fennel seeds

2 pounds ground chicken

1 tablespoon fresh chopped sage leaves

2 teaspoons sweet paprika

1/4 teaspoon cayenne pepper

1/4 teaspoon nutmeg

2 teaspoons salt

1 teaspoon white pepper

INSTRUCTIONS

❶ Using a cheese grater, grate the apple and onion into shreds, reserving any extracted juices.

❷ Heat 2 tablespoons of the extra light tasting olive oil in a small skillet over medium heat. Add grated apples, onions, and fennel seeds. Gently sauté the mixture until apples and onions begin to soften, about 3 to 5 minutes. Set aside and allow mixture to cool.

❸ Meanwhile, combine ground chicken and remaining ingredients in a large mixing bowl. Add cooled apple mixture. Using your hands, knead and squeeze the mixture until well blended.

❹ Form the mixture into thin patties measuring approximately 2-1/2 inches across, yielding about 16 to 20 patties.

❺ Heat remaining oil in a large, non-stick skillet over medium heat. Cook patties 3 to 4 minutes per side, or until cooked through. Serve warm.

RECIPE NOTES

Uncooked sausage patties will keep refrigerated for 3 days or frozen up to 3 months. Cooked patties can be frozen up to 2 months.

Serves: 4. Preparation Time is 10 minutes. Cooking Time is 15 minutes.

Heavenly Hash

⅋◎⍾

INGREDIENTS

1-1/2 pounds russet potatoes, about 2 to 3 medium potatoes

12 ounces cooked roast beef

1 medium red onion, diced

1 medium green pepper, diced

1 teaspoon dried thyme

3/4 teaspoon salt

1/2 teaspoon pepper

1/4 cup canola oil

1 tablespoon fresh chopped parsley

INSTRUCTIONS

❶ Rinse and peel potatoes. Pierce potatoes with a fork and cook on high in microwave for 5 minutes. Remove potatoes from microwave oven and allow to cool slightly before handling. The potatoes should not be completely cooked at this point, or they will fall apart during grating process. They will finish cooking in steps 3 and 4.

❷ Grate cooked beef and potatoes using a cheese grater, or preferably a meat grinder. Toss together with diced onion, green pepper, thyme, salt, and pepper.

❸ Heat olive oil in a heavy medium skillet over medium-high heat. Add beef-potato mixture. Allow to cook for 3 to 5 minutes until peppers and onions begin to soften.

❹ Press mixture flat against the pan. Cook the hash, covered, for 5 minutes. The bottom should begin to brown and become slightly crispy.

❺ Using a spatula, turn over hash and continue to cook, uncovered, for 5 to 7 more minutes. Remove from heat; garnish with parsley and serve immediately.

RECIPE NOTES

A fabulous way to make traditional hash is to use an old-fashioned meat grinder to grind the meat and potatoes. Otherwise, a cheese grater works well. Alternatively, chop the meat and potatoes into small 1/2-inch pieces.

Serves: 4. Preparation Time is 5 minutes. Cooking Time is 20 minutes.

Southwestern Hash

This dish is a fantastic, low-fat, scrumptious way to jolt your palate awake for the day. One advantage to preparing your own hash rather than opening a can is your ability to control the amount of ingredients to meet individual dietary needs, such as daily salt intake.

INGREDIENTS

12 ounces boneless, skinless chicken breast

1 pound boiling potatoes

1-1/2 teaspoons dried parsley

1 teaspoon chili powder

1 teaspoon paprika

1 teaspoon ground cumin

1 teaspoon ground coriander

1/2 teaspoon garlic powder

1/8 teaspoon cayenne pepper

1 teaspoon salt

1/4 teaspoon black pepper

2 tablespoons extra light tasting olive oil

1 medium red bell pepper, chopped

1/2 large red onion, chopped

INSTRUCTIONS

❶ Cook chicken breast; cool and chop into bite-size pieces.

❷ Slice potatoes, with skins, into 1/2-inch cubes. Boil potatoes until 3/4 of the way done, about 5 minutes. Drain and set aside.

❸ Combine all the spices, salt, and pepper into a small dish and set aside.

❹ Heat oil in a large, heavy skillet over medium-high heat. Add red peppers and onions. Cook until peppers soften and onions begin to brown, about 10 minutes.

❺ Reduce heat to medium and add cooked chicken, potatoes, and spice mixture. Stir until ingredients are thoroughly coated. Using a spatula, press down on the mixture to compress into a single layer. Cook without disturbing for 10 to 12 minutes, or until the bottom is golden brown and slightly crispy.

❻ Remove from heat and carefully invert the hash onto a serving plate. Serve hot or warm.

Serves: 4. Preparation Time is 10 minutes. Cooking Time is 40 minutes.

Skillet Home Fries

¡◎¡↑

INGREDIENTS

2 pounds red boiling potatoes

1 medium yellow onion

1 medium green bell pepper

1 medium red bell pepper

1 large poblano pepper, diced

3 tablespoons extra light tasting olive oil

1 teaspoon salt

1/2 teaspoon pepper

INSTRUCTIONS

❶ Add potatoes to a large pot and cover with water. Boil until tender but not completely cooked through, about 10 to 12 minutes. Drain and set aside to cool.

❷ Meanwhile, halve the onion and brush the onion and the outside of the peppers with 1 tablespoon of olive oil. Roast on a grill or open flame for 2 to 3 minutes per side until cooked through and charred on all sides. Place peppers in a covered bowl and allow to steam for 5 minutes (this will help remove the skins.) Once cooled, remove skins of peppers, chop into 1/2-inch pieces, and toss with salt and pepper.

❸ Heat remaining 2 tablespoons of olive oil in a large skillet over high heat. Chop cooled potatoes into quarters and add to pan. Allow potatoes to sear, untouched, until the edges begin to brown, about 3 minutes. Reduce heat to medium and flip. Add peppers and onion to pan and continue to sauté, untouched, for another 3 to 5 minutes. Remove from heat and serve.

Serves: 4. Preparation Time is 5 minutes. Cooking Time is 25 minutes.

Oven-Roasted New Potatoes

¡©¡¡

INGREDIENTS

1/4 cup olive oil

4 cloves garlic, minced

1 teaspoon dried dill

1 teaspoon salt

2 pounds small new or red potatoes (boiling potatoes)

INSTRUCTIONS

Preheat oven to 375°F.

❶ Combine the olive oil, garlic, dill, and salt in a small food processor or blender. Pulse a few times to incorporate and set aside.

❷ Using a vegetable peeler, pare a narrow strip of peel around the middle of each potato, forming a continuous circle of open potato. Toss the pared potatoes together with the olive oil mixture, ensuring all potatoes are evenly coated.

❸ Transfer coated potatoes to a baking dish or rimmed baking sheet. Roast in oven until potatoes are cooked through and beginning to brown, about 40 minutes, turning potatoes one or two times during the roasting. Serve warm.

Serves: 4. Preparation Time is 10 minutes. Cooking Time is 40 minutes.

Baked Potato Chips

The following two potato recipes produce undoubtedly scrumptious potato sides using minimal ingredients. Mix up the recipes with different varieties of potatoes or try sprinkling them with some of the zesty spice mixes found in Chapter 7.

†◎†

INGREDIENTS

2 large Idaho potatoes

3 tablespoons olive oil

1/2 teaspoon salt

INSTRUCTIONS

Preheat oven to 375°F.

❶ Cut the potatoes into 1/16-inch slices using a mandolin. Spread slices on a lightly oiled, nonstick baking sheet and brush with olive oil. Sprinkle with salt.

❷ Bake for 15 minutes or until golden brown.

Serves: 4. Preparation Time is 5 minutes. Cooking Time is 15 minutes.

Sweet Potato Matchsticks

†◎|†

INGREDIENTS

2 large sweet potatoes, peeled

2 cups canola oil

1-1/2 teaspoons salt

1 teaspoon lime zest

INSTRUCTIONS

❶ Using a vegetable peeler, shave the sweet potatoes into long strips.

❷ Meanwhile, heat oil in a large skillet over medium-high heat. The oil should measure about 1 inch deep; more or less oil may be needed.

❸ Working in batches, fry the sweet potato shavings until lightly browned, about 2 minutes. Drain on paper towels and toss with salt and lime zest. Serve immediately.

Serves: 6. Preparation Time is 5 minutes. Cooking Time is 5 minutes.

Confetti Rice

Not only is this confetti rice an entertaining side dish for the eyes, the combination of lemon zest and mint produces a mini-party in your mouth with every bite.

⍾◎⍾

INGREDIENTS

2-1/4 cups water

2 tablespoons lemon juice

1 cup long-grain white rice

1/4 cup extra light tasting olive oil

2 cloves garlic, minced

1 medium white onion, diced

2 medium carrots, diced

1 teaspoon salt

1/2 tablespoon lemon zest

1/4 cup fresh chopped mint leaves

INSTRUCTIONS

❶ Bring water and lemon juice to a boil. Add rice, reduce heat to low, and simmer, covered, until rice is cooked, about 20 minutes.

❷ Meanwhile, heat oil in a sauté pan over medium heat. Add the garlic and sauté for 2 minutes. Add the onion and carrots and sauté until onions become translucent and carrots soften, about 5 minutes.

❸ Add vegetables to cooked rice along with salt, lemon zest, and mint. Fluff with fork and serve warm or chilled.

Serves: 4. Preparation Time is 5 minutes. Cooking Time is 20 minutes.

Brown Rice Pilaf

🍴◎🍴

INGREDIENTS

4 ounces dried porcini mushrooms

4 cups hot water

2 teaspoons salt, divided

2 cups brown rice

2-1/4 cups canola oil

1 cup shredded carrots

1/2 cup chopped green onions

1 teaspoon dried marjoram

2 tablespoons fresh chopped parsley

1/2 teaspoon pepper

INSTRUCTIONS

❶ Place dried porcini mushrooms in a bowl and cover with hot water. Allow to steep for 30 minutes. After 30 minutes, drain the mushrooms and reserve all of the mushroom stock. Strain the liquid through a paper towel to remove any dirt or particles. Add 1 teaspoon of salt directly to the stock, stir to dissolve, and set aside. Rinse mushrooms, chop, and set aside.

❷ Heat a dry sauté pan over low-medium heat. Add rice and toast for 2 to 3 minutes to bring out the nutty flavor. Remove from heat and set rice aside in a separate bowl.

❸ In the same sauté pan, heat canola oil over medium heat. Add carrots and green onions and sauté until vegetables soften, about 3 to 5 minutes. Add toasted rice, mushrooms, and marjoram. Stir to coat everything and sauté for another 2 minutes.

❹ Add mushroom stock and remaining 1 teaspoon of salt. Bring mixture to a boil. Reduce heat to low and simmer the rice, covered, for 20 minutes, or until rice is cooked. Stir in fresh parsley and pepper, fluff with fork, and serve.

RECIPE NOTES

▫ To make a pilaf out of completely natural, minimally processed ingredients, a natural mushroom stock is used, which marries well with the brown rice. Since this recipe is composed entirely of natural ingredients, it calls for a fair amount of salt. However, this amount can be altered to fit individual dietary needs.

▫ Add heated peas, toasted flax seeds, or raisins to spice up this recipe.

Serves: 8. Preparation Time is 30 minutes. Cooking Time is 20 minutes.

Stuffed Tomatoes

¡◎¡↑

INGREDIENTS

1 cup arborio rice

1/4 cup olive oil, plus more for drizzling

1 clove garlic, minced

1 medium shallot, minced

4 large beef steak (or other large) tomatoes

1/4 cup fresh chopped basil

2 tablespoons fresh chopped parsley

1/2 teaspoon salt

1/4 teaspoon pepper

INSTRUCTIONS

Preheat oven to 350°F.

❶ Bring a large pot of water to boiling. Cook rice in water until just cooked through. Drain and rinse rice, and set aside.

❷ Meanwhile, heat oil in a small sauté pan over medium heat. Sauté the garlic and shallots until they begin to sweat, about 3 to 5 minutes. Remove from heat and set aside.

❸ Slice off the top of each tomato and scoop out the inner flesh. Reserve about 1/3 cup of the flesh. Drizzle a little olive oil in a baking dish and place tomatoes upright in the dish.

❹ Mix the reserved pulp together with the cooked rice, garlic, and shallots. Add the fresh basil and parsley, salt, and pepper. Stuff each tomato with the rice mixture and drizzle with a little olive oil. Replace the tomato lids and bake in preheated oven for 25 minutes, or until the tomatoes begin to shrivel and the rice is heated through. Serve warm or refrigerate for up to 8 hours and serve chilled.

Serves: 4. Preparation Time is 15 minutes. Cooking Time is 30 minutes.

Pan-Seared Mushrooms

Searing is not just for steak. Creating a seared dish is quick and easy, and it's the perfect way to cook on busy weeknights. Searing is the technique of cooking something hot and fast in order to brown the surface and seal in the juices. Both of these tactics increase the flavor impact of the ingredient being seared.

🍴◎🍴

INGREDIENTS

16 ounces cremini mushrooms, sliced

1/4 cup chopped flat leaf parsley

1 teaspoon fresh oregano

1 teaspoon fresh thyme leaves

1 clove garlic, minced

1/4 cup olive oil

INSTRUCTIONS

❶ Combine all ingredients in a medium bowl and set aside.

❷ Heat a medium cast iron skillet (or nonstick pan) over high heat. Add seasoned mushrooms and sear in the pan without touching for approximately 3 minutes. Flip once and continue cooking for 2 more minutes. Remove from heat and serve warm.

Serves: 4. Preparation Time is 5 minutes. Cooking Time is 5 minutes.

Oven-Roasted Asparagus and Leeks

⏐◎⏐⏐

INGREDIENTS

1/4 cup olive oil

1 clove garlic, chopped

1 teaspoon fresh thyme leaves

1 teaspoon lemon zest

1/2 teaspoon salt

8 medium leeks, washed and trimmed of roots and green tops

1 pound asparagus, chopped into 1-inch pieces

INSTRUCTIONS

Preheat oven to 400°F.

❶ Combine the olive oil, garlic, thyme, lemon zest, and salt in a small bowl. Set aside.

❷ Arrange the leeks and asparagus on a 9×13-inch rimmed baking sheet or baking dish. Drizzle with olive oil mixture and toss vegetables to ensure even coating.

❸ Roast until vegetables are tender and slightly charred, about 20 minutes.

Serves: 6. Preparation Time is 5 minutes. Cooking Time is 20 minutes.

Green Beans with Summer Herbs

¡◎¡¡

INGREDIENTS

2 pounds green beans, stems trimmed

2 teaspoons salt, divided

1 tablespoon lemon juice

1 clove garlic, crushed

3 tablespoons olive oil

1/4 cup chopped fresh basil

1/4 cup chopped fresh mint

INSTRUCTIONS

❶ Bring a large pot of water to a boil. Add green beans, 1 teaspoon of salt, and lemon juice. Boil the beans until tender, but still vibrant green, about 6 to 8 minutes. Drain and rinse with cool water. Set aside.

❷ Meanwhile, sprinkle 1/2 teaspoon of salt onto the clove of garlic. Mash the clove into a paste by alternating mincing and mashing motions with the side of the knife.

❸ Combine the garlic paste in a large bowl with the remaining 1/2 teaspoon of salt, olive oil, and fresh herbs. Add the cooked green beans, toss, and serve at room temperature or chilled.

Serves: 6. Preparation time is 5 minutes. Cooking Time is 10 minutes.

Homemade Chicken Stock

¡◎¡¡

INGREDIENTS

2 celery stalks

2 large carrots

1 large yellow onion

1 medium parsnip

1 large leek

3-1/2 pounds chicken parts

4 quarts water

4 cloves garlic

2 medium bay leaves

2 sprigs fresh thyme leaves

2 teaspoons salt

1 teaspoon peppercorns

INSTRUCTIONS

❶ Coarsely chop celery, carrots, onion, parsnip, and leek into large pieces.

❷ In a large stockpot, combine all the ingredients and bring to a boil. Reduce heat to low and simmer, uncovered, for about 2 hours. Skim off any fat that forms on the top.

❸ Remove the chicken parts and remove meat from the bones. Save meat for another use.

❹ Remove from the heat and let the stock cool completely. Strain through a fine sieve, or a colander double-lined with paper towels. Be sure to press down on the solids to extract juices and maximize the flavor. Discard the solids.

❺ Store stock in airtight containers for up to 3 days until ready to use. Scrape off and discard any fat that has risen to top prior to use.

RECIPE NOTES

I prefer to make chicken stock with chicken parts rather than a carcass. It is an easier method that lends to a more flavorful stock, and provides fantastic leftover, pre-cooked chicken for another use.

Freeze up to 3 months.

Serves: 8. Preparation Time is 5 minutes. Cooking Time is 2 hours.

Homemade Beef Stock

🍴◎🍴

INGREDIENTS

2 tablespoons olive oil

4 pounds beef shanks

1 large white onion

2 large carrots

1 large leek

1 celery stalk

4 cloves garlic

2 teaspoons salt, divided

12 cups water

8 sprigs flat leaf parsley

4 sprigs thyme

1 medium bay leaf

1 tablespoon whole black peppercorns

INSTRUCTIONS

Preheat oven to 400°F.

❶ Using olive oil, lightly coat a roasting pan. Place beef shanks in roasting pan and roast in oven for 15 minutes.

❷ Meanwhile, coarsely chop the onion, carrots, leek, and celery. Add these vegetables, along with garlic cloves, to the roasting pan. Season beef and vegetables with 1 teaspoon of salt and roast, turning occasionally, until the bones are well browned, about 40 minutes.

❸ Transfer the meat, bones, and vegetables to a large stockpot. Add 2 to 3 cups of water to roasting pan and scrape up any brown bits. Pour caramelized cooking juices into soup pot with remaining 9 to 10 cups of water, herbs, peppercorns, and remaining salt.

❹ Bring stockpot to a boil. Reduce heat and simmer for about 2 hours, occasionally skimming off any foam and fat from top.

❺ Remove from heat and allow to cool. Strain through a fine sieve, or a colander double-lined with paper towels. Be sure to press down on the solids to extract juices and maximize the flavor. Discard the solids.

❻ Store stock in airtight containers until ready to use. Store in refrigerator up to 3 days. Scrape off and discard any fat that has risen to top prior to use.

RECIPE NOTES

Roasting the beef bones and vegetables prior to simmering them in the water provides a full-bodied and healthy flavor far surpassing that of any store-bought version.

 Freeze up to 3 months.

Serves: 8. Preparation Time is 5 minutes. Cooking Time is 3 hours.

Homemade Vegetable Stock

🍽

INGREDIENTS

2 tablespoons olive oil

1 large white onion

2 large carrots

2 medium parsnips

2 large leeks

8 ounces mushrooms

8 sprigs flat leaf parsley

4 sprigs fresh dill

1 tablespoon peppercorns

2 teaspoons salt

INSTRUCTIONS

❶ Wash and coarsely chop vegetables. In a large stockpot, heat oil on medium-high heat. Add onion, cooking until caramelized, about 15 minutes.

❷ Add carrots, parsnips, and leeks. Cook until tender, about 10 minutes.

❸ Add 12 cups of water along with remaining ingredients. Bring to a boil. Reduce heat and simmer, uncovered, for about 2 hours.

❹ Remove from heat and allow to cool completely, about 1 hour. Strain through a fine sieve, or a colander double-lined with paper towels. Be sure to press down on the solids to extract juices and maximize the flavor. Discard the solids.

❺ Store stock in airtight containers until ready to use. Store in refrigerator up to 3 days.

RECIPE NOTES

Allowing the stock to cool completely before straining achieves two important tasks. Not only do you minimize any burn catastrophes, but you get the maximal flavor out of all the ingredients.

Freeze up to 3 months.

Serves: 8. Preparation Time is 10 minutes. Inactive Preparation Time is 1 hour. Cooking Time is 2 hours 25 minutes.

Homemade Marinara Sauce

†◎⑂

INGREDIENTS

2-1/2 pounds vine-ripe tomatoes

1/4 cup olive oil

3 cloves garlic, minced

1/4 cup chopped onion

2 tablespoons fresh chopped basil

3/4 teaspoon salt

1/4 teaspoon pepper

INSTRUCTIONS

❶ Prepare an ice-water bath by filling a large bowl with 1/3 ice and 2/3 water and set aside.

❷ Bring a large pot of water to a boil. Cut an X in the bottom of each tomato and place tomatoes in boiling water until skins just begin to loosen, about 10 to 20 seconds. Remove tomatoes and immediately transfer to ice-water bath. Remove tomatoes from water and peel away the skins. Slice tomatoes in half. Remove and discard seeds and liquid. Cut the flesh into 1/2-inch pieces.

❸ Heat olive oil in a large skillet over medium-low heat. Add garlic and onion and cook until onions are translucent, about 3 to 4 minutes.

❹ Add chopped tomatoes, basil, salt, and pepper. Reduce heat to low-medium and simmer sauce until tomatoes break down somewhat to a saucy consistency, about 15 minutes. Remove from heat and, if desired, place in a food processor and pulse until smooth. The tomato sauce can be stored in an airtight container in the refrigerator for up to 3 days.

RECIPE NOTES

It's easy to over-blanch tomatoes, causing the flesh to become mushy. To test, simply remove a tomato from the water after ten seconds and gently pinch with two fingers. The skin should have just a slight give and feel slightly less taut than when raw. To avoid over-blanching, it is best to work in batches so as not to drastically alter the waters temperature by adding too many tomatoes at once.

Up to 3 months.

Serves: 4. Preparation Time is 15 minutes. Cooking Time is 30 minutes.

"As a teacher I am amazed by how many children have food allergies. And, it seems there are more and more each year."

BENHAM LATIMER, 4TH GRADE TEACHER, NEW YORK, NY

Chapter ❷

Appetizers

Whether meeting friends for drinks and making appetizers into an impromptu dinner or ordering a delicious starter course as part of a festive dinner for two, everyone loves appetizers. This chapter provides you with tasty options when entertaining in your home, bringing a dish to a social engagement, or simply fancying a light meal for yourself. The majority of recipes call for readily available ingredients, while others slowly incorporate alternative products. All are meant to ease you into hypoallergenic cooking.

Honey-Roasted Chickpeas

¶○¶

INGREDIENTS

1 teaspoon extra light tasting olive oil

2 tablespoons honey

2 tablespoons sugar

1 tablespoon brown sugar

1 teaspoon salt

2 15-ounce cans garbanzo beans, drained and rinsed

INSTRUCTIONS

Preheat oven to 325°F.

❶ Oil a large, nonstick, rimmed baking sheet with the extra light tasting olive oil.

❷ In a separate bowl, microwave the honey on high for 20 seconds. Immediately add the sugars and salt. Toss honey mixture together with the garbanzo beans and spread evenly in a single layer on the prepared pan.

❸ Roast on the bottom rack of the oven until browned and crunchy, about 1 hour. Be sure to shake the pan every 10 to 15 minutes to ensure an even roasting.

RECIPE NOTES

Chili Chickpeas: Toss chickpeas with 2 tablespoons extra light tasting olive oil, 1/2 teaspoon chili powder, 1/2 teaspoon cumin, and 1 teaspoon salt.

Cajun-roasted Chickpeas: Toss chickpeas with 2 tablespoons extra light tasting olive oil and 2 teaspoons of the cajun spice rub on page 234.

Serves: 8. Preparation Time is 5 minutes. Cooking Time is 1 hour.

Salsa I

¶◎↾↾

INGREDIENTS

1 tablespoon olive oil

1 clove garlic, minced

1 medium jalapeno pepper, seeded and coarsely chopped

1 medium poblano pepper, seeded and coarsely chopped

8 medium roma tomatoes, seeded and chopped

1 large yellow onion, chopped

1/2 teaspoon sugar

1/2 teaspoon celery salt

1/4 teaspoon oregano

1 teaspoon salt

1/2 teaspoon pepper

1/2 cup water

1/4 cup fresh chopped cilantro

INSTRUCTIONS

❶ Heat oil in a large skillet over high heat. Add garlic and peppers. Sauté until the garlic and pepper skins begin to brown, about 3 to 5 minutes.

❷ Reduce heat to medium. Add tomatoes and onion and sauté for another 3 to 5 minutes. Remove from heat and allow to cool.

❸ Meanwhile, combine the sugar, spices, salt, pepper, and water in a food processor or blender. Add the pepper and tomato mixture and pulse a few times to a chunky consistency. Transfer to a serving bowl, stir in cilantro, and serve or store in refrigerator up to 3 days.

Serves: 4. Preparation Time is 10 minutes. Cooking Time is 10 minutes.

Salsa II

While not as fresh-tasting as the previous recipe, this salsa packs tons of flavor and can be made in 5 minutes with items stocked in your pantry.

¶◎¶

INGREDIENTS

1 medium yellow onion, chopped

1 tablespoon canned, diced jalapeno peppers

1 28-ounce can whole peeled tomatoes in juice

1/4 teaspoon celery salt

1/2 teaspoon garlic salt

1/2 teaspoon sugar

INSTRUCTIONS

❶ In a food processor or blender, combine the onion and jalapeno peppers. Pulse a few times until onions are finely diced.

❷ Add tomatoes with juice and remaining ingredients. Pulse until well blended, but still a little bit chunky. For best results, chill a few hours before serving. Store in refrigerator up to 5 days.

Serves: 8. Preparation Time is 5 minutes.

Pico de Gallo

†◎⋕

INGREDIENTS

3 large vine-ripe tomatoes, seeded and diced

1 large onion, diced

1 small jalapeno pepper, seeded and diced

1/4 cup fresh chopped cilantro

1 teaspoon salt

1/2 teaspoon black pepper

1/2 teaspoon garlic powder

1 tablespoon olive oil

1 tablespoon white wine vinegar

INSTRUCTIONS

❶ Combine all ingredients in a large bowl. Stir until all ingredients are well blended. Refrigerate for at least 4 to 6 hours before serving, preferably overnight. Serve as a topping for any dish or alongside tortilla chips.

RECIPE NOTES

For a milder version, substitute 1/2 green pepper for the jalapeno.

Serves: 4. Preparation Time is 10 minutes.

Guacamole

¡◎⫯

INGREDIENTS

1 head garlic

1 teaspoon olive oil

3 medium avocados

1 tablespoon lime juice

1/2 teaspoon green pepper Tabasco sauce

1 teaspoon coarse sea salt

1/2 cup chopped tomatoes

1/2 cup chopped white onions

INSTRUCTIONS

Preheat oven to 400°F.

❶ Cut and discard the top third of the head of garlic. Loosely wrap garlic in aluminum foil and drizzle olive oil on exposed garlic. Roast in oven for approximately 50 minutes, or until garlic is golden brown and caramelized. Remove from oven and set aside until cool enough to handle. Once cool, grasp the root end of garlic head and gently squeeze to remove the caramelized cloves from the skin. Extract about 4 to 6 cloves and set aside.

❷ Peel and pit avocados and transfer to a blender. Add roasted garlic, lime juice, green pepper Tabasco sauce, and sea salt. Pulse a few times to desired consistency.

❸ Transfer avocado mixture to a bowl. Add chopped tomatoes and onions and stir until well mixed. Serve immediately.

RECIPE NOTES

The key to this version of guacamole is the roasted garlic and coarse sea salt. While roasting the garlic takes about 50 minutes, the combination of the roasted garlic and the green pepper Tabasco sauce adds just the right amount of zing and keeps everyone wondering why your guacamole is so delicious.

Serves: 8. Preparation Time is 5 minutes. Cooking Time is 50 minutes.

Tuscan Bean Dip

❢◎❢

INGREDIENTS

1 head garlic

1/3 cup olive oil, divided

1 15-ounce can cannellini beans, drained and rinsed

2 tablespoons fresh lemon juice

1/8 cup fresh chopped parsley

1 teaspoon salt

1/4 teaspoon pepper

INSTRUCTIONS

Preheat oven to 400°F.

❶ Cut and discard the top third of the head of garlic. Loosely wrap garlic in aluminum foil and drizzle 1 tablespoon of olive oil on exposed garlic. Roast in oven for approximately 50 minutes, or until garlic is golden brown and caramelized. Remove from oven and set aside until cool enough to handle. Once cool, grasp the root end of garlic head and gently squeeze to remove the caramelized cloves from the skin. Reserve about 8 cloves.

❷ Place the roasted garlic cloves, beans, lemon juice, parsley, salt, and pepper in a food processor. Add remaining olive oil continuously as you puree until the mixture is smooth. Transfer bean dip to a small bowl and serve with crackers, toasted bread, or vegetables. Dip can be stored in refrigerator, covered, up to 3 days.

Serves: 6. Preparation Time is 5 minutes. Cooking Time is 50 minutes.

Eight Layer Dip

The eight layers of this dip are as follows: refried beans, grated onion, tomatoes, avocado, lettuce, scallions, olives, and jalapenos.

🍽

INGREDIENTS

3 large avocados

3/4 teaspoon garlic salt

1 medium lime

1 15-ounce can refried beans (or 1/2 recipe on page 206)

1 teaspoon cumin (optional)

1 tablespoon water (optional)

1/2 medium white onion, grated

3 medium vine-ripe tomatoes, seeded and diced

1 teaspoon salt, divided

4 medium scallions, chopped

1/3 head iceberg lettuce, shredded

1/2 cup black olives, sliced

3 tablespoons canned, diced jalapeno peppers

INSTRUCTIONS

❶ Peel and chop avocados. Combine avocados with garlic salt and juice from 1/2 the lime in a small mixing bowl. Mash the avocados with a fork until you reach the consistency of guacamole. Set aside.

❷ Mix the can of refried beans with cumin and water (omit this step if you are using refried beans from recipe on page 206). Spread evenly on the bottom of an 8- or 9-inch square casserole dish.

❸ Next, being layering. Spread the grated onion, with any residual juices, on top of the beans. Layer the tomatoes on top of the onions. Sprinkle 1/2 teaspoon of salt on top of the tomatoes.

❹ Next, spread the avocados evenly over the tomatoes. Layer on the chopped scallions, followed by the shredded lettuce, sliced black olives, and finally the diced jalapenos.

❺ Sprinkle the remaining 1/2 teaspoon of salt over the top, along with the juice from the remaining 1/2 lime. Garnish with a few sprigs of cilantro and serve with tortilla chips or your favorite cracker.

Serves: 8. Preparation Time is 15 minutes.

Caponata

ꞮꙶꞮꞮ

INGREDIENTS

1 large eggplant, diced

1-1/4 teaspoons salt, divided

1/4 cup olive oil

2 cloves garlic, minced

1 large cubanelle pepper, seeded and diced

1/2 medium red onion, diced

2 medium roma tomatoes, seeded and diced

1/2 cup sliced olives

1/3 cup golden raisins

3 tablespoons capers, drained

2 tablespoons pimientos, drained

1/4 cup red wine vinegar

1 28-ounce can crushed tomatoes

1/2 teaspoon pepper

1/2 teaspoon red pepper flakes

2 tablespoons fresh chopped basil

INSTRUCTIONS

❶ Sprinkle 3/4 teaspoon of salt over diced eggplant and set aside.

❷ Heat oil in a medium soup pot over medium heat. Add garlic and sauté for 3 minutes. Add pepper and onion. Sauté until vegetables soften, about 5 minutes.

❸ Add the eggplant and roma tomatoes and sauté for 5 minutes.

❹ Add the olives, raisins, capers, pimientos, vinegar, canned tomatoes, remaining 1/2 teaspoon of salt, pepper, and red pepper flakes. Stir, cover the pot, and cook for 20 minutes until vegetables are tender.

❺ Remove pot from heat, stir in fresh basil, and serve warm or chilled with slices of grilled bread, on top of polenta wedges, or in individual lettuce cups. Store in refrigerator up to 3 days.

Serves: 8. Preparation Time is 10 minutes. Cooking Time is 30 minutes.

Tapenade

†◎‖

INGREDIENTS

3 tablespoons capers, drained

2 cups black olives, pitted

2 tablespoons brandy

3 tablespoons extra virgin olive oil

2 cloves garlic

1 teaspoon thyme

1 teaspoon salt

1/4 teaspoon black pepper

INSTRUCTIONS

❶ Combine all ingredients in a food processor or blender and process until the mixture is still a bit coarse, but of a uniform consistency. Spread on toasted bread, crackers, or serve as a dip for crudités. Tapenade also works well as a topping for grilled chicken served over white rice, or as a spread for sandwiches.

RECIPE NOTES

▢ Brandy is generally distilled from pears, raspberries, cherries, peaches, or other fruits and is often gluten-free. However, check with the manufacture to ensure that your selected brand meets your personal dietary requirements.

▢ Substitute 2 tablespoons of lemon juice for brandy for a less sweet version.

Serves: 8. Preparation Time is 10 minutes.

Vegetable Tempura

￼

INGREDIENTS

4 cups canola oil

3/4 cup white rice flour

2/3 cup potato flour (starch)

1/4 cup tapioca flour

1 cup corn starch

1 teaspoon salt

2 cups club soda

4 cups fresh chopped vegetables of your choice

INSTRUCTIONS

❶ Heat canola oil in a large sauté pan or fryer. The oil should measure about 1 inch deep in the pan; more or less oil may be needed.

❷ Combine the flours, corn starch, and salt in a large mixing bowl. Slowly add in the club soda, being careful that it does not fizz over the top of the bowl. Stir just a few times to obtain a thick batter.

❸ Make sure the oil is hot enough and, working in batches, dip vegetables in batter and place in hot oil. Fry until batter is a golden brown on all sides, about 3 to 5 minutes. Transfer to a plate covered with a paper towel to drain off excess oil. Serve immediately with the Sweet and Sour Dipping Sauce or Smoky Chipotle Dip.

RECIPE NOTES

The best vegetables for this recipe are vegetables containing crevices the batter can seep into, such as broccoli or cauliflower. A simple way to determine if the oil is hot enough for frying is to place the stem of a wooden spoon into the oil. If tiny bubbles emerge along the sides of the spoon stem, the oil is ready.

Potato flour, otherwise known as potato starch flour or potato starch, is a fine-textured, gluten-free flour made from cooked, dried, and ground potatoes. It is quite versatile as it is great for baking or as a thickening agent.

Add 2 teaspoons of creole seasoning to the batter.

Serves: 4. Preparation Time is 10 minutes. Cooking Time is 15 minutes.

Jalapeno Poppers

†◎↟

INGREDIENTS

2 medium baked potatoes

1/4 cup potato flour (starch),
    plus 1 tablespoon

3/4 cup rice milk

2 tablespoons olive oil

1 medium white onion, grated

1-1/2 teaspoons salt, divided

3 cups cooked brown rice

3 tablespoons tomato paste

1/2 teaspoon garlic powder

1/2 teaspoon pepper

1/4 cup canned, diced jalapeno peppers

1-1/2 cups bread crumbs

6 cups canola oil

INSTRUCTIONS

❶ Pierce potatoes with fork and bake in oven until cooked, about 50 minutes (or microwave on high for 8 to 10 minutes). Scoop out the cooked potato flesh and combine with potato flour and rice milk in a large mixing bowl.

❷ Meanwhile, heat olive oil in a small sauté pan. Add grated onion and 1/2 teaspoon of salt. Sauté just until the onions begin to sweat, about 3 to 5 minutes. Remove from heat and add to mashed potatoes.

❸ Add the cooked rice, tomato paste, garlic powder, remaining salt, and pepper to the mixing bowl. Using your hands, knead the mixture together to incorporate all the ingredients. Add jalapenos and stir just a few times to evenly disperse the peppers.

❹ Roll the mixture into 1-inch balls and coat with bread crumbs. If necessary, refrigerate filling for up to 2 hours to ease the rolling.

❺ Heat oil in a large skillet. The oil should measure at least 1 inch deep; more or less oil may be needed. Working in batches, fry the poppers until golden brown on all sides, about 3 to 5 minutes. Transfer to a paper towel to drain. Serve with Enchilada/Taco Sauce as a dip.

RECIPE NOTES

💡 Substitute 1-1/2 cups of leftover mashed potatoes for the baked potatoes, potato flour, and rice milk.

🍲 For a lower-fat version, bake frozen poppers in a 375°F oven for 45 minutes, or until outside is well browned and crispy and poppers are heated through.

🍲 To alter the amount of heat, add more or less jalapeno peppers. Additionally, add up to 1 tablespoon of hot sauce or Tabasco sauce.

▢ Up to 3 months. Freeze poppers prior to frying, after step 4. When ready to use, heat oil and fry frozen poppers for 5 to 7 minutes until golden brown and heated through.

Serves: 8. Preparation Time is 15 minutes. Inactive Preparation Time is 2 hours. Cooking Time is 1 hour 15 minutes.

Buffalo Wings

❦◎❦

INGREDIENTS

1 tablespoon lard

1/4 cup hot pepper or Tabasco sauce

1 tablespoon honey

1/2 cup bread crumbs

1/2 cup potato flour (starch)

1 teaspoon paprika

1/4 teaspoon cayenne pepper

1/2 teaspoon salt

2 pounds chicken wings (or drumsticks)

4 cups canola oil

INSTRUCTIONS

Preheat oven to 350°F.

❶ Heat lard in a small saucepan over medium heat. Add hot pepper or Tabasco sauce and honey. Stir together until ingredients are well combined, remove from heat, and set aside.

❷ Combine bread crumbs, potato flour, paprika, cayenne pepper, and salt in a large resealable bag. Add chicken wings (or drumsticks) and toss together until wings are evenly coated.

❸ Heat canola oil in a large frying pan. The oil should be high enough to cover the wings entirely; more or less oil may be needed. Fry coated wings (working in batches if necessary) for 3 to 5 minutes per side, or until wings begin to brown. Remove from heat and transfer to a casserole dish. Pour hot sauce mixture over and bake in oven for 15 minutes, or until wings are cooked through. Serve warm with Sweet and Spicy Dipping Sauce alongside carrot or celery sticks.

RECIPE NOTES

Serves: 8. Preparation Time is 5 minutes. Cooking Time is 25 minutes.

Sweet and Sour Wings

¡◎¡ᵼ

INGREDIENTS

4 cups canola oil

3/4 cup tapioca flour, plus 2 tablespoons, divided

20 ounces chicken wings

1/2 cup honey

1/4 cup fresh lime juice

1 tablespoon lemon zest

1 clove garlic, minced

1 teaspoon salt

1/2 teaspoon pepper

INSTRUCTIONS

❶ Heat oil in a large skillet over medium-high heat. The oil should measure at least 1-inch deep; more or less oil may be needed.

❷ Place 3/4 cup of tapioca flour in a large resealable bag. Shake the chicken wings in the flour to coat. Place coated wings in oil and fry until cooked through, about 5 to 7 minutes.

❸ Meanwhile, place the honey in a microwaveable bowl and microwave on high for 30 seconds. Immediately add the lime juice, lemon zest, garlic, salt, and pepper. Whisk in the remaining 2 tablespoons of tapioca starch and return to microwave for another 30 seconds. Stir.

❹ Place cooked wings in a baking dish and cover with the honey mixture. Toss to ensure even coating. Serve warm.

RECIPE NOTES

🖽 Tapioca flour is a great complement to the honey in this recipe. The tapioca thickens the sauce but allows the sauce to retain a clear finish.

Serves: 8. Preparation Time is 5 minutes. Cooking Time is 15 minutes.

Honey Mustard Wings

⦙◎⦙

INGREDIENTS

1 tablespoon lard

2/3 cup honey

1/4 cup Dijon mustard

1/4 cup rice vinegar

1 teaspoon curry powder

1/2 cup bread crumbs

1/2 cup potato flour (starch)

1/2 teaspoon cumin

1/2 teaspoon salt

2 pounds chicken wings (or drumsticks)

4 cups canola oil

INSTRUCTIONS

Preheat oven to 350°F.

❶ Heat lard in a small saucepan over medium heat. Add honey, mustard, vinegar, and curry powder. Stir together until ingredients are well incorporated, remove from heat, and set aside.

❷ Combine bread crumbs, potato flour, cumin, and salt in a large resealable bag. Add chicken wings (or drumsticks) and toss together until wings are evenly coated.

❸ Heat canola oil in a large frying pan. The oil should be high enough to cover the wings entirely; more or less oil may be needed. Working in batches, fry coated wings for 3 to 5 minutes per side, or until wings begin to brown. Remove from heat and transfer to a casserole dish. Pour honey mustard sauce over and bake in oven for 15 minutes, or until wings are cooked through. Serve warm.

Serves: 4. Preparation Time is 5 minutes. Cooking Time is 25 minutes.

Baked Stuffed Mushrooms

¶◎↿

INGREDIENTS

24 large stuffing mushrooms, stems removed and reserved

3 tablespoons olive oil, divided

2 cloves garlic, minced

20 ounces ground Italian sausage

1/2 medium green bell pepper, diced

1/2 medium white onion, grated

3/4 cup bread crumbs

1 tablespoon dried parsley

1/2 teaspoon salt

INSTRUCTIONS

Preheat oven to 400°F.

❶ Using your hands, lightly rub mushroom caps with 1 tablespoon of olive oil. Place oiled caps in a single layer in a baking dish.

❷ Chop about 1/2 of the reserved mushroom stems and set aside. Toss remaining stems or reserve for another use.

❸ Heat remaining 2 tablespoons of olive oil in a large sauté pan. Add garlic and sauté for 2 minutes. Add sausage and cook until browned and no longer pink.

❹ Add pepper, onion, and chopped mushroom stems. Continue to cook until vegetables soften, about 3 to 5 minutes.

❺ Remove pan from heat and stir in bread crumbs, parsley, and salt until thoroughly combined.

❻ Fill mushroom caps with stuffing using a small scoop or large spoon. Bake in middle of oven for 15 minutes, or until heated through. Serve warm.

Serves: 8. Preparation Time is 15 minutes. Cooking Time is 30 minutes.

Gyro Kabobs

¡◎¦ᵢ

INGREDIENTS

4 medium shallots, minced

1 clove garlic, minced

1-1/2 teaspoons salt, divided

1-1/2 pounds ground lamb

1/4 cup dried parsley

1 tablespoon ground coriander

1 teaspoon ground ginger

1 tablespoon olive oil

INSTRUCTIONS

❶ Combine the shallots and garlic. Sprinkle 1 teaspoon of the salt over the shallots and garlic and mince the mixture even more finely. The salt will create a nice friction making it easier to mince, while simultaneously releasing juices from the shallots and garlic and smoothing the consistency. Set aside for 10 minutes to allow natural juices to extract.

❷ Combine remaining salt with the ground lamb, parsley, coriander, and ginger in a large bowl of an electric mixer. Add minced shallots and garlic and mix on low speed until smooth and well blended. Be sure to mix on a low speed, otherwise the mixture will be too fluffy to hold on a skewer.

❸ Take a fistful of the meat and shape into a ball. Put a skewer in the center. Begin turning the skewer and meat in opposite directions, carefully squeezing meat so it moves along the skewer and becomes the shape of a flattened sausage. Kabobs should be about 1-1/2 inches wide, and 4 to 6 inches long. Repeat the process with remaining meat.

❹ Brush kabobs with olive oil and grill over medium-high heat for 8 to 10 minutes, turning skewers once during the cooking process. Serve warm.

RECIPE NOTES

▦ "Mincing" is the term used for the process of cutting garlic or onions with a very sharp knife into the smallest pieces possible. It is the opinion of many cooks that cutting garlic with a knife, as opposed to crushing or pressing, better preserves the nutty flavor of the garlic. Many kitchen pros use the following method when mincing or chopping garlic: make vertical cuts in a peeled clove very close together for mincing, further apart for chopping, but don't cut the clove completely apart; leave the root part intact. Make similar horizontal cuts and then cut crosswise. If you think the pieces still aren't small enough, use your knife in a rocking or chopping motion to cut the garlic even more finely.

▦ Metal skewers are generally used when grilling. If you use wooden skewers, soak skewers in water for 30 minutes before using to prevent them from burning.

Serves: 4. Preparation Time is 20 minutes. Cooking Time is 10 minutes.

Risotto Croquettes

¡◎¡¡

INGREDIENTS

4 cups risotto Milanese, refrigerated, recipe on page 175

2 cups bread crumbs

6 cups canola oil

1 teaspoon salt

INSTRUCTIONS

❶ If necessary, prepare Risotto Milanese (page 175) and refrigerate for 4 to 6 hours.

❷ Using a melon baller, form risotto into individual balls. Using hands, roll balls to firm up, then roll in bread crumbs. Refrigerate balls until ready to use.

❸ Heat oil in a large skillet. The oil should measure at least 1 inch deep; more or less oil may be needed. Working in batches, fry the risotto croquettes until golden brown on all sides, about 3 to 5 minutes. Transfer to a paper towel to drain and sprinkle with salt. Serve with marinara sauce as a dip.

RECIPE NOTES

Up to 3 months. Freeze croquettes prior to frying, after step 2. When ready to use, heat oil and fry frozen croquettes for 6 to 8 minutes until golden brown and heated through.

Serves: 12. Preparation Time is 15 minutes. Cooking Time is 10 minutes.

Asparagus Wrapped with Prosciutto

¶◎�

INGREDIENTS

1 cup balsamic vinegar

1/3 cup sugar

2 pounds asparagus

2 tablespoons lemon juice

1 teaspoon salt

16 slices prosciutto

INSTRUCTIONS

❶ Combine vinegar and sugar in a small saucepan over medium-high heat. Stir to dissolve the sugar and bring to a boil. Reduce heat to low and simmer until the vinegar reduces to 1/3 cup, about 20 minutes.

❷ Meanwhile, prepare a large ice bath of water and ice cubes.

❸ Bring a large pot of water to a boil over high heat. Trim the asparagus spears so that they are all the same length. When the water is boiling, add the lemon juice, salt, and asparagus spears and cook until just tender, about 3 minutes. Plunge the asparagus into the ice bath to stop them from cooking. When the spears are cold, remove from ice bath and lay them out onto a paper towel.

❹ To assemble, lay 2 or 3 spears together on the end of a piece of prosciutto. Roll up the prosciutto with the spears tucked snugly inside. Drizzle the wrapped spears with the reduced balsamic vinegar just prior to serving.

RECIPE NOTES

▤ Reduced balsamic and asparagus may be prepared and refrigerated up to 1 day in advance. Wrap with prosciutto just prior to serving to retain freshness.

Serves: 8. Preparation Time is 10 minutes. Cooking Time is 20 minutes.

"As a pediatric registered nurse, I felt that I had a lot of knowledge and experience working with patients who have food allergies. After learning my infant daughter was allergic to milk, soy, eggs, and peanuts, I quickly realized that the day to day implications of living with food allergies was significantly more challenging than I had previously thought. So many of life's holidays and major events are celebrated with food, and in my family, we are unable to simply eat something without first checking every ingredient."

SARA PAINE (MOTHER TO JULIA), REGISTERED NURSE, NEW CANAAN, CT.

Chapter ❸

Soups and Salads

In loving memory of Grandma Komlyn

One of my most vivid childhood memories is of piling out of the car after the nine-hour road trip from Connecticut, where my family lived, to Pittsburgh, the hometown of my father's family. It is not the journey I remember but the destination. Upon our arrival, my grandmother was always waiting at the door, even if we arrived in the middle of the night, which happened often. Regardless of the time of our arrival, the minute we emerged from the car we'd see my grandmother standing in the doorway, the delicious aroma from the simmering, stovetop pot of chicken soup filling the air behind her. Grandma's chicken soup – my father's favorite. After our arrival, we would laze around, talking and sipping soup, unwinding from the long journey as we watched my dad eat bowl after bowl of Grandma's homemade chicken soup.

We made the trip to Pittsburgh once or twice a year until I was nine years old and my grandmother passed away. She died from complications arising from an allergic reaction to the blood-thinning drug Coumadin. (An allergic reaction – go figure.) I recently learned through my dad's siblings that my dad probably suffered from multiple food allergies as a young child. Their most vivid recollections of him can be summed up in one sentence: *"Tony was either throwing up or eating bananas."*

My father was the youngest of six, although he only knew three of his siblings. My grandmother's first child was born stillborn. Then came Barbara, Rosemary, Donna, Nicholas, and finally Anthony, my dad. Rosemary died from pneumonia at the tender age of two-and-a-half. My heart dropped ten stories when my father told me this. Eerily, my daughter, Piper, suffered from several bouts of what we presumed was "pneumonia" throughout her second and third years of life. In Piper's case, extensive testing eventually contradicted our doctor's immediate diagnosis of pneumonia. We ultimately discovered that Piper was experiencing severe asthma attacks, often complicated by her food allergies. I can't help but wonder if Rosemary had asthma and/or severe allergies – not pneumonia – when she died in the early 1940s. Unfortunately, Rosemary lived her infant life during a time when we didn't have the capabilities to accurately diagnose, or the medical technology to rapidly treat, asthmatic symptoms.

I can only imagine the "life" my grandmother had. As difficult as it may be to have a child with severe food allergies today, I count my blessings that Piper was born in 2003. Instead of complaining about our situation, I know how lucky I am to have cooking conveniences, such as all-inclusive supermarkets, store-to-door grocery services, large freezers, dishwashers, microwaves, access to a multitude of alternative products, and inexpensive food storage containers. And these available cooking conveniences do not compare to the medical advances achieved over the past decades. Medical and other health-related advances have come so far in the last sixty years that, although we still have a long road ahead of us, many lives are saved every day that might have been lost years ago. And we all benefit from increased awareness and stringent regulations concerning food manufacturing and labeling practices.

Perhaps my grandmother and baby Rosemary might have survived longer had we known more about allergies back then. This chapter is dedicated to my grandmother who was taken from us way too soon, and for baby Rosemary who was taken even sooner. As an adult, I never had a chance to really get to know my grandmother. But I feel a very strong connection to her, as I know she labored over the stove for every meal. And I know that she did not complain. Quite simply, she did the best she could with what she had. As I cook I envision the kind of life she had and the type of person she was. As I watch my son Theo eagerly gobble up every batch of soup I make, I feel a very strong bond to my grandmother. I know she watched my father with the same adoring eyes. She loved her children dearly and did whatever was necessary to provide for them. By doing so she was a pioneer, unknowingly paving a smoother path for me.

Third-Generation Chicken Noodle Soup

This soup is so therapeutic when battling the flu. The ginger and spinach provide addition-al nourishment without adding extra sugar or carbohydrates.It is a great soup to always have on hand in the freezer ready to combat the first sign of any virus in the house.

🍴◎🍴

INGREDIENTS

12 cups water

2 pounds chicken parts

1 tablespoon salt

2 tablespoons olive oil

2 cloves garlic, crushed

1 tablespoon ginger root, grated

1 cup white onion, coarsely chopped

1 cup chopped carrots

1 cup chopped broccoli

2 cups rice noodles

1 cup spinach leaves, loosely packed

INSTRUCTIONS

❶ Add water to a large cooking pot and bring to a boil.

❷ Add chicken parts and salt. Simmer for 45 minutes to one hour, until chick-en is cooked. Remove cooked chicken to a platter and let cool. Once chicken has cooled, cut off chicken meat and return meat to pot of stock.

❸ Meanwhile, heat oil in large sauté pan. Add garlic and ginger and cook for 2 to 3 minutes.

❹ Add onion and carrots and continue to cook over medium heat until veg-etables begin to soften. Add cooked vegetables to chicken stock, along with chopped broccoli, and continue to simmer for 30 minutes.

❺ Bring soup to a boil and add rice noodles. Continue to boil until noodles become tender.

❻ Stir in spinach leaves and serve immediately.

RECIPE NOTES

There are many brands of rice noodles on the market today. Rice noodles have a slightly blander taste than do wheat-based noodles, but are quite ver-satile and can be substituted anywhere for a wheat-based noodle. Cooking times vary according to particular brands. However, one universal trait of rice noodles is that they disintegrate if overcooked. Consequently, the best cooked rice noodles are cooked to al dente.

(continued)

First Generation: This version, used by my Grandmother, maintains a clear broth. Additionally, you can use portion control to everyone's liking. Cook noodles separately and ladle noodles into each bowl. Top with broth, chicken, and vegetables.

Second Generation: This version, used by my Aunt Barbara, yields a lower-fat base. After step 4, allow pot to cool and then refrigerate overnight, allowing the fat to solidify. Skim fat off the top of the soup, bring to a boil, and add noodles.

To freeze, skip steps 5 and 6. Rice noodles cannot withstand too much heat before they begin to disintegrate. Freezing and reheating the soup with noodles will turn the noodles into mush. Accordingly, freeze the soup in batches after step 4. Reheat soup on the stove top. Bring soup to a boil then add the noodles.

Serves: 12. Preparation Time is 20 minutes. Cooking Time is 1 hour 30 minutes.

Roasted Tomato Basil Soup

¡◎¡¡

INGREDIENTS

2 pounds vine-ripe tomatoes

1 pound carrots

1 large white onion

4 cloves garlic

1/4 cup olive oil

2 cups rice milk, divided

1-1/2 teaspoons salt

1/2 teaspoon white pepper

2 tablespoons chopped fresh basil

INSTRUCTIONS

Preheat oven to 425°F.

❶ Coarsely chop and seed the tomatoes. Coarsely chop carrots, onion, and garlic. Toss all vegetables together with olive oil.

❷ Using one large or two small rimmed baking sheets, spread vegetable mixture in a single layer over pan(s.) The rim will prevent cooking juices from dripping into your oven.

❸ Roast on top rack of oven for 40 minutes, turning once. The vegetables should be well browned, but not burned.

❹ Cool slightly and transfer roasted vegetables, including any brown bits, to a blender. Slowly add 1 cup of the rice milk and puree until smooth.

❺ Pour pureed soup into a soup pot. Add up to 1 cup of the remaining rice milk to reach desired consistency. Stir in salt and pepper. Heat to a low simmer. Remove from heat; stir in basil. Serve warm or chilled.

RECIPE NOTES

This fabulous soup is creamy, vibrant, and effortless. It is so thick that rice milk is needed to thin it out. Classical cooking turns to a few usual suspects for thickening soups such as glutinous flour, butter, or cream. But there are other ways to thicken soup and sauces naturally. This soup is a perfect example of how well-cooked carrots and onions act as thickening agents when pureed. Other unsuspecting ingredients that work well as thickening agents when pureed include well-cooked celery and cannellini beans.

Serves: 4. Preparation Time is 10 minutes. Cooking Time is 50 minutes.

Cream of Chicken Soup

Cream of chicken soup? You betcha! You simply must try this recipe to believe that you can enjoy such a rich and creamy soup without eating an ounce of dairy. It is truly fabulous.

🍴◎🍴

INGREDIENTS

8 cups chicken stock

4 cups water

1-1/2 cups crushed rice noodles

2 teaspoons salt, divided

2 tablespoons olive oil

3 cloves garlic, minced

1 medium yellow onion, diced

1 cup shredded carrots

1 stalk celery, diced

2 tablespoons dry sherry

20 ounces cooked chicken breast, diced

INSTRUCTIONS

❶ Heat chicken stock and water in a large soup pot and bring to a boil. Add crushed rice noodles and 1 teaspoon of salt. Boil over low heat, stirring occasionally to prevent noodles from sticking to the bottom of the pot. Continue to boil the soup until noodles disintegrate and liquid thickens, about 40 minutes.

❷ Meanwhile, heat olive oil in a small sauté pan over medium-high heat. Add garlic and sauté until garlic begins to brown. Reduce heat to medium and add onion, carrots, and 1/2 teaspoon of salt. Sauté until vegetables soften, about 5 minutes. Add celery and sauté for 5 more minutes. Add sherry, remove from heat, and set aside.

❸ When soup is thick, puree the soup until smooth using a handheld immersion blender. (Alternatively, allow contents to cool, transfer to a blender, and puree.) Return to soup pot; add vegetable mixture, cooked chicken breast, and remaining 1/2 teaspoon of salt. Serve warm.

RECIPE NOTES

🗔 Similar to any soup thickened with crushed rice noodles, this soup will continue to thicken as it ages. To thin soup, use water or rice milk.

💡 Substitute water plus 1 teaspoon salt for the chicken stock.

❄ Freeze soup up to 3 months. Reheat over stovetop and thin with rice milk.

Serves: 6. Preparation Time is 30 minutes. Cooking Time is 45 minutes.

Cream of Mushroom Soup

It took six years of living in Minnesota before I gave in and made my husband a hotdish. Similar to grits in the South, hotdish is an acquired taste that you may need to develop in childhood. I made the beloved hotdish and conveniently stopped making it when my daughter was diagnosed with food allergies, as virtually every Minnesotan hotdish recipe calls for 1 can of condensed cream of mushroom soup. But since my children are being raised in Minnesota, I did not want them to be deprived of a genuine, Minnesotan childhood delicacy. And so, I embarked on a mission to make a tasty, allergen-free cream of mushroom soup. The results were unbelievable. If you are rooted in Minnesota or wanting to try a new recipe from the Sunday paper, your prayers have been answered. This soup is amazing by the bowl and also works fabulously in recipes calling for cream of mushroom soup.

🍴◎🍴

INGREDIENTS
1 cup dried mushrooms (1 ounce)

1 cup hot water

6 cups beef stock

8 cups rice milk, divided

1-1/2 cups crushed rice noodles

1-1/2 teaspoons salt

2 tablespoons canola oil

2 medium shallots, chopped

8 ounces button mushrooms, sliced (about 2 cups)

2 tablespoons dry sherry

INSTRUCTIONS
❶ Place dried mushrooms in a bowl and add hot water. Let steep for 30 minutes. After 30 minutes, drain the mushrooms and reserve all the mushroom stock. Strain the liquid through a paper towel to remove any dirt or particles and set aside.

❷ Heat beef stock and 4 cups of rice milk in a large soup pot and bring to a boil. Add crushed rice noodles and salt. Continue to boil over low heat, stirring occasionally to prevent noodles from sticking to the bottom of the pot. Continue to boil the soup until noodles disintegrate and liquid thickens, about 50 minutes.

❸ Meanwhile, heat canola oil in a small sauté pan. Add shallots, sliced mushrooms, and rehydrated mushrooms. Sauté for about 5 minutes. Add sherry and 1/2 of the reserved mushroom liquid. Continue to cook until liquid evaporates. Remove pan from heat, add remaining mushroom liquid, and set aside.

❹ When soup is thick, using a handheld immersion blender, puree the soup until smooth. (Alternatively, allow contents to cool, transfer to a blender, and puree.) Add mushroom mixture.

(continued)

5 Stir in 2 to 4 cups of rice milk to bring soup to desired consistency. Season with 1 teaspoon salt and white pepper. Serve warm.

RECIPE NOTES

The creaminess of this soup is achieved by slowly boiling the crushed rice noodles. As the rice noodles cook, their starches are slowly released into the broth. Crushing the noodles results in more starch released per noodle in less time. Approximately 2 cups of dry rice noodles are needed to obtain 1-1/2 cups of crushed noodles. Crush the noodles to 1/8-inch pieces, being careful not to crush them all to a dust.

For a lighter-colored soup, use chicken stock in lieu of the beef stock.

Substitute an additional 8 ounces of fresh mushrooms and an additional 1 tablespoon of sherry for the dried mushrooms.

Condensed Cream of Mushroom Soup. Skip step 5. Add the mushroom mixture in step 3 and puree with the other ingredients. Store in convenient 10- to 12-ounce portions so there is always a "can of condensed soup" ready when a recipes calls for it.

Freeze soup for up to 3 months.

Serves: 6. Preparation Time is 30 minutes. Cooking Time is 1 hour.

Creamy Artichoke Soup

INGREDIENTS

2 tablespoons olive oil

2 cloves garlic, minced

2 medium leeks, coarsely chopped

1 medium baked potato, scrubbed, peeled, and chopped

1 14-ounce can artichoke hearts, drained

2 cups vegetable stock

1 teaspoon salt

1/2 teaspoon white pepper

1 tablespoon chives, dried

INSTRUCTIONS

❶ Heat olive oil in a large soup pot over medium heat. Add the garlic and sauté for 2 minutes. Add the leeks and sauté until the leeks soften, about 3 minutes.

❷ Add the chopped potato and cook for 5 minutes, stirring often.

❸ Add the artichokes, stock, salt, and pepper and cook until the vegetables are tender, about 15 minutes.

❹ Puree the soup until smooth using a handheld immersion blender. (Alternatively, allow contents to cool, transfer to a blender in batches, and puree.)

❺ Spoon into bowls and sprinkle with chives. Serve warm.

RECIPE NOTES

Potatoes are a great option for thickening soups. However, I have discovered that potatoes do not produce the creamy, rich texture achievable when using rice noodles. Nevertheless, the texture and flavor of the potatoes are a wonderful complement to the artichokes.

Serves: 4. Preparation Time is 10 minutes. Cooking Time is 25 minutes.

Creamy Turkey Asparagus Soup

This soup is a family favorite, especially during runny-nose season. Without an ounce of dairy, this recipe provides all the comfort you seek without any added congestion.

🍴◎🍴

INGREDIENTS

12 cups water

1-1/2 cups crushed rice noodles

2 teaspoons salt, divided

1/4 cup olive oil

4 cloves garlic, chopped

16 ounces turkey cutlet(s)

1 pound asparagus, chopped into 1-inch pieces

INSTRUCTIONS

❶ Bring 12 cups of water to a boil. Add crushed rice noodles and 1 teaspoon of salt. Cook until rice noodles are well cooked and begin to disintegrate, about 20 minutes. Stir periodically to prevent noodles from sticking to the bottom of the pot.

❷ Meanwhile, heat olive oil in a large sauté pan over medium-high heat. Add garlic and cook until garlic begins to brown, about 5 to 7 minutes.

❸ Season turkey cutlets with about 1/2 teaspoon salt. Working in batches, cook turkey cutlets in sauté pan with browned garlic until turkey is cooked through, about 3 minutes per side. Remove turkey from heat and set aside to cool. (Be sure to reserve the residual garlic and oil, a wonderful flavor enhancer for the soup.) When the turkey is cool enough to handle, cut cutlets into 3/4-inch strips.

❹ Add approximately 1/3 of the sliced turkey and 1/3 of the asparagus to the pot of well-cooked noodles. Puree the noodles, turkey, and asparagus until smooth using a handheld immersion blender. (Alternatively, allow contents to cool, transfer to a blender, and puree.) If soup becomes too thick, gradually add a little water to thin.

❺ Add remaining turkey slices, asparagus, and 1/2 teaspoon of salt to the soup stock. Bring to a low boil and then simmer, uncovered, for 5 minutes or until the asparagus pieces are tender. Serve warm. Garnish with croutons or garlic toast.

RECIPE NOTES

🍲 Creamy Chicken and Broccoli Soup. Substitute 16 ounces of chicken for turkey and 1 pound of broccoli for asparagus.

Serves: 6. Preparation Time is 5 minutes. Cooking Time is 40 minutes.

Lentil Soup

¶◎⊩

INGREDIENTS

1 pound dried lentils

2 tablespoons grapeseed oil

1 clove garlic

1 pound Italian sausage

1 large yellow onion, chopped

8 cups beef stock

4 cups water

2 medium vine-ripe tomatoes, diced

2 tablespoons fresh chopped sage leaves

1 teaspoon salt

INSTRUCTIONS

❶ Rinse lentils and drain.

❷ Heat grapeseed oil in a medium sauté pan. Add garlic and sauté for 2 to 3 minutes. Add sausage and onion and continue to sauté until sausage is cooked through. Set aside.

❸ In a large soup pot, bring beef stock and water to a boil. Add rinsed lentils and sausage mixture. Reduce heat to low-medium and allow soup to simmer until the soup thickens and lentils soften, about 45 minutes.

❹ Remove from heat, stir in tomatoes, sage, and salt. Serve in individual bowls.

RECIPE NOTES

🍲 Vegetarian Lentil Soup. Substitute vegetable stock for the beef stock and omit the sausage. Stir in one 15-ounce can of black beans, rinsed and drained, with the chopped tomatoes in step 4.

Serves: 6. Preparation Time is 5 minutes. Cooking Time is 55 minutes.

Roasted Tortilla Soup

INGREDIENTS

2 medium orange bell peppers,
    seeded and coarsely chopped

1 medium jalapeno pepper,
    seeded and coarsely chopped

5 medium vine-ripe tomatoes,
    seeded and coarsely chopped

1 medium white onion, coarsely chopped

6 cloves garlic

2 tablespoons olive oil

1 teaspoon salt, divided

1 28-ounce can crushed tomatoes

4 cups chicken stock

2 teaspoons ground cumin

1 teaspoon paprika

1/2 teaspoon white pepper

12 ounces tortilla chips, broken,
    (approximately 4 cups)

12 ounces cooked chicken breast,
    shredded (optional)

INSTRUCTIONS

Preheat oven to 425°F.

❶ Spread chopped peppers, tomatoes, onion, and garlic in a single layer onto one large or two small rimmed baking sheets. Drizzle with olive oil and 1/2 teaspoon salt. Roast in oven until vegetables begin to brown, turning once, about 20 minutes.

❷ Add roasted vegetables to a large soup pot. Add 2 to 3 tablespoons of water to the baking sheet to scrape up any brown bits and add these to the pot.

❸ Add the can of crushed tomatoes and chicken stock. Bring to a boil. Reduce heat to low-medium simmer. Add spices and remaining 1/2 teaspoon of salt and pepper.

❹ Add tortilla chips and allow soup to continue to simmer for 10 to 15 minutes or until tortilla chips are very soft and disintegrating in the broth.

❺ Puree the soup until well combined using a handheld immersion blender. (Alternatively, allow soup to cool slightly, transfer to a blender, and puree.)

❻ Divide shredded chicken among four large soup bowls (optional). Ladle soup over chicken and serve warm. Garnish with additional tortilla chips or fresh chopped cilantro.

RECIPE NOTES

Substitute 2 cups of cooked black beans for the chicken. Divide equally among four bowls and ladle soup over top.

Blend 1/2 cup of leftover soup with a 15-ounce can of drained and rinsed pinto beans in a food processor for a simple version of homemade refried beans.

Up to 3 months.

Serves: 4. Preparation Time is 20 minutes. Cooking Time is 20 minutes.

Mulligatawny Soup

¡◎¡†

INGREDIENTS

1/4 cup canola oil

1 medium carrot, peeled and chopped

1 medium onion, thinly sliced

2 tablespoons grated fresh ginger root

1 tablespoon curry powder

1 teaspoon coriander

2 pounds chicken thighs, skinned and boned, cut into bite-size pieces

4 cups chicken stock

1 teaspoon salt

2 tablespoons sugar

1-1/2 cups rice milk

2 cups cooked white basmati rice

1 large Granny Smith apple or other tart apple, chopped (optional)

1 tablespoon fresh cilantro (optional)

INSTRUCTIONS

❶ Heat oil in a soup pot over medium heat. Add chopped carrot and sauté until softened, about 5 minutes. Add onion and ginger root. Sauté for another 5 minutes.

❷ Add curry powder and coriander. Blend well and cook for 1 minute.

❸ Add chicken and cook until the chicken loses its raw appearance, about 3 to 5 minutes.

❹ Add chicken stock and salt. Bring to a boil, then reduce heat and simmer until chicken is cooked through, about 25 minutes.

❺ Stir sugar into rice milk until it dissolves. Add rice milk mixture to soup and heat to a simmer.

❻ To serve, spoon approximately 1/2 cup cooked rice into individual bowls, top with a spoonful of chopped apples (optional,) and ladle the soup on top. Garnish with cilantro leaves.

Serves: 4. Preparation Time is 5 minutes. Cooking Time is 40 minutes.

Gumbo

Gumbo. So many versions, so many recipes, so many contradictions. Some recipes require a roux with poultry, while others command filé (ground sassafras leaves) and seafood. Some recipes use okra only in the summer and andouille sausage in the winter. But regardless of the ingredient variations, the key foundation of any gumbo is the thickener. This wonderful version of gumbo I created is thickened using the inherent properties of natural ingredients.

❢◎❢❢

INGREDIENTS

1/4 cup grapeseed oil

1 pound boneless, skinless chicken breast

1 pound boneless, skinless chicken thighs

1-1/2 teaspoons salt, divided

1 pound andouille sausage

2 cloves garlic, minced

4 celery stalks, diced

1 large white onion, chopped

2 medium green bell peppers, diced

6 medium vine-ripe tomatoes,
    seeded and diced

2 quarts chicken stock

2 tablespoons tomato paste

2 medium bay leaves

1 teaspoon pepper

1/2 teaspoon onion powder

1/2 teaspoon garlic powder

1 teaspoon thyme

1/2 teaspoon mustard powder

1/4 teaspoon cayenne pepper

1-1/4 pounds okra, fresh or frozen,
    chopped into 1/2-inch pieces

INSTRUCTIONS

❶ Heat grapeseed oil in a large, heavy-bottomed pot or Dutch oven over medium heat. Cut chicken and sausage into bite-size pieces. Season chicken with 1 teaspoon salt and cook the chicken and sausage until browned on all sides, about 2 to 3 minutes. You may need to work this step in batches. Remove meats and set aside.

❷ Add garlic, celery, onion, and green peppers to pot. Cook until vegetables soften, about 3 to 5 minutes.

❸ Add chopped tomatoes, chicken stock, tomato paste, bay leaves, remaining salt, pepper, and seasonings. (Alternatively, you could substitute 2-1/2 teaspoons of Creole seasoning from the recipe on page 234 for the combined onion powder, garlic powder, thyme, mustard, and cayenne pepper.) Stir and bring to a boil.

❹ Reduce heat to a low simmer and add okra along with the reserved chicken and sausage. Simmer for 1 hour, uncovered, until ingredients are well cooked and gumbo becomes thick and luscious. Serve over bowls of white rice.

RECIPE NOTES

Interestingly, the word "Gumbo" is of African origin and means okra. Okra is a popular vegetable in the southern part of the U.S., but can now be found all over year-round. Okra not only thickens a gumbo, it adds flavor. The pods, when cut, exude a mucilaginous juice. When well cooked, the gumminess goes away and it serves as a wonderful thickening agent.

Serves: 6. Preparation Time is 15 minutes. Cooking Time is 1 hour 15 minutes.

Mock Tuna Salad

I'll admit, this recipe may be pushing it slightly, but in order to satisfy persistent crav-ings of off-limit foods, I have found that sometimes cravings can be satisfied by simply combining a few safe ingredients in a creative way. While pregnant with my third child, I created this recipe and found the combination of mustard, relish, and celery enabled me to stop daydreaming about Subway's 6-inch tuna sub.

†◎⋔

INGREDIENTS

16 ounces boneless pork chops, cooked and chopped into small pieces

2/3 cup bread crumbs

1/3 cup olive oil

2 tablespoons Dijon mustard

1 stalk celery, diced

1/2 medium red onion, diced

1/2 cup sweet relish, or minced pickles of your choice

1/2 teaspoon dried dill (optional)

1/4 teaspoon salt

1/4 teaspoon pepper

INSTRUCTIONS

❶ Combine the chopped pork, bread crumbs, olive oil, and Dijon mustard in a food processor or blender. Pulse until pork is shredded and slightly mushy and ingredients are well incorporated. Transfer to a medium mixing bowl.

❷ Add celery, onion, relish, dill (optional), salt, and pepper and stir together. Serve on toasted bread or a bed of red leaf lettuce. For best results, refrigerate for 2 hours before consuming. Can be prepared up to 2 days in advance.

RECIPE NOTES

▤ Based on different textures and consistencies of bread crumbs, you may need a little more or less oil to bind the salad together.

Serves: 4. Preparation Time is 10 minutes.

Pasta Salad

I have yet to find an allergen-free/gluten-free pasta that is edible when refrigerated. Every brand that I have tried has an unsavory texture that crumbles in your mouth when chilled. However, this doesn't mean pasta salads are out of the question. Follow these simple hypoallergenic techniques and you will be able to enjoy a tasty pasta salad once again.

ﾔ◎ﾔ

INGREDIENTS

4 ounces sun-dried tomatoes in oil, drained and chopped

2 ounces sliced olives, drained

1 medium green pepper, diced

1/2 cup shredded carrots

1 small shallot, chopped

1/2 teaspoon salt

1/4 teaspoon pepper

1/2 cup Creamy Italian Dressing, recipe on page 221

1/4 cup canola oil

12 ounces rice tri-color spirals, or any shape of rice pasta

INSTRUCTIONS

❶ Combine sun-dried tomatoes, olives, green pepper, carrots, shallot, salt, pepper, Creamy Italian Dressing, and canola oil in a large mixing bowl. Stir to incorporate all ingredients.

❷ Cook rice noodles according to package. Drain and immediately toss with marinated vegetables while noodles are still warm. Serve immediately. Do not refrigerate. This salad should remain palatable at room temperature for up to 3 hours.

RECIPE NOTES

The condiments can be prepared up to 24 hours in advance and stored in the refrigerator. Add warm, cooked pasta just prior to serving. Not only does this technique enhance the texture of the pasta, but it also enhances the flavor. By adding the pasta to the other ingredients while the pasta is still warm, the pasta absorbs the flavors of the condiments, thereby giving each spiral maximum flavor rather than just coating the noodles with ingredients.

Serves: 6. Preparation Time is 10 minutes. Cooking Time is 10 minutes.

Chicken Salad

In addition to adding a delightful nutty crunch to this salad, flax seeds are rich in heart protective Omega-3 fatty acids, as well as vitamins and minerals such as B6 and magnesium.

¡◎¡¡

INGREDIENTS

16 ounces cooked chicken breast, shredded

1/2 cup sun-dried tomatoes in oil, drained and chopped

1/4 cup red onion, finely sliced

1/4 cup capers, drained

2 tablespoons lemon juice

2 tablespoons Dijon mustard

2/3 cup olive oil

1/2 teaspoon salt

1/4 teaspoon pepper

1/3 cup flax seeds

INSTRUCTIONS

❶ Combine the shredded chicken breast, sun-dried tomatoes, onion, and capers in a medium mixing bowl.

❷ In a small bowl, whisk together lemon juice and mustard. Slowly pour in the olive oil while continuously whisking. Add salt and pepper.

❸ Pour dressing over chicken mixture and toss. The chicken salad can be prepared about 4 hours ahead of time and refrigerated. Sprinkle flax seeds over individual portions just prior to serving. Serve over a bed of greens or individually in butter lettuce leaves.

Serves: 4. Preparation Time is 10 minutes.

Asian Chicken Salad

†◎‖

INGREDIENTS

1 cup rice vinegar

1 cup sugar

2 tablespoons minced ginger root

20 ounces cooked chicken breast, diced

8 ounces shredded cabbage

1/2 cup shredded carrots

1/4 cup chopped scallion

1 celery stalk, diced

2 cups snow peas

18-ounce can water chestnuts, sliced (optional)

1 cup bean sprouts

INSTRUCTIONS

❶ In a small glass bowl, whisk together the vinegar, sugar, and ginger root until sugar is dissolved. Set aside.

❷ Combine the chicken, cabbage, carrots, scallions, and celery together in a large bowl. Pour vinegar mixture over and toss well to combine.

❸ To serve, arrange snow peas and optional water chestnuts in a single layer on a plate. Top with chicken salad and sprinkle with bean sprouts.

Serves: 4. Preparation Time is 15 minutes.

Curried Chicken Salad

¶◎¶

INGREDIENTS

2 tablespoons canola oil

2 small shallots, minced

1/2 cup rice milk

1 tablespoon curry powder

20 ounces cooked chicken breast, diced

1/4 cup golden raisins

1/2 teaspoon salt

1/4 teaspoon pepper

1 tablespoon fresh chopped cilantro

1/4 cup flax seeds (optional)

INSTRUCTIONS

❶ Heat canola oil in a large saucepan over medium heat. Add shallots and sauté until softened, about 3 minutes. Add rice milk and curry powder. Whisk together and bring to a boil. Reduce heat and simmer, uncovered, for 5 minutes.

❷ Add cooked chicken, raisins, salt, and pepper to pan and continue to simmer, uncovered, for 15 minutes, or until mixture thickens.

❸ Remove from heat; stir in cilantro and allow to cool completely before serving. Serve on Bibb lettuce leaves or on top of chilled rice pilaf. Sprinkle optional flax seeds on salad just prior to serving for added crunch. Store salad in airtight container in refrigerator for up to 3 days.

Serves: 4. Preparation Time is 5 minutes. Inactive Preparation Time is 30 minutes. Cooking Time is 25 minutes.

Chopped Salads

Chopped salads are a fabulous way to please a crowd, whether you are making dinner for your family or entertaining party guests. All you need are some fresh, crisp greens and vegetables, a big bowl, and a splash of dressing. The following flavorful salads can be eaten as meals, sides, or even snacks. Better yet, they can be personalized to everyone's taste by segregating ingredients around a bed of lettuce so everyone can take bits of what they like and garnish with their own dressing. This is especially good when entertaining so you don't have to worry about the dressing making the ingredients soggy. I have paired each salad with the type of lettuce and dressing that I feel complements the dish best, but feel free to mix in different lettuce and dressings as personal tastes may dictate.

Chopped Antipasto Salad

¡©¡¡

INGREDIENTS

1/2 head romaine lettuce

1/2 head radicchio

2 cups chopped salami, or other Italian meats such as mortadella, ham, or capicola

1 cup cannellini beans, drained and rinsed

1 cup garbanzo beans, drained and rinsed

12 ounces sun-dried tomatoes in oil, drained and chopped

1/2 cup roasted red peppers, chopped

1 medium red onion, diced

3/4 cup Kalamata olives, pitted and sliced

2 tablespoons capers, drained

1/2 cup Creamy Italian Dressing, recipe on page 221

INSTRUCTIONS

❶ Wash and dry romaine lettuce and radicchio. Slice lettuce into bite-size pieces. Pile together in center of a large platter.

❷ Divide chopped meat into two equal piles and place on either side of lettuce. Place beans on remaining two ends.

❸ Place sun-dried tomatoes, roasted peppers, red onion, and olives into the four remaining spaces between the meat and bean piles.

❹ Garnish with capers over the top. Drizzle with Creamy Italian Dressing, or reserve dressing for the side.

Serves: 8. Preparation Time is 15 minutes.

Chopped Greek Salad

🍴⊚🍴

INGREDIENTS

1 head iceberg lettuce

8 ounces chopped salami, or other Italian meats such as mortadella, ham, or capicola

2 medium cucumbers, peeled and diced

4 large roma tomatoes, seeded and diced

1 medium red onion, finely sliced

1 15-ounce can artichoke hearts, drained and chopped

2 medium green peppers, diced

2 large pepperoncini peppers

1/2 cup Classic Greek Dressing, recipe on page 223

INSTRUCTIONS

❶ Wash, dry, and chop iceberg lettuce. Mound in the center of a large platter. Place salami meat in the center of the lettuce bed.

❷ Place cucumber, tomatoes, red onion, artichoke hearts, and green peppers in piles surrounding the bed of lettuce.

❸ Place the pepperoncini peppers on top. Drizzle Classic Greek Dressing on top or serve with a reserved portion on the side.

Serves: 6. Preparation Time is 10 minutes.

Chopped Mexican Salad

¡◎¡¡

INGREDIENTS

1 large orange bell pepper
1 large red bell pepper
1 large red onion
1 tablespoon olive oil
1/2 teaspoon salt
1 head romaine lettuce, leaves washed and dried
1 15-ounce can black beans, drained and rinsed
1 15-ounce can corn, drained
2 large avocados
1 large lime
2 large vine-ripe tomatoes, seeded and diced
8 medium green onions, chopped
12-ounce can pimientos, drained
3 tablespoons fresh chopped cilantro
1/2 cup Smoky Chipotle Dressing, recipe on page 216

INSTRUCTIONS

Preheat oven to 425°F.

❶ Line a heavy-duty, rimmed baking sheet with aluminum foil. Halve and seed the peppers and lay on the baking sheet, cut side down. Quarter the red onion and place on baking sheet, cut side down. Drizzle peppers and onion with olive oil and sprinkle with salt. Roast in the oven until the peppers begin to shrivel and slightly char, about 20 minutes. Set aside to cool.

❷ Meanwhile, spread the romaine lettuce over the bottom of a large platter. This will serve as a base.

❸ Place a pile of black beans on top of the lettuce at one end of the platter and the corn at the other end.

❹ Scrape away the charred skins on the peppers. Dice the peppers and onions, toss together, and place in one big pile in the middle of the platter.

❺ Slice, peel, and chop the avocados. Squeeze the juice of 1 lime on top and toss together.

❻ Place tomatoes, avocados, and green onions in piles in remaining open spaces on the platter. Sprinkle diced pimientos and chopped cilantro over the top. Serve with Smoky Chipotle Dressing drizzled on top or reserved for the side.

Serves: 6. Preparation Time is 15 minutes. Cooking Time is 20 minutes.

Chopped Chef Salad

†◎†

INGREDIENTS

1-1/2 pounds Boston, Bibb, green, or red leaf lettuce

6 ounces baked ham, cubed

6 ounces turkey breast, cooked and chopped into bite-size pieces

4 ounces roast beef, cooked and sliced into 1/2-inch strips

2 medium avocados, peeled and diced

4 medium roma tomatoes, seeded and diced

1/2 medium red onion, finely sliced

1 cup croutons

1/4 cup fresh chopped parsley

1/2 cup Creamy Herb Dressing, recipe on page 214

INSTRUCTIONS

❶ Wash and dry the lettuce. Tear into bite-size pieces and place in a large salad bowl.

❷ Arrange the ham, turkey breast, and roast beef on top of the lettuce like spokes of a wheel.

❸ Fill the open spaces with diced avocados and tomatoes. Place the sliced onion around the rim of the bowl.

❹ Pile croutons in center of the bowl. Garnish with fresh parsley. Serve with Creamy Herb Dressing on top or alongside.

Serves: 6. Preparation Time is 10 minutes.

Chopped Cobb Salad

And last but not least, the Cobb salad. With its multitude of flavors and textures, the Cobb salad is the quintessential American salad, first pulled together on a whim by Robert Cobb. Cobb created the first Cobb salad at the end of a long day, when he realized he had not had time to eat. Wandering over to one of the restaurant iceboxes, a weary Cobb scrounged around to see what he could fix.(Alas, he must have felt similar to how I often feel at the end of a long day, scrounging the aisles of the market to determine what to make for dinner with limited ingredients that are safe.) While I have invented many recipes this way, I prefer to tinker around with the classics, substituting ingredients to create hypoallergenic versions we can all enjoy without sacrificing taste or appearance.

INGREDIENTS
8 ounces bacon

1 bunch watercress, washed and dried

1/2 head romaine lettuce, leaves washed and dried

12 ounces cooked chicken breast, diced

1 pint cherry tomatoes, diced

2 large avocados, peeled and diced

2 stalks celery, diced

3 tablespoons fresh chopped chives

1/2 cup Derby Dressing, recipe on page 223

INSTRUCTIONS

❶ Cook bacon in a large skillet over medium-high heat. Remove from heat and place strips on a paper towel to drain. When cooled, crumble into tiny pieces. Set aside.

❷ Cut watercress and romaine lettuce into fine, bite-size pieces and arrange on the bottom of a large platter.

❸ Arrange the chicken, bacon, tomatoes, avocados, and celery in strips on top of the greens.

❹ Sprinkle chives over the Cobb salad and garnish with any remaining watercress.

❺ Drizzle Derby Dressing over the top or reserve for on the side.

RECIPE NOTES

💡 Old-fashioned watercress can be difficult to find, but it adds such a nice, distinct peppery bite to this salad. If necessary, use the whole head of romaine in lieu of the watercress.

Serves: 6. Preparation Time is 20 minutes.

Chapter ❹

Lighter Fare

I receive so much enthusiasm when I prepare elaborate entrées such as osso bucco and beef stroganoff that I almost feel obligated to present my family with a culinary masterpiece every evening. Or perhaps I just like the sound of my children jumping for joy and telling their daddy that we are having *"veal malala"* for dinner! But for me, good, wholesome dishes without fancy titles can be equally satisfying and comforting. And anyway, I receive equal amounts of enthusiasm when I make these lighter bites.

These recipes are great options when you don't want to prepare an elaborate entrée but still want to provide a wholesome, homemade meal. Many of the results are freezer-friendly and make great lunches the second time around. I love serving my kids homemade hot lunches without doing more than pressing the reheat button on the microwave. These dishes are also convenient and easily transportable to the office, or anywhere for that matter, for a safe meal. I recently wrapped a couple meatball grinders in aluminum foil, packed them in an insulated bag, and sent them off with my husband and kids to a tailgating event. They were the perfect accompaniment for a crisp, fall day. I've discovered that with these kinds of dishes, my family is not missing out, but rather becomes the envy of others!

Eight Layer Casserole

This is a simple recipe to prepare, one with dynamic flavors and flair. It is one of those dishes that is so easy to make and so very hard to mess up.

INGREDIENTS

1 cup white rice

1 15-ounce can corn, drained

2 cups tomato sauce, divided

1/2 cup water, divided

1 small white onion, diced

1 small green pepper, diced

1/2 cup sliced olives

1 pound ground beef

4 ounces bacon

INSTRUCTIONS

❶ Sprinkle rice on bottom of a 9×13-inch casserole dish and top with corn. Pour 1 cup of tomato sauce and 1/4 cup of water over the first two layers. Layer the onion on top followed by the green pepper, olives, and ground beef. Pour remaining 1 cup of tomato sauce and 1/4 cup of water on top of the beef. Layer the strips of bacon on top of the casserole.

❷ Cover the dish with aluminum foil and bake for 1 hour. Uncover and continue to bake for 30 minutes, or until bacon becomes slightly crispy. Serve warm.

Serves: 4. Preparation Time is 10 minutes. Cooking Time is 1 hour 30 minutes.

Pizza Pockets

The great thing about pizza is that most of the toppings are allergen-free and gluten-free. However without cheese working as a binder, most of the ingredients fall off. An easy solution to this problem is to create pizza pockets! Not only are these a great way to enjoy your favorite pizza, but they are freezer-friendly and portable, allowing you to enjoy homemade pizza anywhere, at anytime. These pockets are perfect to bring to the office or a child's birthday party. Just follow this easy method of preparing the pockets, fill with your favorite "toppings," and enjoy!

The five filling combinations here emphasize complementing flavors while simultaneously producing different textures of ingredients that work well with allergen-free/gluten-free pizza dough. Since these are pockets, you need to be careful, as some traditional pizza ingredients, like tomatoes, will make your pocket quite soggy; the juices will not be able to evaporate during cooking as they do with a traditional pizza. Although different brands of pizza dough will yield different results, the ingredients here should give you enough filling for approximately 12 pizza pockets.

¶◎¶

INGREDIENTS
1/2 cup olive oil, divided
2 packages pizza dough mix
1 cup white rice flour (optional)

INSTRUCTIONS
Preheat oven to 350°F.

❶ Line a large baking sheet with aluminum foil. Generously grease the sheet using about 2 tablespoons of olive oil.

❷ Prepare pizza dough according to the instructions. Using slightly less than half the dough (about 40%), roll out a portion of dough into a large rectangle on the greased baking sheet. If the dough is really sticky, use extra rice flour to ease the process. Brush the surface of the dough with olive oil and bake for 6 to 8 minutes, or until the dough has firmed up but is not completely cooked.

❸ Remove pan and increase oven temperature to 400°F. Using a pizza slicer or sharp knife, cut the pizza dough into 3×5-inch rectangles (or any desired shape.) Use a spatula to gently separate the rectangles from one another.

❹ Place a generous portion of filling on each rectangle. (Filling recipes follow.)

❺ Using remaining dough, roll out individual portions and layer over the top of each filled rectangle, creating the pizza pocket. Use a little extra rice flour for sticky dough, if needed. This top layer should be slightly thinner than the bottom. Press down on edges to seal and brush the top with olive oil. Garnish with seasonings and bake on the top rack of oven for 8 minutes, or until the top begins to brown. Cool and serve immediately or store in freezer for a later use.

(continued)

RECIPE NOTES

Wrap pockets individually in aluminum foil and place in a resealable freezer bag for up to 6 months.

Serves: 6. Preparation Time is 10 minutes. Cooking Time is 15 minutes.

Italian Filling

⫼◎⫼

INGREDIENTS

1/4 cup olive oil

2 medium green bell peppers, diced

1 medium white onion, diced

1/2 teaspoon salt

8 ounces pepperoni, diced

12 ounces tomato paste

INSTRUCTIONS

❶ Heat olive oil in a medium sauté pan over medium heat. Add peppers, onion, and salt. Cook until vegetables soften, about 5 minutes. Remove from heat and allow to cool slightly.

❷ Add the pepperoni and tomato paste to the cooked vegetables. Stir thoroughly.

RECIPE NOTES

Adding salt to the vegetables while cooking draws out the natural juices of the onions and peppers. This liquid will help keep the dough moist in your pizza pocket. Additionally, using tomato paste rather than tomato sauce will work with the dough and give your pocket a sweet, creamy bite without resulting in a soggy crust.

Serves: 12. Preparation Time is 5 minutes. Cooking Time is 5 minutes.

Hawaiian Filling

🍴◎🍴

INGREDIENTS

2 tablespoons canola oil

2 medium red bell peppers, diced

1-1/2 cups canned pineapple chunks, drained

8 ounces Canadian bacon, thinly sliced

1 tablespoon packed brown sugar (optional)

INSTRUCTIONS

❶ Heat canola oil in a small skillet over medium heat. Add peppers and cook until peppers soften, about 5 minutes.

❷ Toss cooked peppers together with remaining ingredients. Use immediately or store in refrigerator up to 1 day in advance.

RECIPE NOTES

Serves: 12. Preparation Time is 5 minutes. Cooking Time is 5 minutes.

Blanca Filling

¡◎¡

INGREDIENTS

1/4 cup olive oil

3 pounds Vidalia onions, or other sweet onions, thinly sliced

1/2 teaspoon salt

2 tablespoons sugar (optional)

2 teaspoons dried rosemary

1-1/2 teaspoons dried thyme

24 ounces mild Italian sausage

4 ounces fresh spinach

6 sprigs fresh rosemary

INSTRUCTIONS

❶ Heat olive oil in a pan over low heat. Add sliced onions and sprinkle with salt. Cook over low heat, covered, for 1 hour.

❷ Stir onions and add sugar, if desired. Continue to cook onions for another 30 minutes, uncovered, stirring occasionally. Remove from heat and stir in the rosemary and thyme.

❸ Meanwhile, cook the sausage. If using links, remove casings and break up the links into bite-size pieces. Add the cooked sausage to the caramelized onions. Stir together and use as a filling for pizza pockets. Filling can be prepared up to 1 day in advance.

❹ To fill the pockets, lay one to two spinach leaves on bottom and top with filling. Garnish the outside of pockets with a small sprig of rosemary.

RECIPE NOTES

This recipe for caramelized onions keeps the temperature low throughout the entire caramelizing process. Covering the onions for the first hour will prevent liquids from evaporating. The onions won't obtain a rich caramel color but, because these are a substantial ingredient for the blanca filling, you actually want the onions to remain somewhat soft and a little soupy to work with the allergen-free crust.

Substitute 2 cups of leftover roasted potatoes or 1-1/2 cups of mashed potatoes for the sausage.

Substitute 1/2 rice flour and 1/2 corn meal for the 1 cup of extra rice flour in the crust recipe. The corn meal adds a delightful color and flavor that compliments the rosemary in this filling beautifully.

Add 1/2 cup of sliced black olives.

Serves: 12. Preparation Time is 5 minutes. Cooking Time is 1 hour 30 minutes.

Rustica Filling

¡◎¡¡

INGREDIENTS
1 large eggplant, cubed

1 medium red onion, chopped

3 cloves garlic, chopped

2 tablespoons olive oil

1/2 teaspoon salt

1/4 teaspoon pepper

1/4 cup capers, drained

1/2 cup sun-dried tomatoes in oil, drained and chopped

1/2 cup roasted red peppers, julienned

8 ounces prosciutto, chopped

8 medium fresh basil leaves, chopped

INSTRUCTIONS
Preheat oven to 400°F.

❶ Place eggplant, onion, and garlic on a rimmed baking sheet. Toss with olive oil, salt, and pepper. Roast in oven for 25 minutes or until the edges begin to char.

❷ Add roasted vegetables to a large bowl and combine with remaining ingredients.

Serves: 12. Preparation Time is 5 minutes. Cooking Time is 25 minutes.

The Works Filling

¡◎¡

INGREDIENTS

2 tablespoons olive oil

1 medium white onion, diced

8 ounces button mushrooms, sliced

6 ounces ground beef

6 ounces ground sausage

3 ounces pepperoni, diced

1/2 cup sliced olives

12 ounces tomato paste

1/2 teaspoon salt

INSTRUCTIONS

❶ Heat olive oil in a medium sauté pan over medium heat. Add onion and mushrooms. Cook until vegetables soften, about 5 minutes. Remove from heat and allow to cool slightly.

❷ Meanwhile, cook beef and sausage.

❸ Combine onion and mushroom mixture, the cooked meats, and remaining ingredients in a large bowl. Stir well. Use immediately or store in refrigerator for up to 1 day.

Serves: 12. Preparation Time is 5 minutes. Cooking Time is 15 minutes.

Chicken Fingers

INGREDIENTS

1-1/2 cups bread crumbs

1 teaspoon salt

1 teaspoon pepper

20 ounces chicken breast strips

1/2 cup corn oil

INSTRUCTIONS

Preheat oven to 350°F.

❶ Combine bread crumbs, salt, and pepper in a small bowl; stir together and set aside.

❷ Place chicken strips in a resealable bag. Briefly tenderize by pounding with a kitchen mallet. Add bread crumbs to bag and, using hands, massage bread crumbs into chicken strips while tossing bag to evenly distribute. For heavily breaded strips, press the bread crumbs into the meat while you massage the chicken by pressing firmly on the chicken with your fingertips, creating small cavities where the breadcrumbs can nestle.

❸ Meanwhile, heat corn oil in a large sauté pan. Working in batches, fry breaded chicken until golden brown, about 2 to 3 minutes per side. Transfer to a 9×12 casserole dish and cook in oven, uncovered, for 15 minutes, or until chicken is cooked through. Serve warm with honey mustard or sweet and sour dipping sauce on the side.

RECIPE NOTES

Corn oil gives these chicken fingers a punch more of flavor than does using canola or grapeseed oil, both of which are viable alternatives. The flavor from the corn oil marries so well with the extra pepper suggested in this recipe and is reminiscent of the Colonel's version at KFC.

Wrap leftover chicken strips in aluminum foil and freeze up to 3 months.

Serves: 4. Preparation Time is 10 minutes. Cooking Time is 20 minutes.

Spaghetti Os, Ps and Qs

Who didn't grow up with the comfort of a hot lunch of Spaghetti Os and Meatballs while sitting at the counter, watching Mom cater to the needs of the kitchen. No child should be denied this simple pleasure and satisfying meal that has become an American classic. A simple addition of mini-meatballs is sure to create vivid memories for your child.

🍴◎🍴

INGREDIENTS

4 cups water

1 cup alphabet rice noodles

1 teaspoon salt, divided

1-1/2 cups tomato sauce

1/2 cup rice milk

INSTRUCTIONS

❶ Bring the water to a boil. Add the rice noodles and 1/2 teaspoon of salt. Cook until the noodles are al dente and the cooking liquid becomes cloudy with the starches released from the pasta, about 3 to 5 minutes. Drain the noodles and reserve 1 cup of the cooking liquid. Return noodles and 1 cup of cooking liquid to the pot.

❷ Add the tomato sauce, rice milk, and remaining 1/2 teaspoon of salt. Bring to a boil, reduce heat, and simmer until noodles are softened and sauce thickens, about 5 to 7 minutes. Serve warm.

RECIPE NOTES

Beefaroni: Substitute macaroni rice noodles for the alphabet noodles and add approximately 1/2 cup cooked ground beef at the end of step 2.

Serves: 4. Cooking Time is 15 minutes.

Hot Dogs and Hamburgers

A recipe for hot dogs and hamburgers? If you are new to hypoallergenic cooking or unfamiliar with gluten-free/allergen-free breads and buns, you will be delighted to find that this recipe provides a way to enjoy these American classics. As good as they may appear, gluten-free/allergen-free breads and buns sometimes need a little tinkering with to be edible. Not only does this method provide edible versions, the results are so great you won't miss the traditional bun or social fun associated with these two American favorites.

†◎|†

INGREDIENTS

4 medium hot dogs
4 medium hamburgers
4 medium hot dog buns
4 medium hamburger buns

INSTRUCTIONS

❶ Cook hot dogs/hamburgers to your preference.

❷ Meanwhile, slice each bun and wrap individually in aluminum foil. Don't wrap them too tightly.

❸ Before hot dogs/hamburgers finish cooking, place wrapped buns in a 325°F oven for approximately 3 minutes. Remove buns from oven and immediately place steaming hot, cooked hot dogs/hamburgers in individual buns. Immediately rewrap each bun tightly. Return filled buns to oven for an additional 3 to 5 minutes. The inner steam from the cooked meat will graciously soften the bun from the inside, while the external heat from the oven will add a nice toasty exterior.

❹ Remove from oven and customize each hot dog/hamburger with everyone's favorite toppings: ketchup, mustard, chopped onion, lettuce, pickles, relish, or chili. Rewrap to seal in toppings and serve.

Serves: 4. Cooking Time is 5 minutes.

Corn Dogs

🍴◎🍴

INGREDIENTS

3 cups water

1 pound hot dogs, about 8 total

4 cups canola oil for frying

1/4 cup sweet white rice flour

1/4 cup potato flour (starch)

1/2 cup cornmeal

1 teaspoon baking powder

1/2 teaspoon salt

1/2 teaspoon sugar

1 tablespoon shortening (or lard)

1/3 cup rice milk

INSTRUCTIONS

❶ Bring approximately 3 cups of water to a boil in a large saucepan. Add hot dogs and bring back to boiling. Remove from heat and cover for 20 minutes.

❷ Heat canola oil in a large skillet. The oil should measure at least 2 inches deep; more or less oil may be needed.

❸ Meanwhile, combine flours, cornmeal, baking powder, salt, and sugar in a medium-size bowl and blend with fork. Add shortening and cut in with a knife until the size of small peas.

❹ Add rice milk to cornmeal mixture; stir until well combined. Pour mixture into a tall glass.

❺ Remove cooked hot dogs from pan and pat dry. Insert a skewer into the hot dog and dip hot dog into batter. Immediately transfer to the hot oil and fry until golden brown on all sides, about 3 minutes. Remove and drain on paper towels. Serve warm.

Serves: 6. Preparation Time is 20 minutes. Cooking Time is 5 minutes.

Veggie Burgers

These burgers are fabulous on a bun with a dollop of Smoky Chipotle Dressing or alone as a side dish.

🍽️

INGREDIENTS

3-1/2 cups water

1-1/2 cups short grain brown rice

1 cup shredded carrots

1/2 medium white onion

2 tablespoons arrowroot starch

1/2 teaspoon dried thyme

1/2 teaspoon dried marjoram

1/2 teaspoon dried oregano

1-1/2 teaspoons salt

1/4 teaspoon black pepper

8 ounces mushrooms, sliced

2 cloves garlic, minced

2 tablespoons olive oil, divided

INSTRUCTIONS

Preheat oven to 375°F.

❶ In large saucepan, bring water to boil. Add rice, carrots, and onion. Stir, reduce heat, and cover. Allow rice and vegetables to simmer for approximately 30 minutes, or until all water is dissolved.

❷ Meanwhile, combine the arrowroot starch, thyme, marjoram, oregano, salt, and pepper in a small bowl and set aside.

❸ Add the mushrooms, garlic, and 1 tablespoon of olive oil to a food processor and chop. Add about 1/3 of the cooked rice mixture and pulse quickly about three times. The texture should remain somewhat chunky. Transfer rice mixture to a large mixing bowl.

❹ Working in batches, add remaining cooked rice to the food processor and pulse each batch about 3 times. Transfer processed rice to the large mixing bowl.

❺ When all the rice has been added to the mixing bowl, add the arrowroot starch and spices. Mix just until all ingredients are incorporated.

❻ Spread remaining 1 tablespoon of olive oil on a non-stick baking pan. Form small patties out of the rice mixture and place on the non-stick baking sheet.

❼ Cook burgers for 15 minutes. Flip the burgers and continue baking for 10 minutes.

RECIPE NOTES

Be careful not to overblend or overmix the rice mixture. Otherwise, the burgers won't stick together. To create uniformly round burgers, press rice mixture into a circular cookie cutter and lift up the cookie cutter. Lightly press down on patty if necessary.

Freeze burgers in an airtight container or freezer bag for up to 4 months.

Serves: 4. Preparation Time is 5 minutes. Cooking Time is 45 minutes.

Turkey Burgers

¡◎¦

INGREDIENTS

1/4 cup chicken stock (or water)

2 cloves garlic, minced

1 large shallot, chopped

1/2 small orange bell pepper, chopped

1 medium serrano pepper, seeded and chopped

1 teaspoon dried thyme

1 teaspoon dried parsley

1 teaspoon ground cumin

1/2 teaspoon dried chipotle

1 teaspoon Tabasco sauce

1 teaspoon salt

1/2 teaspoon pepper

1-1/3 pounds ground turkey

INSTRUCTIONS

❶ Combine chicken stock, garlic, shallot, bell pepper, serrano pepper, spices, Tabasco sauce, salt, and pepper in a food processor. Pulse until well blended, but still a little chunky.

❷ Add the vegetable mixture to a large mixing bowl and add the ground turkey. Mix with hands until ingredients are well distributed.

❸ Form turkey mixture into 4 patties. Grill over medium heat for 5 to 7 minutes per side depending on thickness of patties.

❹ Garnish with desired toppings and serve warm on top of hamburger buns or corn tortillas.

RECIPE NOTES

Freeze burgers in an airtight container or freezer bag for up to 3 months.

Serves: 4. Preparation Time is 5 minutes. Cooking Time is 10 minutes.

Meatball Grinders

¶◎¶

INGREDIENTS

1/2 medium white onion, grated

1 clove garlic, minced

1/2 cup bread crumbs

1/4 cup ketchup

1/2 teaspoon fennel seed

1/4 teaspoon dried oregano

1/2 teaspoon salt

1/4 teaspoon pepper

1/2 pound ground beef

1/4 pound ground veal

1/4 pound ground pork

1/4 cup olive oil

2 cups marinara sauce, jarred or see recipe on pages 224 or 57

2 tablespoons fresh chopped basil

2 tablespoons fresh chopped parsley

INSTRUCTIONS

❶ In a large bowl, combine the grated onion, garlic, bread crumbs, ketchup, spices, salt, and pepper. Mix to incorporate ingredients.

❷ Using your hands, mix in the ground meats. Knead the meat to incorporate all the ingredients, but be careful not to overmix.

❸ Roll the meat mixture into 1-inch balls, yielding about 12 to 15 meatballs.

❹ Heat olive oil in a large skillet over medium-high heat. Sauté the meatballs until they are well browned on all sides.

❺ Reduce heat to medium and add marinara sauce directly to the skillet. Simmer over medium heat until meatballs are cooked through, about 15 minutes.

❻ Slice and individually wrap 4 gluten-free/allergen-free hotdog buns in aluminum foil. Warm in a 325°F oven for 3 minutes. Remove buns and promptly place 3 steaming hot meatballs in each bun. Spoon a little sauce over meatballs, garnish with fresh chopped basil and parsley. Quickly rewrap the grinder and return to oven for 3 to 5 minutes. Serve warm.

RECIPE NOTES

Freeze meatballs (with sauce) in an airtight container for up to 3 months.

Serves: 4. Preparation Time is 15 minutes. Cooking Time is 25 minutes.

Sausage, Peppers, and Onions

⫯◎⫯

INGREDIENTS

1/4 cup olive oil

16 ounces Italian sausage

4 cloves garlic, chopped

2 large red bell peppers, julienned

1 large yellow onion, thinly sliced

1 teaspoon salt

6 ounces tomato paste

3/4 cup Marsala wine

1 14.5-ounce can diced tomatoes

3/4 cup loosely packed fresh basil leaves, chopped (about 3/4 ounce)

4 to 6 hotdog buns

INSTRUCTIONS

❶ Heat olive oil in a large skillet over medium heat. Add sausage links and cook until brown on all sides, about 8 to 10 minutes. Remove sausages from pan and cover with aluminum foil to keep warm.

❷ Add the garlic, peppers, onion, and salt to the pan and cook over medium heat until the peppers soften and the onions begin to brown, about 5 minutes.

❸ Add the tomato paste and stir until the paste is well distributed. Add the Marsala wine and canned tomatoes. Stir until ingredients are well incorporated.

❹ Add the sausages back to the pan and bring to a boil. Reduce heat to low and continue to simmer, uncovered, until the sauce thickens, about 15 minutes.

❺ Add basil and continue to simmer for 2 to 3 more minutes.

❻ If using allergen-free buns, wrap buns in foil and preheat in 325°F oven for 3 minutes.

❼ Hollow out the bread from the bottom side of each bun and nestle a sausage in place. Top with ample peppers and onions. For allergen-free buns, reassemble, wrap with aluminum foil, and return to oven for 3 to 5 minutes. Allow sandwiches to sit for 3 to 5 minutes. Serve warm.

Serves: 4. Preparation Time is 5 minutes. Cooking Time is 40 minutes.

Steak Bake

¶◎¶

INGREDIENTS

4 medium baking potatoes

2 tablespoons grapeseed oil

16 ounces flank steak, cut into 1-inch strips

1/2 teaspoon salt

1/4 teaspoon pepper

1/2 cup Creamy Italian Dressing, recipe on page 221

2 cups fresh spinach

2 medium tomatoes, chopped

INSTRUCTIONS

Preheat oven to 400°F.

❶ Wash potatoes and pierce with a fork. Bake in oven until softened, about 50 minutes. Remove from oven and allow to cool for a few minutes before handling.

❷ Heat oil in a medium skillet. Season steak with salt and pepper. Cook steak until browned on outside, but still pink on inside, about 3 to 5 minutes. Remove from heat and set aside.

❸ Cut an X in the top of each potato. Press in and up on the ends. Drizzle a little salad dressing on each potato. Top with spinach, cooked steak, and tomatoes. Drizzle remaining dressing on top of tomatoes and serve.

RECIPE NOTES

Substitute chicken and Cajun Seasoning for the steak and dressing.

Serves: 4. Preparation Time is 10 minutes. Cooking Time is 50 minutes.

Chili-Stuffed Baked Potatoes

¡©!¡

INGREDIENTS

1 head garlic

1/2 teaspoon olive oil

4 large russet potatoes, about 2 pounds

1/2 cup rice milk

2 ounces scallions, chopped

1 teaspoon salt

1/2 teaspoon pepper

2 cups chili con carne, recipe on page 133

2 tablespoons fresh chopped chives

INSTRUCTIONS

Preheat oven to 400°F.

❶ Cut and discard the top third of the head of garlic. Loosely wrap garlic in aluminum foil and drizzle olive oil on exposed garlic. Roast in oven for approximately 50 minutes, or until garlic is golden brown and caramelized. Remove from oven and set aside until cool enough to handle. Once cool, grasp the root end of garlic head and gently squeeze to remove the caramelized cloves from the skin. Extract the cloves and set aside.

❷ At the same time, rinse and scrub potatoes. Pat dry with paper towel and pierce each potato once with a fork. Bake potatoes in oven with garlic for 45 minutes. Remove from oven and allow to cool slightly before handling.

❸ Slice each potato lengthwise. Scoop out the flesh of two potatoes and transfer to a large mixing bowl. Scoop out the flesh of the remaining potatoes and toss or reserve for another use. Add reserved garlic cloves to bowl. Using an electric mixer, beat the potato mixture while slowly adding rice milk.

❹ Add chopped scallions to potatoes and stir together by hand.

❺ Lightly season each potato shell with salt and pepper. Begin to stuff the shells by first adding potato mixture. Be sure to press it in firmly to the bottom and sides of the shell, leaving a little boat for the chili. Next add approximately 1/2 cup of chili to each potato shell and top with chives. Return to oven and bake for approximately 15 minutes until heated through. Garnish with chopped onions, tomatoes, or fresh chopped cilantro.

Serves: 4. Preparation Time is 15 minutes. Cooking Time is 1 hour 10 minutes.

Swedish Meatballs

On Christmas Eve in Swedish homes throughout the Midwest, lutefisk assumes a prominent place on the traditional dinner table. For those who never acquired the taste for the salty cod dish and for those who cannot eat fish, these Swedish meatballs will undoubtedly reposition the lutefisk to the end of the table.

¡◎¡¡

INGREDIENTS

1 cup bread crumbs

1/4 medium white onion, grated

1/2 teaspoon ground cardamom

1/4 teaspoon ground nutmeg

1/4 teaspoon ground ginger

1 teaspoon salt

1/4 teaspoon pepper

1 pound ground beef

1/2 pound ground pork

1/2 pound ground veal

1-1/4 cups water

1/4 cup grapeseed oil

2 cups beef stock

1 tablespoon Dijon mustard

1 tablespoon potato flour (starch)

INSTRUCTIONS

Preheat oven to 375°F.

❶ Combine the bread crumbs with the grated onion, spices, salt, and pepper in a large mixing bowl. Stir with a fork to incorporate all the ingredients.

❷ Add the ground meat and water and beat with an electric mixer on low speed until the mixture is somewhat smooth. Increase the speed to high and beat until the meat becomes light and fluffy, about 5 to 7 minutes.

❸ Using your hands, roll mixed meat into 1-inch balls.

❹ Heat grapeseed oil in a large skillet over medium heat. Working in batches, sauté meatballs until they are well browned on all sides. Transfer meatballs to a baking dish and continue baking in an oven, covered, for about 10 minutes or until meatballs are cooked through. Keep cooked meatballs warm and covered.

❺ Whisk together the beef stock, Dijon mustard, and potato starch and pour directly into skillet used to cook meatballs. Continue whisking and heat over low-medium heat until sauce simmers. Continue to simmer and whisk until sauce thickens, about 3 to 5 minutes. Pour sauce over cooked meatball and serve warm.

RECIPE NOTES

The key to making these Swedish meatballs is to use an electric mixer to ensure a smooth yet fluffy texture.

Freeze meatballs (without sauce) in resealable freezer bags up to 3 months.

Serves: 6. Preparation Time is 15 minutes. Cooking Time is 30 minutes.

Tacos

¡◎¡

INGREDIENTS

2 tablespoons corn oil

1 small red onion, chopped

16 ounces ground beef

1 tablespoon chili powder

2 teaspoons ground cumin

2 teaspoons ground coriander

1 teaspoon salt

1 cup tomato sauce

12 medium corn tortillas or corn tortilla shells

INSTRUCTIONS

❶ Heat corn oil in a medium skillet over medium heat. Add chopped onion and cook until softened, about 5 minutes. Add ground beef and cook until meat is well cooked and no longer pink.

❷ Meanwhile, combine chili powder, cumin, coriander, salt, and tomato sauce. Stir well until spices are well incorporated.

❸ Add tomato mixture to meat and continue to cook until it thickens slightly, about 2 to 3 minutes.

❹ Heat corn tortillas or taco shells in oven at 325°F for 5 minutes. Spoon meat mixture onto tortillas or into shells and garnish with toppings: shredded lettuce, chopped tomato, chopped onion, sliced jalapenos, chopped avocado, salsa, or fresh chopped cilantro.

RECIPE NOTES

Freeze taco meat in airtight containers up to 3 months.

Serves: 4. Preparation Time is 5 minutes. Cooking Time is 15 minutes.

Steak Fajitas

¡◎¡¡

INGREDIENTS

1 pound flank steak

1/3 cup lime juice

1 teaspoon chili powder

1 teaspoon paprika

1 teaspoon ground cumin

1/8 teaspoon cayenne pepper

1/2 teaspoon garlic powder

1-1/2 teaspoons dried parsley

1 teaspoon salt

1/4 teaspoon pepper

3 tablespoons grapeseed oil

1 medium red bell pepper, julienned

1 medium orange bell pepper, julienned

1 medium yellow bell pepper, julienned

1 large white onion, sliced

INSTRUCTIONS

❶ Cut flank steak into 3-inch strips. Combine the lime juice with all the spices, salt, and pepper. Whisk together and toss in a resealable bag with the flank steak. Marinate in the refrigerator for 12 to 24 hours, tossing occasionally.

❷ Heat the oil in a large sauté pan over medium-high heat. Remove steak from marinade and cook in pan until steak begins to brown, but is not quite cooked through, about 3 minutes. Add peppers and onion and continue to cook until vegetables soften and steak is cooked, about 5 to 7 minutes. Serve warm with warm corn tortillas or over shredded lettuce with the smoky chipotle dressing for a fajita salad. Top with favorite garnish.

RECIPE NOTES

♀ Substitute 1 pound of boneless, skinless chicken breast for the flank steak. However, do not marinate the chicken for more than 3 hours.

♀ Substitute 2-1/2 tablespoons of the Southwest Spice Rub in lieu of all the spices to create the marinade.

Serves: 4. Preparation Time is 12 hours. Cooking Time is 10 minutes.

Chicken Enchiladas

The robust flavors and simple techniques introduced in this recipe yield chicken enchiladas so scrumptious that you won't even notice the omission of one main ingredient present in most enchilada recipes: cheese.

¶◎¦¦

INGREDIENTS

2 tablespoons corn oil

1 teaspoon cumin

1 teaspoon garlic powder

1 teaspoon salt, divided

1 pound boneless, skinless chicken breast

1 medium white onion, chopped

1 clove garlic, minced

3 medium vine-ripe tomatoes, seeded and diced

1 11-ounce can corn, drained

2 small chipotle peppers in adobo sauce, diced

1 tablespoon white wine vinegar

1 tablespoon grapeseed oil

2 cups enchilada sauce, divided, recipe on page 228

10 corn tortillas

1 14-ounce can diced green chiles

1 12-ounce can diced jalapeno peppers (optional)

1 12-ounce can sliced olives (optional)

INSTRUCTIONS

Preheat oven to 350°F.

❶ Heat corn oil in a medium skillet over medium-high heat. Combine the cumin, garlic powder, and 1/2 teaspoon of salt in a small bowl. Season chicken breasts with spice mixture and brown chicken in pan for 6 to 8 minutes per side, or until no longer pink. Transfer chicken to a plate to cool.

❷ Reduce heat to medium. Add onion and garlic to pan with residual chicken drippings. Sauté until translucent, about 3 to 5 minutes.

❸ Add tomatoes, corn, chipotle peppers, and remaining 1/2 teaspoon of salt. Sauté for 3 to 5 minutes.

❹ Meanwhile, pull apart the chicken breast and add the shredded pieces back to the pan along with any residual juices or spices on the plate. Stir to incorporate all ingredients and remove from heat.

❺ Transfer approximately 1/2 of the chicken mixture to a food processor or blender. Add the vinegar and puree ingredients. Add pureed chicken mixture back to the remaining chicken mixture, stir together, and set aside.

(continued)

6   Prepare the tortillas. Heat grapeseed oil in a small skillet over medium heat. Place approximately 1/2 cup of the enchilada sauce on a large plate or into a shallow bowl. Dip a tortilla in the sauce to lightly coat both sides. Place the tortilla in the skillet for approximately 30 seconds or until the tortilla begins to bubble. Flip the tortilla over for another 30 seconds. Transfer heated tortilla to a plate and cover with aluminum foil. Repeat with remaining tortillas. (Alternatively, wrap tortillas in aluminum foil with a dab of oil on each tortilla and place in preheated oven for 3 to 5 minutes to soften the tortillas and make them more pliable before assembling.)

7   Ladle approximately 3/4 cup of enchilada sauce into a 9×13-inch baking dish. Assemble the enchiladas by placing a few spoonfuls of the chicken mixture in each tortilla. Roll the tortillas and place in prepared baking dish. Top assembled tortillas with remaining enchilada sauce, green chiles, optional jalapenos, and optional olives. Bake in oven for 15 minutes. Serve warm alongside Spanish rice and beans.

RECIPE NOTES

Cooking all the ingredients in the same pan rather than cooking the chicken separately in the oven and then adding it to the vegetables will maximize the flavors derived from all ingredients. Additionally, the extra step of pureeing 1/2 of the chicken mixture with 1 tablespoon of vinegar will serve as a binder for the chicken filling inside the tortillas. Finally, preparing the tortillas in the suggested manner infuses the flavors of the sauce directly into the tortillas, resulting in a much richer and spicier flavor for both the sauce and the tortilla.

Substitute 2 cups of leftover Slow-Roasted Chipotle Pork for the chicken.

Serves: 4. Preparation Time is 25 minutes. Cooking Time is 50 minutes.

Burrito Bake

¡◎¦

INGREDIENTS

1 pound ground beef

1 cup salsa

1 cup pancake mix

1 cup water

1 15-ounce can refried beans

1 teaspoon chipotle chile powder

1/4 cup canned diced jalapeno peppers

INSTRUCTIONS

Preheat oven to 350°F.

❶ Cook ground beef until browned and cooked through. Remove from heat, stir in salsa, and set aside.

❷ Meanwhile, combine pancake mix, water, refried beans, and chipotle chile powder together. Mix well and transfer to the bottom of a greased pie plate. Add ground beef mixture and top with diced jalapenos.

❸ Bake, uncovered, for 30 minutes. Serve with extra salsa, guacamole, or tortilla chips and garnish with lime slices.

Serves: 4. Preparation Time is 5 minutes. Cooking Time is 35 minutes.

Sloppy Joes

¶◎¶

INGREDIENTS

2 tablespoons grapeseed oil

1 clove garlic, minced

1 medium red bell pepper, diced

1 small white onion, chopped

1 medium tomato, seeded and chopped

16 ounces ground beef

4 tablespoons tomato paste

2 tablespoons brown sugar

3 tablespoons sugar

2 tablespoons red wine vinegar

1/2 teaspoon salt

1/4 cup water

4 to 6 hamburger buns

INSTRUCTIONS

1 Heat oil in a large sauté pan. Add garlic and sauté for 2 minutes.

2 Add chopped pepper, onion, and tomato. Sauté until vegetables begin to soften, about 5 minutes.

3 Add ground beef and continue to cook until meat is well browned.

4 Add remaining ingredients and stir until ingredients are well mixed and sugar is dissolved. Continue to simmer, uncovered, over low heat for 20 minutes.

5 To serve, spoon meat mixture onto toasted hamburger buns and serve. Alternatively try serving over biscuits or white rice.

RECIPE NOTES

Grapeseed oil is a flavorless oil that literally evaporates while cooking. Consequently, it is used often in dishes where all the ingredients end up in one pan. If unable to locate or use grapeseed oil, substitute another flavorless oil such as canola oil or extra light tasting olive oil. Just be sure to drain the meat or use separate pans if your dishes are too oily.

Freeze meat in airtight containers up to 3 months.

Serves: 4. Preparation Time is 5 minutes. Cooking Time is 35 minutes.

Vegetarian Chili I

¡◎!!

INGREDIENTS

1 15-ounce can red kidney beans
1 15-ounce can black beans, drained and rinsed
1 15-ounce can garbanzo beans, drained and rinsed
1 15-ounce can corn, drained
1 28-ounce can diced tomatoes
3 cups salsa, jarred or recipe on page 61 or 62
2 medium chipotle peppers in adobo sauce, diced
1 teaspoon salt
1/2 teaspoon pepper

INSTRUCTIONS

❶ Place beans in a colander; drain and rinse.
❷ Place all ingredients in a large Dutch oven or soup pot. Heat to boiling.
❸ Reduce heat to low-medium and continue to simmer for 10 minutes. Serve warm and garnish with toppings: guacamole, tortilla chips, diced onion, shredded lettuce, or serve alongside corn bread.

Serves: 4. Preparation Time is 5 minutes. Cooking Time is 10 minutes.

Vegetarian Chili II

🍴◎🍴

INGREDIENTS

1/4 cup grapeseed oil

2 large carrots, peeled and chopped

1 medium yellow onion, chopped

2 medium red bell peppers, chopped

1 medium green bell pepper, chopped

2 cloves garlic, minced

1 medium chipotle pepper in adobo sauce, diced

2 tablespoons chili powder

1 tablespoon ground cumin

1 teaspoon ground coriander

1 teaspoon salt

1/2 teaspoon pepper

1 28-ounce can crushed tomatoes

2 15-ounce can red kidney beans, drained and rinsed

1 15-ounce can cannellini beans, drained and rinsed

1 cup refried beans (or lima beans)

1 cup water

1 teaspoon Tabasco sauce

INSTRUCTIONS

❶ Heat grapeseed oil in a large skillet over medium heat. Add chopped carrots, onion, peppers, and garlic. Cook until vegetables soften and onions are translucent, about 10 minutes.

❷ Add chipotle pepper, chili powder, cumin, coriander, salt, and pepper. Stir until vegetables are well coated. Cook for 1 minute.

❸ Add crushed tomatoes, beans, and water. Bring to a boil. Reduce heat to low and simmer, uncovered, for approximately 45 minutes. You may need to periodically add more water depending on desired thickness.

❹ Add Tabasco sauce and simmer for 5 more minutes. Ladle into bowls and serve warm with white rice or corn bread. Garnish with chopped onions, tomatoes, diced jalapeno peppers, guacamole, or fresh chopped cilantro.

RECIPE NOTES

💡 Refried beans are a wonderful thickener for this chili. If you cannot find refried beans that meet your needs, substitute with 1 cup of lima beans and 1 tablespoon of tomato paste.

🍲 Substitute 1 can of dark red kidney beans and 1 can of light red kidney beans for the 2 cans of kidney beans for added variety and color.

Serves: 6. Preparation Time is 10 minutes. Cooking Time is 1 hour.

Chili con Carne

¶☺¶

INGREDIENTS

3 pieces bacon, chopped into 1-inch pieces

1 large red onion, diced

1 large red bell pepper, diced

2 pounds ground beef chuck

2 tablespoons chili powder

2 teaspoons ground cumin

1 teaspoon ground coriander

1 teaspoon salt, divided

2 28-ounce cans whole peeled tomatoes in juice, drained

2 tablespoons tomato paste

3 medium chipotle peppers in adobo sauce, diced

2 tablespoons adobo sauce from the canned peppers

2 15-ounce cans kidney beans (optional)

INSTRUCTIONS

❶ Cook bacon in a large soup pot over medium heat. Add onions and peppers and cook until slightly tender, about 5 minutes.

❷ Add the ground chuck, chili powder, cumin, coriander, and 1/2 teaspoon of salt. Cook until the meat is well browned and cooked through.

❸ Using your hands, crush the canned tomatoes and add them to the pot.

❹ Add the tomato paste, chipotle peppers, adobo sauce, and remaining salt. Stir to fully incorporate the ingredients.

❺ Optional: drain and rinse the beans and add to the pot.

❻ Bring the chili to a boil. Lower heat and simmer, stirring occasionally, until chili becomes thick and fragrant, about 20 minutes (10 minutes with beans.) Ladle into bowls and serve warm with white rice or corn bread. Garnish with chopped onions, tomatoes, diced jalapeno peppers, guacamole, or fresh chopped cilantro.

RECIPE NOTES

👁 Spoon leftover chili over burgers for a southwestern burger or over the top of french fries for chili fries. Alternatively use leftovers to make Chili-Stuffed Baked Potatoes, recipe on page 123.

Serves: 8. Preparation Time is 5 minutes. Cooking Time is 40 minutes.

Southern Barbecue

The word "barbecue" conjures up different images for everyone. For many, it entails a gas or charcoal grill with various meats, laughter, and good conversation. But if you are in the south-eastern part of the U.S., the word "barbecue" means so much more. The varied history of barbecue reflects the varied history of the South and barbecue has become a cultural icon for Southerners of every race, class, and sex. Here is a simple recipe for a sampling of Southern tradition, whether you are in search of flavors rooted deep in heritage or simply looking to try a new recipe. This one is sure to please all.

🍽️

INGREDIENTS
1 medium white onion, chopped
1 cup shredded carrots
1 cup water
1/2 cup ketchup
1/4 cup balsamic vinegar
2 teaspoons brown sugar
2 teaspoons chili powder
1/2 teaspoon salt
2 pounds boneless pork loin chop, cooked and cut into 3/4-inch slices
1 tablespoon corn starch
1 tablespoon water
4 hamburger buns

INSTRUCTIONS
❶ In a medium saucepan, combine onion, carrots, water, ketchup, vinegar, brown sugar, chili powder, and salt. Bring mixture to a boil, reduce heat, cover, and simmer for 15 minutes, or until carrots are soft.

❷ Add pork and simmer, uncovered for 5 more minutes, or until pork is heated through.

❸ Whisk together corn starch with 1 tablespoon of water. Pour into barbecue and stir until thickened, about 2 minutes. Serve warm the traditional way, slathered over hamburger buns. Alternatively, serve with warm corn tortillas or polenta wedges.

Serves: 4. Preparation Time is 5 minutes. Cooking Time is 20 minutes.

Chapter ❺

Entrées

"What is for dinner?"

Whether you have food sensitivities or not, this is the burning question that haunts everyone, every day. When you have food sensitivities complicating the task, preparing dinner can seem daunting. This chapter is full of family favorites, as well as eclectic dishes, to bring both familiarity and flair to your table. All recipes yield extremely satisfying results; you probably won't even remember how you used to make their conventional counterparts.

This chapter takes the fundamentals of hypoallergenic cooking up a degree. Once you have prepared a few of these dishes you will be well on your way to mastering the trade. Pay particular attention to the variety of interchangeable ingredients, or products that you may not be familiar with, such as different cooking oils. In addition to olive oil and canola oil, you will find recipes made with grapeseed oil and safflower oil, for example. While I know that individuals with food sensitivities must experiment cautiously with new ingredients, I introduce a variety of interchangeable ingredients for many reasons. When you cook every single meal, regardless of what you cook, you may feel as you are always eating the same thing. This occurs when we use one ingredient, such as olive oil, for everything. But by alternating oils you can achieve different tastes and textures due to the varied properties of different oils. Accordingly, I like to use many different oils in my cooking. You will find information regarding these oils as you test the recipes. Of course you will want to seek out brands that meet your personal and dietary needs as well.

In addition to switching up the oils used in cooking, these recipes call for various hypoallergenic products such as gluten-free pastas made from rice, quinoa, corn, or beans. Similar to the diversity of oils, these grains have diverse tastes. I have made these recipes with the particular product that I feel best enhances the dish. If you are unable to use the recommended grain, the information on these hypoallergenic products provided should enable you to choose a suitable substitute.

Chicken Piccata

Chicken piccata is an Italian dish accompanied by a tart sauce of lemon juice, white wine, and capers. Traditionally, it is served alongside rice pilaf or herbed pasta and steamed vegetables. I have provided two versions here. I love the chicken piccata pasta, as it provides a complete meal in the same amount of time.

🍽

INGREDIENTS

20 ounces boneless, skinless chicken breast

1/2 teaspoon salt, divided

1/4 teaspoon pepper

1/2 cup tapioca flour

1/3 cup olive oil

1/2 cup dry white wine

2 tablespoons fresh lemon juice

1/4 cup capers, drained

1/3 cup fresh chopped parsley

INSTRUCTIONS

❶ Lightly pound chicken between sheets of plastic wrap to about 1/4 inch thick. Pat chicken dry; season with 1/4 teaspoon of salt and pepper. Dredge chicken in tapioca flour and shake off excess.

❷ In a large skillet over medium high heat, heat olive oil. Working in batches so as not to overcrowd the pan, add chicken and cook for 3 to 5 minutes per side, or until browned and cooked through. Remove cooked chicken, transfer to a plate, and loosely cover with foil to keep warm.

❸ In the same skillet used to cook the chicken, add wine and lemon juice and deglaze skillet over medium heat by stirring and scraping up brown bits. Simmer for 2 minutes until liquid reduces by about half. Add capers and remaining 1/4 teaspoon of salt and remove from heat.

❹ Spoon sauce over cooked chicken and garnish with parsley. Serve alongside herbed rice and steamed vegetables.

RECIPE NOTES

Tapioca flour, otherwise known as tapioca starch or Cassava starch, works particularly well with this dish. This white, starchy, fine-ground flour browns quickly, providing a nice texture and color to the chicken. Additionally, residual traces help thicken the sauce, similar to cornstarch. However using tapioca starch as a thickener results in a sauce with a much clearer consistency than when using corn starch and hence, it is my preferred choice for lighter sauces.

Serves: 4. Preparation Time is 5 minutes. Cooking Time is 15 minutes.

Chicken Piccata Pasta

¶◎¶

INGREDIENTS

20 ounces boneless, skinless chicken breast

1/4 teaspoon salt

1/4 teaspoon pepper

1/2 cup tapioca flour

2/3 cup olive oil, divided

16 ounces rice fettuccine pasta

1/2 cup dry white wine

2 tablespoons fresh lemon juice

1/4 cup capers, drained

5 medium roma tomatoes (about 1 pound)

1/2 teaspoon coarse sea salt

1/3 cup fresh chopped parsley

INSTRUCTIONS

❶ Lightly pound chicken between sheets of plastic wrap to about 1/8 inch thick. Pat chicken dry; season with salt and pepper. Dredge chicken in tapioca flour and shake off excess.

❷ In a large skillet over medium high heat, heat 1/3 cup of olive oil. Working in batches so as not to overcrowd the pan, add chicken and cook for 3 to 5 minutes per side, or until browned and cooked through. Remove cooked chicken, transfer to a plate, and loosely cover with foil to keep warm.

❸ Cook fettuccine pasta according to instructions.

❹ Meanwhile, in the same skillet used to cook the chicken, add wine and lemon juice and deglaze skillet over medium heat by stirring and scraping up brown bits. Simmer for 2 minutes until liquid reduces by about half. Add capers, chopped tomatoes, and remaining 1/3 cup olive oil. Continue to cook until tomatoes soften, about 3 to 4 minutes.

❺ Add cooked fettuccine directly to pan, along with coarse sea salt. Remove from heat. Stir until well coated. Mound a plate with a serving of fettuccine on each plate and top with chicken. Garnish with parsley and serve.

Serves: 4. Preparation Time is 5 minutes. Cooking Time is 15 minutes.

Chicken Marinara

¡◎¡¡

INGREDIENTS

1-1/2 cups bread crumbs

1 teaspoon salt

1/2 teaspoon pepper

4 medium chicken breasts, about 20 ounces

1/4 cup grapeseed oil

1/2 medium lemon

2 cups chunky marinara sauce, jarred or see recipe on pages 224 or 57

1/3 cup sliced olives (optional)

2 tablespoons capers, drained (optional)

4 medium fresh basil leaves

INSTRUCTIONS

Preheat oven to 350°F.

❶ Combine bread crumbs, salt, and pepper in a small bowl; stir together and set aside.

❷ Place chicken breasts in a large resealable plastic bag. Briefly tenderize by pounding with a kitchen mallet. Add bread crumb mixture to bag and, using hands, massage bread crumbs into chicken breasts while tossing bag to evenly distribute.

❸ Heat grapeseed oil in a large sauté pan. Working in batches, fry breaded chicken until golden brown, about 2 to 3 minutes per side. Transfer chicken to a 9×13 casserole dish and drizzle with juice of 1/2 lemon. Cover with aluminum foil and place in preheated oven for 15 minutes, or until chicken is cooked through.

❹ Meanwhile, heat marinara sauce over low-medium heat. If desired, add sliced olives and capers.

❺ Remove chicken from oven. Place one breast on each plate and top with 1/2 cup marinara sauce. Garnish each serving with one basil leaf and serve on top of rice pasta.

RECIPE NOTES

◉ Leftover cutlets are very versatile and an enormous time saver. Simply reheat in microwave and serve on a toasted bun with mustard, bacon, and tomato for a delicious chicken cutlet sandwich or slice over the top of a salad and drizzle with honey.

▢ Wrap leftover cooked chicken cutlets (without sauce) in aluminum foil and freeze for up to 3 months.

Serves: 4. Preparation Time is 10 minutes. Cooking Time is 20 minutes.

Chicken Scaloppine with Tarragon Wine Sauce

 ¡◎¡¡

INGREDIENTS

20 ounces boneless, skinless chicken breast

1/2 cup potato flour (starch)

3 tablespoons olive oil

1 medium shallot, minced

16 ounces button mushrooms, sliced

1/2 cup white wine

1-1/2 cups chicken stock

2 small roma tomatoes, seeded and chopped

1 tablespoon fresh chopped tarragon

1/2 teaspoon salt

1/4 teaspoon pepper

INSTRUCTIONS

❶ Using a meat mallet, pound the chicken breasts to approximately 1/2 inch thick. Lightly dredge breasts in potato flour and shake off excess.

❷ Heat olive oil in a large sauté pan over medium-high heat. Sauté the chicken breasts until lightly browned on both sides and cooked through, about 3 to 5 minutes per side. Remove chicken and cover to keep warm.

❸ Add shallots and mushrooms to pan. Sauté for 2 minutes.

❹ Add wine to pan and simmer while scraping up any brown bits. Continue to simmer until most of the liquid has evaporated, about 5 minutes.

❺ Add the chicken stock, tomatoes, tarragon, salt, and pepper. Bring to a simmer and continue to cook until the liquid has reduced by half. To serve, slice a chicken breast diagonally into 2-inch strips and ladle tarragon wine sauce over top. Garnish with lemon wedges and serve alongside rice and steamed vegetables.

Serves: 4. Preparation Time is 5 minutes. Cooking Time is 20 minutes.

Bourbon Chicken

🍴⊙🍴

INGREDIENTS

1 cup white grape juice, divided

1/2 cup bourbon whiskey

3 tablespoons packed brown sugar

1/2 teaspoon ground ginger

1/4 teaspoon salt

20 ounces boneless, skinless chicken breast

1/4 cup grapeseed oil

1 tablespoon sugar

1/4 cup water

1 tablespoon dark corn syrup

INSTRUCTIONS

❶ Combine 1/2 cup white grape juice, bourbon, brown sugar, ginger, and salt. Stir until thoroughly blended. Pour 1/2 of the marinade over chicken and seal in a resealable plastic bag. Refrigerate for up to 3 hours. Reserve remaining marinade in refrigerator.

❷ Heat grapeseed oil in a large sauté pan over medium heat. Sear the chicken breasts until browned and cooked through, about 5 minutes per side.

❸ Meanwhile, combine the reserved marinade with the remaining 1/2 cup grape juice, sugar, water, and corn syrup in a small saucepan. Bring to a simmer and stir until sugar dissolves and the bourbon sauce thickens. Pour over the cooked chicken in pan and allow to simmer over medium heat until a glaze forms on the chicken, about 3 minutes. Serve warm.

RECIPE NOTES

◉ Wrap leftover chicken and store in refrigerator for up to 2 days. Slice leftovers and layer over a green salad. Or cube the chicken and toss with sautéed vegetables and serve over white rice for a tasty stir-fry.

▢ Freeze in airtight containers up to 3 months.

Serves: 4. Preparation Time is 5 minutes. Inactive Preparation Time is 3 hours. Cooking Time is 15 minutes.

Turkey Tetrazzini

🍴◎🍴

INGREDIENTS

4 cups rice milk

8 ounces quinoa pasta, spaghetti style

2 tablespoons canola oil

8 ounces button mushrooms,
    sliced (about 2 cups)

1 medium white onion,
    chopped (about 1 cup)

1 cup chicken stock

2 tablespoons dry sherry

1 tablespoon cornstarch

1 tablespoon dried tarragon

1 teaspoon salt

20 ounces cooked turkey meat,
    sliced into 1/2-inch bite-size strips
    (about 3 cups)

1/2 cup bread crumbs

2 tablespoons olive oil

INSTRUCTIONS

Preheat oven to 375°F.

❶ Lightly grease a 9×13-inch baking pan or other shallow baking dish using a dab of canola oil or other allowed shortening.

❷ Heat rice milk in a pot until boiling. Add quinoa pasta and cook until pasta is al dente, being careful not to overcook as the pasta will finish cooking in the oven. Drain pasta and reserve 1-1/2 cups of the cooking liquid.

❸ Meanwhile, heat canola oil in a large skillet. Add mushrooms and onion and sauté over medium heat. Cook until mushrooms and onions become softened, about 5 minutes. Remove from heat and set aside.

❹ Add the 1-1/2 cups of reserved cooking liquid to the mushrooms and onions, stir, and heat over medium heat.

❺ Whisk together the chicken stock, sherry, cornstarch, tarragon, and salt and add to the mushroom sauce. Bring sauce to a boil and continue boiling for 1 minute until sauce begins to thicken. Remove from heat and add the cooked pasta and turkey directly to the mushroom sauce.

❻ Pour the mixture into the prepared pan and sprinkle with bread crumbs. Drizzle with olive oil and bake on top rack of oven until sauce is bubbly, about 15 to 20 minutes. Serve warm.

RECIPE NOTES

 Ancient Harvest's corn and quinoa spaghetti pasta gives this dish vibrant color and an added punch of flavor. However a rice-based spaghetti pasta will work as well. Similar to rice pasta, the quinoa pasta will disintegrate slightly when cooking. By cooking the pasta directly in the rice milk, the natural flavors of the ingredients work together to maximize the intensity and produce an amazing result. The pasta will absorb the sweet flavor and nutrients of the rice milk during the cooking. At the same time, as the pasta cooks, it will thicken the rice milk, giving the mushroom sauce a nice and creamy consistency.

Serves: 4. Preparation Time is 5 minutes. Cooking Time is 45 minutes.

Roasted Cornish Game Hens with Rhubarb Compote

⅋⊚⅋

INGREDIENTS

4 cups chopped rhubarb,
    cut into 1-inch pieces

1/3 cup sugar

1 tablespoon orange zest

4 medium Cornish game hens,
    thawed, rinsed, and patted dry

1/4 cup extra light tasting olive oil

1 tablespoon orange juice

1 teaspoon salt

1/4 teaspoon pepper

4 medium bay leaves

INSTRUCTIONS

Preheat oven to 375°F.

❶ Combine chopped rhubarb and sugar in a medium saucepan. Let stand at room temperature for 15 minutes so the natural juices begin to extract. Then heat the rhubarb over medium-high heat until boiling, stirring constantly to prevent the sugar from burning. Reduce heat to low and simmer, covered, until the rhubarb is tender and the sauce is thickened, about 10 minutes.

❷ Add the orange zest, stir a few times, remove from heat, and cool without stirring for 10 to 15 minutes before transferring to the refrigerator. Refrigerate for 2 hours to allow compote to thicken properly.

❸ Meanwhile, prepare the hens. Whisk together the extra light tasting olive oil, orange juice, salt, and pepper and brush hens inside and out with mixture. Place hens in a shallow roasting pan, breast side up, and place one bay leaf on top of each breast. Roast in oven for approximately 50 minutes or until the thickest part of the thigh reaches an internal temperature of 175°F and the outer skin is well browned. Remove from oven and allow to cool for 10 minutes. To serve, plate each bird with a spoonful of rhubarb compote over the top. Serve alongside wild rice.

RECIPE NOTES

For those who suffer from multiple food allergies to fruits, a sweet sauce may be out of the question. Contrary to what it may seem, rhubarb is actually a perennial vegetable and a member of the buckwheat family. By adding a little sugar, the natural sweetness comes out and cuts through any tartness, adding a wonderful complement to pork and poultry. Additionally, it is extremely simple to prepare. Remember, only the stalks are edible; don't eat the leaves or roots. Add a bowl of this compote to your Thanksgiving table and you will be swimming in compliments.

Store leftover rhubarb compote in refrigerator for up to 3 days or in freezer up to 3 months. Spoon over toast, spread on a turkey sandwich, or place a dollop on roasted pork.

Serves: 4. Preparation Time is 15 minutes. Inactive Preparation Time is 2 hours. Cooking Time is 1 hour 20 minutes.

Pan-Seared Duck Breast with Cherry Wine Sauce

¡◎¡†

INGREDIENTS

4 duck breasts (about 6 ounce each)

1/4 teaspoon salt

2 tablespoons grapeseed oil

1 cup dried cherries

1/2 cup unsulfured molasses

4 cups chicken stock, divided

2 tablespoons arrowroot starch

1/2 cup Madeira wine

2 teaspoons sherry wine vinegar

INSTRUCTIONS

Preheat oven to 375°F.

❶ Place the duck breasts skin (fat) side up. Using a sharp knife, score 4 cuts across the skin for each breast. Turn over and season meat side with salt.

❷ Heat the grapeseed oil in a nonstick skillet over high heat. Sear the duck breasts, skin side down, until skin is brown and crispy, about 3 to 5 minutes. Turn and cook meat side for 2 to 3 more minutes. Remove from heat. Transfer duck breasts to a baking dish or rimmed baking sheet and finish cooking on top rack of preheated oven, skin side up, for 6 to 8 minutes, or until desired doneness. Remove from oven and keep warm.

❸ To the original pan with duck drippings, add the dried cherries, molasses, and 3-1/2 cups of chicken stock. Bring to a boil, reduce heat, and simmer for 15 minutes.

❹ Whisk the arrowroot starch into the remaining 1/2 cup chicken stock and add to the pan, along with the Madeira wine. Continue to simmer the sauce until slightly thickened, about 3 to 4 minutes. Add sherry vinegar and simmer for 2 to 3 more minutes. To serve, slice each duck breast at a 45° angle into 1/2-inch thick slices and spoon warm cherry wine sauce on top. Serve with a side of wild rice and Glazed Baby Carrots.

RECIPE NOTES

▣ Grapeseed oil is fabulous for searing the duck breasts as it literally evaporates while cooking. Not only does it allow the fat from the duck breast to flavor the dish rather than the oil, but it results in a sauce that is less oily.

▣ Arrowroot starch is a wonderful thickening agent that results in a clear yet somewhat shimmery consistency, which is the perfect complement to the cherry color. This starch works better than cornstarch when thickening an acidic liquid. Alternatively you could use tapioca starch, which will also give the sauce a glossy sheen.

Serves: 4. Preparation Time is 10 minutes. Cooking Time is 35 minutes.

Braised Pork Chops

A simple dish with vibrant flavor, this recipe pairs wonderfully with the Fruited Acorn Squash Bake or even better, a simple side of applesauce or the Spiced Pear Compote.

🍴◎🍴

INGREDIENTS

2 teaspoons Dijon mustard

1/4 cup brown sugar

2 tablespoons red wine vinegar

1/3 cup beef stock

1/3 cup water

2 teaspoons garlic salt

2 tablespoons grapeseed oil

2 pounds boneless center-cut pork chops

INSTRUCTIONS

❶ In a small bowl, combine mustard, brown sugar, vinegar, beef stock, water, and garlic salt. Stir well and set aside.

❷ Heat oil in a large skillet over medium-high heat. Brown pork chops on all sides, about 2 to 3 minutes per side. Reduce heat to low and pour prepared sauce over pork chops. Cover and simmer until the pork chops are tender and cooked through, about 50 minutes.

❸ Transfer pork to a platter. Raise heat to medium-high and bring sauce to a low, steady boil. Continue to cook until it thickens, about 5 minutes. Pour sauce over pork chops and serve alongside cinnamon apples or acorn squash and wild rice.

RECIPE NOTES

Freeze in airtight containers up to 3 months.

Serves: 4. Preparation Time is 5 minutes. Cooking Time is 1 hour.

Sweet and Sour Pork

¶◎∥

INGREDIENTS

1 tablespoon arrowroot starch

1/4 cup pineapple juice

1 cup sliced strawberries (fresh or frozen and thawed)

3/4 cup apple juice

24 ounces pork loin

1/2 teaspoon salt

1/2 teaspoon pepper

3 tablespoons canola oil

1/2 teaspoon grated fresh ginger root

1 medium red bell pepper, julienned

1 tablespoon brown sugar

2 tablespoons cider vinegar

1/2 cup pineapple chunks

1/2 cup maraschino cherries (optional)

INSTRUCTIONS

❶ In a small bowl, whisk arrowroot starch into pineapple juice and set aside.

❷ Using a food processor, puree strawberries with apple juice until smooth. Set aside.

❸ Cut pork loin into 1-1/2-inch cubes. Season with salt and pepper. Heat canola oil in a heavy skillet over medium heat. Cook pork cubes in oil until browned on the outside and cooked through, about 4 to 5 minutes per side. Transfer cooked pork to a platter and keep warm.

❹ In same skillet, add grated ginger and red pepper. Sauté until pepper begins to soften, about 3 minutes. Add strawberry-apple puree and bring to a boil. Add brown sugar and vinegar. Continue to boil until sugar dissolves, about 1 minute.

❺ Add arrowroot starch mixture and reduce heat to low. Stir continuously over a low simmer until mixture thickens.

❻ Add pineapple chunks and cherries (optional). Spoon sweet and sour sauce over pork. Serve with white or brown rice.

RECIPE NOTES

Arrowroot starch (flour) thickens sauces at a lower temperature than does cornstarch or ordinary flour without adding chalky flavor. Consequently it is a great thickening agent to use for sauces you don't want to boil to thicken.

Serves: 4. Preparation Time is 10 minutes. Cooking Time is 15 minutes.

Slow-Roasted Chipotle Pork

†◎†

INGREDIENTS

2 tablespoons extra light tasting olive oil

1-1/2 tablespoons coarse sea salt

1 tablespoon chipotle chile powder

3-1/2 pounds pork shoulder roast

INSTRUCTIONS

Preheat oven to 300°F.

❶ Combine olive oil, sea salt, and chipotle powder and rub all over the pork, massaging the pork as you work. Be sure to cover the entire surface of the meat with the rub.

❷ Place roast in a large roasting pan, cover, and roast in oven for about 3-1/2 hours. To test the doneness, press the pork with the back of a fork; it should fall apart when done. Remove roast from oven and allow to cool at room temperature, covered, for 20 minutes.

❸ Transfer pork to a large serving platter and, using two forks, pull apart the pork, shredding it into chunks. Serve over white rice or with warm corn tortillas and garnish with lime slices.

RECIPE NOTES

◉ Refrigerate leftovers up to 3 days. Toss with barbecue sauce and serve on toasted buns for a scrumptious pulled pork sandwich.

Serves: 6. Preparation Time is 5 minutes. Cooking Time is 3 hours 30 minutes.

Meat Loaf

¶◎¡↑

INGREDIENTS

1 cup chopped green bell pepper

1 cup chopped yellow onion

2 cloves garlic

1 teaspoon salt

1 cup bread crumbs

1/4 cup dried parsley

1/3 cup ketchup

1/2 teaspoon ground mustard

2 pounds ground meat

GLAZE

3 tablespoons packed brown sugar

1/3 cup ketchup

1 tablespoon minced onion

1 teaspoon coarse sea salt

INSTRUCTIONS

Preheat oven to 400°F.

❶ Add green pepper, onion, garlic, and salt to a food processor and chop until pieces are well minced. Set aside for 10 minutes to allow the natural juices to release.

❷ Meanwhile, combine the bread crumbs, parsley, ketchup, and ground mustard. Add the minced peppers and onions to this mixture and combine.

❸ Using hands, knead the meat into the loaf mixture just until ingredients are well combined. Transfer meat loaf to a nonstick loaf pan.

❹ For the glaze, combine the brown sugar, ketchup, minced onion, and sea salt until smooth. Brush glaze over meat loaf. Bake, uncovered, for 45 to 50 minutes. Remove from oven, cover with foil, and let meat loaf rest for another 10 minutes before serving.

RECIPE NOTES

Most conventional meat loaf recipes use eggs as binders. Unfortunately, most egg-replacement products are formulated to work well in baking recipes and do not work well in meat recipes. However, by employing certain techniques and working with the other ingredients' natural cooking properties, you can make a fabulous version of meat loaf without eggs or egg replacement products.

Adding salt to the peppers and onions will naturally draw out the juices of these ingredients, which will assist in binding the other ingredients together. Well-cooked onions are a wonderful thickening agent which fill in open spaces of the meat loaf and actually hold it together. Just be careful not to overmix the meat or the onion juices will become too sparse to work their magic.

Slice meat loaf and wrap individual slices in aluminum foil. Place in a resealable freezer bag and freeze up to 3 months.

Serves: 6. Preparation Time is 10 minutes. Cooking Time is 50 minutes.

Beef Stroganoff

¡◎¡¡

INGREDIENTS

3 tablespoons grapeseed oil

1 pound beef tenderloin tips

1/2 medium red onion, chopped

8 ounces cremini mushrooms, sliced

1-1/2 cups beef broth

1 tablespoon cornstarch

1 teaspoon salt

3 tablespoons rice milk

1 teaspoon Dijon mustard

INSTRUCTIONS

❶ Heat grapeseed oil in a large skillet over medium-high heat. Add beef tips and red onion. Sauté until meat is evenly browned, 3 to 4 minutes total. The meat should remain pink in the center.

❷ Add mushrooms and continue cooking for 1 to 2 minutes.

❸ Reduce heat to low. Whisk the beef broth, cornstarch, and salt together and add to the beef. Continue simmering until sauce thickens, about 5 minutes.

❹ Add rice milk and mustard. Stir and remove from heat. Spoon over quinoa noodles or rice.

RECIPE NOTES

Beef Stroganoff pairs wonderfully with a quinoa and corn pasta. The combination of the two grains gives this noodle a buttery, egg flavor that really complements this dish. Compared to other grains, quinoa is high in protein, calcium, and iron.

For a more succulent version, substitute 1 ounce of dried porcini mushrooms for the cremini mushrooms. Rehydrate the dried mushrooms in 1 cup of hot water for 30 minutes, rinse, and add in step 2.

Serves: 4. Preparation Time is 10 minutes. Cooking Time is 15 minutes.

Butter-Knife Short Ribs

These short ribs require a lot of time, time which you probably don't have. However, the recipe requires minimal attention and the ribs just seem to come out perfect every time. They are so succulent and flavorful, allowing you a little indulgence without a lot of effort.

🍴◎🍴

INGREDIENTS

1/4 cup grapeseed oil

3 pounds bone-in beef short ribs

1 teaspoon salt, divided

3 cloves garlic, chopped

1 medium white onion, chopped

2 medium carrots, chopped

2 celery stalks, chopped

1 bottle dry red wine (750 ml)

6 cups beef stock

INSTRUCTIONS

Preheat oven to 350°F.

❶ Heat grapeseed oil in a large, heavy-bottomed ovenproof pan or Dutch oven over high heat. Season short ribs with 1/2 teaspoon of salt. Working in batches, sear the ribs until browned on all sides; remove from heat and set aside in refrigerator.

❷ Add the garlic and onion to the pan and sauté until lightly browned, about 2 to 3 minutes. Reduce heat to medium and add the carrots, celery, and remaining 1/2 teaspoon of salt. Cook until vegetables are softened, about 5 minutes.

❸ Add the entire bottle of wine to the pan, scraping up any brown bits that have accumulated on the bottom. Bring to a boil and then reduce heat to low-medium and continue to simmer, uncovered, until the liquid reduces by about 75%, about 30 minutes.

❹ Return short ribs to pan and add enough stock so that the ribs are completely covered. Bring to a boil, cover, and transfer to oven. Cook until meat is tender and falling away from the bone, about 2 hours. Remove from oven and let stand for 20 minutes.

❺ Transfer short ribs to plates. Strain cooked vegetables from remaining stock and puree in a blender until smooth. Thin with residual cooking stock if desired. Pour gravy over ribs and serve alongside mashed potatoes or polenta.

RECIPE NOTES

This dish can be prepared up to 2 days in advance and is one of those dishes that actually improves with time. Allowing the meat to cool in its juices really intensifies the flavor. After step 4, allow meat to cool in the liquid, then refrigerate for up to 48 hours. Scrape off solidified fat from top and reheat on stove, uncovered, at a low simmer for about 30 minutes, while occasionally spooning sauce over the ribs to create a thin glaze. This extra step will give you a melt-in-the-mouth effect with such a robust flavor you will suddenly have time to make this over and over.

Serves: 6. Preparation Time is 10 minutes. Cooking Time is 3 hours.

Beef Burgundy

As winds of winter blow at your door, nothing warms the soul like a pot of stew simmering on the stove. This hearty beef dish is an adaptation of the classic French concoction and, like any stew, it tastes better the next day.

†◎††

INGREDIENTS
1-1/2 pounds boneless beef bottom round
1-1/2 cups dry red wine
1/4 cup olive oil
1 clove garlic, chopped
1 teaspoon salt, divided
4 ounces bacon, chopped
1 medium red onion, chopped
1 medium carrot, peeled and chopped
1 medium bay leaf
8 ounces button mushrooms, sliced
8 ounces pearl onions
2 tablespoons fresh chopped parsley
1/2 teaspoon dried thyme
1/2 teaspoon dried marjoram

INSTRUCTIONS
1. Cut beef into 1-inch cubes. Combine the wine with the olive oil, garlic, and 1/2 teaspoon of salt and pour over meat. Refrigerate for at least one hour, preferably overnight. When finished marinating, remove beef and pat dry. Save the wine marinade.
2. Meanwhile cook the bacon in a large Dutch oven over medium-high heat until well browned. Remove the bacon with a slotted spoon and save for later.
3. Reduce heat to medium and add the onion and carrot to the bacon fat. Sauté for 3 to 5 minutes until vegetables soften. Add the marinade, beef, bacon, and bay leaf to pot. Bring to a boil then reduce heat to low and simmer, covered, for 1-1/2 hours.
4. Add the mushrooms and pearl onions and continue to cook over low heat, covered, for another 30 minutes.
5. Remove the bay leaf and stir in the remaining 1/2 teaspoon of salt, parsley, thyme, and marjoram. Allow the stew to cool in its own juices for 20 minutes before serving. Serve over noodles, rice, or boiled new potatoes.

RECIPE NOTES
Freeze in airtight containers for up to 3 months.

Serves: 4. Preparation Time is 10 minutes. Inactive Preparation Time is 1 hour 20 minutes. Cooking Time is 2 hours 15 minutes.

Veal Marsala

This dish is a simple yet elegant entrée that can be made in a matter of minutes. Veal cutlets are a wonderful staple to maintain in your freezer as they thaw rather quickly.

¶◎¶

INGREDIENTS

1 pound veal scallopine (cutlet)

3/4 teaspoons salt

1/4 teaspoon pepper

3/4 cup potato flour (starch)

1/4 cup grapeseed oil

2 cloves garlic, chopped

16 ounces mushrooms, sliced

1 cup dry Marsala wine

2 tablespoons tapioca flour

1/4 cup beef stock

2 tablespoons fresh chopped parsley

INSTRUCTIONS

❶ Sprinkle the veal cutlets with salt and pepper. Dredge each slice in potato flour and shake off the excess.

❷ Heat the grapeseed oil in a heavy large skillet over medium-high heat. Add the veal cutlets and cook until golden brown, about 2 minutes per side. Transfer the veal to a plate and cover with foil.

❸ Add the garlic to the skillet and sauté until fragrant, about 1 minute. If necessary, add another tablespoon of oil. Add the mushrooms and sauté until tender, about 3 to 5 minutes.

❹ Add the Marsala wine and simmer about 3 minutes or until liquid reduces by about half.

❺ Meanwhile, whisk the tapioca starch into the beef stock until dissolved. Add to the skillet and continue to simmer until sauce begins to thicken.

❻ Return veal to the pan and continue to cook until the veal is heated through, about 1 to 2 minutes.

❼ To serve, place a piece of veal on a plate and spoon the sauce over the veal. Garnish with a sprig of fresh parsley.

RECIPE NOTES

This recipe calls for two different starches, potato and tapioca. The potato flour (starch) gives the veal a rich, golden brown flavor while maintaining the tenderness of the dish. The tapioca starch is a great thickener to use to enhance this sauce as it maintains a clear consistency, adding to the elegance of the dish. The potato flour (starch) can be used in lieu of the tapioca in step 4 if you desire a thicker sauce with a creamier texture.

Serves: 4. Preparation Time is 5 minutes. Cooking Time is 15 minutes.

Stuffed Veal Rolls

¶◎⑇

INGREDIENTS

1 large red bell pepper, diced
2 medium green onions, chopped
1 clove garlic, minced
1-1/2 cup chicken stock, divided
1 cup bread crumbs
1/2 teaspoon salt
1-1/2 pounds veal scallopine (cutlet)
4 ounces prosciutto
1/3 cup olive oil

INSTRUCTIONS

❶ In a small saucepan, combine the pepper, green onions, garlic, and 1 cup of chicken stock. Heat over medium heat, covered for 5 to 7 minutes, or until vegetables are tender. Remove from heat and stir in bread crumbs and salt. Use your hands to lightly press the stuffing together. Set aside.

❷ Lay veal cutlets on a flat working surface. Lay a slice of prosciutto on each cutlet, followed by a scoop of the bread crumb mixture. Roll up the stuffed cutlets, folding in the sides and securing with wooden toothpicks.

❸ Meanwhile, heat oil in a large skillet over medium-high heat. Sauté the cutlets until browned on all sides, about 3 minutes per side. Reduce heat to medium, add the remaining 1/2 cup of chicken stock to the skillet, cover, and simmer for 15 minutes or until veal is cooked and tender. Serve stuffed veal rolls with quinoa pilaf or herbed rice and a steamed vegetable. If desired, spoon extra sauce over veal rolls and garnish with fresh chopped parsley.

Serves: 4. Preparation Time is 10 minutes. Cooking Time is 30 minutes.

Osso Buco

¶◎↾↿

INGREDIENTS

1 cup dried porcini mushrooms (1 ounce)

1 cup hot water

4 veal shanks, 2 inches thick
 (about 2 pounds total)

3/4 teaspoon salt, divided

1/2 teaspoon pepper, divided

1/2 cup olive oil

1 large red onion, chopped

1 cup chopped carrots

4 cloves garlic, chopped

1 can (14-1/2 ounces) whole tomatoes

1/2 tablespoon fresh chopped rosemary

2 tablespoons cornstarch

1 cup beef stock

1 cup dry red wine

INSTRUCTIONS

Preheat oven to 325°F.

❶ Place dried porcini mushrooms in a bowl and cover with hot water. Let sit for 30 minutes. After 30 minutes, drain the mushrooms and reserve about 1/2 of the mushroom stock. Strain the stock through a paper towel to remove any dirt or particles and set aside.

❷ Season the shanks with 1/4 teaspoon of salt and pepper. Heat olive oil in large Dutch oven or large heatproof casserole. Sauté shanks on both sides until golden brown, about 3 minutes per side. Remove shanks and set aside.

❸ Reduce heat to low-medium and in the same pan, sauté the onion, carrots, and garlic until softened, about 5 minutes.

❹ Remove pan from heat and add tomatoes with juice, rosemary, rehydrated mushrooms, 1/2 strained mushroom stock, remaining 1/2 teaspoon salt, and 1/4 teaspoon pepper to the pan.

❺ Whisk cornstarch into beef stock and add to the pan. Return the veal shanks to pan and add the red wine. The liquid should come up to about 3/4 of the shanks. If not, add additional equal parts of stock and wine.

❻ Cover and bake in oven for 2 hours, or until veal is tender and pulls away from the bone.

❼ To serve, spoon risotto (or other suggested accompaniment) onto a large serving dish and top with shanks. Generously moisten with some of the sauce. Garnish with gremolata (optional).

RECIPE NOTES

Risotto Milanese is the ideal accompaniment to this dish. But polenta is also quite complementary and can be prepared quickly and easily. Mashed potatoes are another favorite. Basically, any starch that will help sop up the succulent sauce pairs well with osso buco.

Serves: 4. Preparation Time is 40 minutes. Cooking Time is 2 hours.

Lamb Curry

ᵧ◎ᵧ

INGREDIENTS

2 tablespoons grapeseed oil

1-1/2 pounds boneless lean lamb, cut into 1-inch pieces

1 tablespoon curry powder

1/2 teaspoon salt

1 clove garlic, minced

1 medium white onion, chopped

1 medium carrot, diced

1 celery stalk, diced

1/2 cup water

1/2 cup apple juice or white grape juice

1/3 cup golden raisins

1 tablespoon corn starch

1 cup water

INSTRUCTIONS

❶ Heat grapeseed oil in a large sauté pan over medium-high heat. Season the lamb with curry powder and salt. Sauté until browned, about 5 minutes. Remove lamb from pan.

❷ Reduce heat to medium. Add garlic and onion to pan. Sauté until translucent, about 3 minutes. Add carrot and celery and sauté for 2 minutes.

❸ Return meat along with any residual juices to the pan. Stir in water, apple juice, and raisins. Bring mixture to a boil, reduce heat, and simmer, covered, for 30 minutes or until lamb is tender.

❹ Whisk the corn starch into the water and add to the pan. Simmer the curry just until the sauce becomes thickened, about 5 minutes. Remove from heat. Serve warm over white rice.

Serves: 4. Preparation Time is 5 minutes. Cooking Time is 55 minutes.

Shepherd's Pie

¶◎¶

INGREDIENTS

3 large baking potatoes (about 2 pounds)

2 tablespoons extra light tasting olive oil

1 cup rice milk (hot)

2 teaspoons salt, divided

1/4 cup canola oil

1 medium onion, chopped

1 large carrot, diced

1 celery stalk, diced

1 clove garlic, chopped

1 pound ground lamb

1/2 cup dry red wine

1 tablespoon potato flour (starch)

1/2 cup beef stock

1/2 cup frozen peas

1 teaspoon dried thyme

1/2 teaspoon dried rosemary

1/2 teaspoon pepper

INSTRUCTIONS

Preheat oven to 375°F.

❶ Rinse, peel, and quarter potatoes. Place in large pot of water and bring to a boil. Cook until tender, about 20 minutes. Drain and transfer to a large mixing bowl. Add olive oil and begin to mash potatoes. Using a wire fork, mix in enough hot rice milk to make a creamy puree (you may not need all the milk.) Fluff with fork, add 1 teaspoon of salt, and set aside. The consistency of the potato topping should not be as creamy as mashed potatoes. They should be drier and fluffy, lending a cloud-like texture to the top of the meat while baking.

❷ Meanwhile, heat oil in a large frying pan over medium heat. Add onion, carrot, celery, and garlic. Sauté until vegetables are softened, about 5 to 7 minutes.

❸ Add ground lamb and continue to sauté until lamb is cooked through, about 10 minutes.

❹ Add red wine and bring to a boil, scraping up any brown bits. Continue to simmer until liquid is reduced by half.

❺ Whisk potato starch into beef stock and add to pan. Stir in frozen peas, remaining salt, and spices. Reduce heat to low and simmer until sauce is thickened, about 5 minutes.

❻ Transfer lamb mixture to a 9-inch loaf pan or pie plate. Spread mashed potato mixture over top. Bake in oven until potatoes peaks are golden brown, about 40 minutes. Serve hot.

(continued)

RECIPE NOTES

While I often recommend using grapeseed oil when cooking all ingredients together due to its evaporating characteristic, this recipe actually benefits from a heavier, flavorless oil like canola oil. Some of the oil will evaporate while cooking, while the remainder will act as a binder to hold the pie together.

Cottage Pie: Substitute ground beef for the ground lamb.

Freeze in airtight container up to 3 months. Alternatively, prepare pie in a disposable foil pan and wrap with aluminum foil.

Serves: 4. Preparation Time is 10 minutes. Cooking Time is 1 hour 25 minutes.

Baked Stuffed Zucchini

¡◎⁉

INGREDIENTS

4 large zucchini, about 6 inches in length

1/2 cup water

4 tablespoons olive oil, divided

1/4 teaspoon salt

2 medium canned artichoke hearts

1/4 cup tomato sauce

1/2 teaspoon onion powder

1/2 teaspoon garlic salt

1 teaspoon dried parsley

1/8 teaspoon cayenne pepper (optional)

1/2 pound ground turkey

1 cup bread crumbs, divided

INSTRUCTIONS

Preheat oven to 350°F.

❶ Split zucchini lengthwise. Scoop out pulp using a melon baller and set aside. Place zucchini shells in a baking dish and add water to the bottom of the dish.

❷ Heat 2 tablespoons of oil in a medium saucepan over medium heat. Add zucchini pulp and salt. Sauté until the zucchini softens, about 3 minutes. Transfer zucchini to a food processor and add the artichoke hearts, tomato sauce, onion powder, garlic salt, parsley, and optional cayenne pepper. Puree ingredients and transfer to a large mixing bowl.

❸ Meanwhile cook the ground turkey in the same pan used to sauté the zucchini. Transfer cooked turkey to the mixing bowl along with 1/2 cup bread crumbs. Use hands to incorporate ingredients.

❹ Stuff the zucchini shells with the turkey filling. Sprinkle remaining 1/2 cup bread crumbs over the top and drizzle with remaining 2 tablespoons of olive oil. Bake in oven, uncovered, for 25 minutes. Serve warm with extra tomato sauce drizzled over the top.

Serves: 4. Preparation Time is 10 minutes. Cooking Time is 25 minutes.

Eggplant Marinara

INGREDIENTS

2 large eggplants (about 1 pound each)

5 tablespoons olive oil, divided

1/2 teaspoon salt

1/4 teaspoon pepper

1 small white onion, chopped

2 cloves garlic, chopped

1 pound ground beef

1/2 teaspoon dried oregano

2 cups marinara sauce, divided, jarred or see recipe on page 57

1/2 cup bread crumbs, divided

1/3 cup loosely packed fresh basil leaves, chopped (about 3/4 ounce)

INSTRUCTIONS

Preheat oven to 450°F.

❶ Slice eggplants lengthwise, about 3/4-inch thick. Arrange eggplant slices in a single layer on two rimmed baking sheets. Brush about 3 tablespoons of olive oil on both sides of the slices and season with salt and pepper. Roast in oven for 25 minutes or until eggplant is tender and golden, turning once halfway through.

❷ Meanwhile, heat remaining 2 tablespoons of olive oil in a medium sauté pan. Add onion and garlic and sauté for 3 minutes. Add ground beef and continue to cook until meat is no longer pink. Stir in oregano and set aside.

❸ Ladle approximately 1/2 cup of marinara sauce into a 9×13-inch baking dish. Lay approximately 1/3 of the eggplant slices on the bottom and spread 1/2 of the meat mixture on top of the eggplant. Sprinkle 1/4 cup of bread crumbs on top, followed by another 1/2 cup of marinara sauce. Repeat layers, ending with the final 1/3 of the eggplant slices. Ladle the remaining 1/2 cup marinara sauce over the top layer of eggplant slices and top with basil leaves.

❹ Reduce oven temperature to 350°F and bake, covered, for 20 minutes or until heated through.

Serves: 4. Preparation Time is 10 minutes. Cooking Time is 45 minutes.

Eggplant Marinara – Vegetarian

¡◎¡↑

INGREDIENTS

2 large eggplants (about 1 pound each)

5 tablespoons olive oil, divided

1/2 teaspoon salt

1/4 teaspoon pepper

1 small white onion, chopped

2 cloves garlic, chopped

2 medium tomatoes, seeded and chopped

1 15-ounce can artichoke hearts, drained and chopped

1/2 cup white wine

1 15-ounce can garbanzo beans, drained and rinsed

1/2 cup golden raisins

1/2 teaspoon dried oregano

2 cups marinara sauce, divided, jarred or see recipe on page 57

1/2 cup bread crumbs, divided

1/3 cup loosely packed fresh basil leaves, chopped (about 3/4 ounce)

INSTRUCTIONS

Preheat oven to 450°F.

❶ Slice eggplants lengthwise, about 3/4-inch thick. Arrange eggplant slices in a single layer on two rimmed baking sheets. Brush about 3 tablespoons of olive oil on both sides of the slices and season with salt and pepper. Roast in oven for 25 minutes or until eggplant is tender and golden, turning once halfway through.

❷ Meanwhile, heat remaining 2 tablespoons of olive oil in a medium sauté pan. Add onion and garlic and sauté for 3 minutes. Add tomatoes, artichoke hearts, and wine. Cook until tomatoes soften and most of the liquid has evaporated, about 10 minutes. Stir in garbanzo beans, golden raisins, and oregano and set aside.

❸ Ladle approximately 1/2 cup of marinara sauce into a 9×13-inch baking dish. Lay approximately 1/3 of the eggplant slices on the bottom and spread 1/2 of the bean mixture on top of the eggplant. Sprinkle 1/4 cup of bread crumbs on top, followed by another 1/2 cup of marinara sauce. Repeat layers, ending with the final 1/3 of the eggplant slices. Ladle the remaining 1/2 cup marinara sauce over the top layer of eggplant slices and top with basil leaves.

❹ Reduce oven temperature to 350°F and bake, covered, for 20 minutes or until heated through.

Serves: 4. Preparation Time is 10 minutes. Cooking Time is 45 minutes.

Spaghetti with Tomatoes, Basil, and Capers

This is a light and simple dish that can be made in the amount of time it takes to cook a pot of pasta.

¡◎į

INGREDIENTS

16 ounces rice spaghetti

1/3 cup olive oil

3 cloves garlic

6 medium roma tomatoes, seeded and chopped

1/4 cup chopped Kalamata olives, pits removed

2 small dried red hot chilies, chopped

3 tablespoons capers

1/4 cup fresh chopped basil

1/2 teaspoon sea salt

1/4 teaspoon pepper

INSTRUCTIONS

❶ Cook spaghetti in large pot of boiling water.

❷ Meanwhile, heat olive oil in a large sauté pan over medium heat. Sauté garlic for 5 minutes. Remove from heat and add tomatoes, olives, chilies, and capers to pan.

❸ When spaghetti is tender, but still firm, drain and add to tomato mixture. Toss together with basil, salt, and pepper. Serve warm.

RECIPE NOTES

Serves: 4. Preparation Time is 5 minutes. Cooking Time is 10 minutes.

Rotini à la Vodka Sauce

This hearty, robust sauce is the perfect complement for the distinctive flavor of the buckwheat noodle.

†◎††

INGREDIENTS

1 medium carrot, peeled and chopped

1/2 medium white onion, coarsely chopped

2 cloves garlic

2 tablespoons olive oil

1/4 teaspoon salt

1 28-ounce can crushed tomatoes

1/3 cup vodka (optional)

1/4 cup rice milk

1/2 teaspoon garlic salt

1/4 teaspoon red pepper flakes

3/4 pound mild Italian sausage, cooked

1 pound buckwheat spirals (or any preferred noodle)

1/2 cup pasta water

2 tablespoons fresh chopped parsley

INSTRUCTIONS

Preheat oven to 425°F.

❶ Toss the carrot, onion, and garlic together with olive oil and salt. Roast in oven for 30 minutes, turning once during the process. Allow vegetables to cool and transfer to a blender. Add the crushed tomatoes and puree until smooth.

❷ Transfer the sauce to a large sauté pan, along with the optional vodka, rice milk, garlic salt, and red pepper flakes. Heat over low heat to a simmer. Continue to simmer until sauce reduces by about 1/3. Add cooked sausage and continue to simmer for another 2 to 3 minutes.

❸ Meanwhile, cook the pasta in a large pot of boiling salted water until al dente (tender but still firm to the bite.) Drain and reserve 1/2 cup of the cooking liquid. Add the drained pasta to the sauce and sausage. If necessary, use the reserved cooking liquid to moisten the sauce. Garnish with fresh parsley and serve.

(continued)

RECISE NOTES

RECIPE NOTES

In spite of its name, buckwheat is not related to wheat but is actually the seed of a broadleaf plant related to rhubarb. Buckwheat has more protein than do rice, wheat, millet, or corn, and it is high in the essential amino acids lysine and arginine. This unique amino acid profile gives buckwheat the power to boost the protein value of beans and cereal grains eaten the same day. It is high in minerals as well, especially zinc, copper, and manganese. Unlike true grains, buckwheat's low-fat content is skewed toward monounsaturated fatty acids, similar to the type that makes olive oil so heart-healthful.

However, buckwheat can have a strong-tasting, earth-like flavor that many are not accustomed to. Accordingly, it pairs well with robust sauces that can mask the strong flavor, or with sugary-sweet substances like syrups that take the bite out of the flavor, making buckwheat grits and buckwheat flour a favorite addition to pancakes.

The vodka really unites this sauce together by balancing out the sweetness of the carrots and onion, the acidity of the tomatoes, the creaminess of the rice milk, and the peppery hints of the sausage and red pepper. Vodka is said to have been originally created from potatoes in Russia for medicinal purposes. However, nowadays Vodka is distilled from barley, wheat, and rye as well. Be sure to use a potato-based Vodka. Not only will this ensure your sauce is gluten-free, but it will produce a smoother sauce, as vodka made from potatoes tends to have a smoother taste than do those made from grains.

Serves: 4. Preparation Time is 15 minutes. Cooking Time is 30 minutes.

Creamy Penne with Sun-Dried Tomatoes and Broccoli

This pasta is creamy and savory, yet light and healthy.

¶◎¶

INGREDIENTS

16 ounces rice penne, or any desired shape of pasta

1-1/2 ounces sun-dried tomatoes

1/2 cup olive oil

3 cloves garlic, minced

1 cup pasta water

3 cups chopped broccoli

1/2 cup rice milk

1/2 teaspoon sea salt

1/2 teaspoon pepper

INSTRUCTIONS

❶ Bring large pot of water to boil. Add penne pasta and sun-dried tomatoes. Cook until pasta is al dente.

❷ Meanwhile, heat olive oil in a small sauté pan. Add garlic and sauté until garlic softens, about 5 minutes. Remove from heat.

❸ When pasta is al dente, add 1 cup of the pasta water directly to the garlic oil. Put the broccoli in the colander and drain the pasta over the top.

❹ Return drained pasta and broccoli to cooking pot along with the garlic oil, rice milk, sea salt, and pepper. Heat over low-medium heat and simmer, uncovered, for 3 to 5 minutes until sauce thickens. Serve warm.

RECIPE NOTES

▢ Adding the sun-dried tomatoes to the pasta while cooking will flavor the noodles as well as the sauce. Placing the chopped broccoli in the colander is a quick and easy way to blanch the broccoli, lending a crunchy bite to this wonderful dish.

▢ For best results, note the cooking time of pasta on the package and subtract at least 2 minutes to ensure that the pasta is al dente, tender on the outside, and firm on the inside. This allows the pasta to finish cooking in the sauce, which will help thicken the sauce. For a super-creamy sauce, err on the side of undercooked noodles and allow more time to finish cooking in step 4.

▢ Add 8 ounces cooked chicken breast in step 4. Reduce pasta to 12 ounces.

▢ Substitute 1/4 teaspoon red pepper flakes for 1/4 teaspoon of black pepper.

Serves: 4. Preparation Time is 5 minutes. Cooking Time is 15 minutes.

Creamy Fusilli
with Asparagus and Mushrooms

🍴◎🍴

INGREDIENTS

16 ounces rice penne, or any desired shape of pasta

1/2 cup olive oil

3 cloves garlic, minced

1 pound asparagus, chopped into 1-inch pieces

8 ounces cremini mushrooms, sliced

1 cup pasta water

1/4 cup rice milk

1/2 teaspoon sea salt

1/2 teaspoon pepper

INSTRUCTIONS

❶ Bring large pot of water to boil. Add fusilli pasta. Cook until pasta is al dente.

❷ Meanwhile, heat olive oil in a small sauté pan over medium heat. Add garlic and sauté for 3 minutes.

❸ Add asparagus and mushrooms. Sauté for 3 to 5 minutes or until asparagus is cooked but still firm.

❹ When pasta is al dente, add 1 cup of the pasta water directly to the asparagus and mushrooms.

❺ Drain pasta and add directly to the asparagus along with the rice milk, sea salt, and pepper. Heat over low-medium heat and simmer, uncovered, for 3 to 5 minutes, until sauce thickens. Serve warm.

Serves: 4. Preparation Time is 5 minutes. Cooking Time is 15 minutes.

Pasta Primavera

Pasta primavera is a simple-to-prepare dish that utilizes the fresh vegetables of the season. This recipe not only uses the fresh produce available in mid-summer, but allows each vegetable to be fairly represented with its beautiful color.

🍴◎🍴

INGREDIENTS

2 medium carrots, diced

2 small yellow squash, diced

2 small zucchini, diced

1/2 medium eggplant, cubed

1 large red bell pepper, julienned

1/4 cup olive oil

1 teaspoon salt, divided

1/2 teaspoon pepper

1 pound rice pasta

1 tablespoon tomato paste

1/2 teaspoon herbes de Provence (or dried Italian herbs)

1 pint cherry tomatoes, halved

2 tablespoons fresh chopped basil

INSTRUCTIONS

Preheat the oven to 425°F.

❶ On one large (or two small) rimmed baking sheet, toss the carrots, squash, zucchini, eggplant, and pepper together with the olive oil and 1/2 teaspoon of salt and pepper, and spread in a single layer. Roast in the oven for 25 minutes, or until the vegetables are tender and begin to char, stirring once during the process.

❷ Meanwhile, cook the pasta in a large pot of boiling, salted water until al dente (tender but still firm to the bite). Drain pasta and reserve 1 cup of the cooking liquid.

❸ Toss the cooked pasta together with the roasted vegetables in a large bowl. Add tomato paste, herbs, and remaining 1/2 teaspoon of salt. Stir in reserved cooking liquid 1/4 cup at a time to moisten pasta to desired consistency.

❹ Gently mix in the cherry tomatoes and basil. Serve warm.

Serves: 4. Preparation Time is 10 minutes. Cooking Time is 25 minutes.

Tortilla Casserole

¡◎¡¡

INGREDIENTS

16 ounces boneless, skinless chicken
    thighs, cut into 1-inch pieces

1/3 cup cornmeal

1/2 teaspoon cumin

1/2 teaspoon chili powder

1/2 teaspoon salt

3 tablespoons corn oil, divided

1 small red onion, diced

1 small red bell pepper, diced

1-1/2 pounds tomatillos, husks removed,
    sliced into 1-inch pieces

1/3 cup water

1 15-ounce can diced tomatoes with basil

4 ounces canned, diced jalapeno peppers

16 medium corn tortillas

INSTRUCTIONS

❶ Combine the chicken pieces with the cornmeal, cumin, chili powder, and salt in a large resealable bag. Shake to evenly coat chicken pieces.

❷ Meanwhile, heat 2 tablespoons of corn oil in a large sauté pan over medium-high heat. Add the coated chicken until well browned and cooked through, about 6 to 8 minutes. Transfer chicken to plate and store in refrigerator.

❸ Add onion and red pepper to pan. Sauté until vegetables are softened, about 3 to 5 minutes. Add the tomatillos and water. Reduce heat to low and simmer, covered, until tomatillos are tender, about 20 minutes. Remove lid, increase heat to medium-high, and cook until most of the liquid has evaporated. Remove from heat and allow to cool.

❹ Transfer mixture to food processor or blender along with diced tomatoes and 1/3 reserved chicken. Process mixture until blended with a few chunks.

❺ Grease the bottom of a pie dish or 8×8-inch baking dish with remaining 1 tablespoon of corn oil. Place 3 to 4 tortillas on the bottom of the dish. Spread 1/2 of the blended tomatillo mixture over the tortillas. Place 3 to 4 tortillas on top of the mixture. Evenly spread remaining chicken and jalapenos over the top. Top the chicken with 3 to 4 more tortillas and cover with remaining tomatillo mixture. Cover with remaining tortillas and drizzle with corn oil.

❻ Bake for 25 minutes. Serve warm.

RECIPE NOTES

Tomatillos, also known as tomate verde (green tomato), are considered a staple in Mexico and Mexican cooking. The tomatillo is a member of the nightshade family and related to tomatoes. Fresh, ripe tomatillos will keep in the refrigerator for about two weeks. They will keep even longer if the husks are removed and the fruits are placed in sealed plastic bags stored in the refrigerator. They can also be frozen whole or sliced and enjoyed year-round.

Serves: 4. Preparation Time is 10 minutes. Cooking Time is 1 hour 10 minutes.

Wild Mushroom Ragu

¶◎↟

INGREDIENTS

1 ounce dried porcini mushrooms

1 cup hot water

2 tablespoons olive oil

3 cups assorted wild mushrooms (cremini, oyster, or shiitake, for example)

2 medium green onions, chopped

2 medium roma tomatoes, seeded and diced

1 small shallot, minced

2 cloves garlic, minced

1 teaspoon salt, divided

1/2 cup Marsala wine

1/2 cup vegetable stock or water

1 tablespoon tapioca flour

2 tablespoons fresh chopped parsley

INSTRUCTIONS

❶ Place dried porcini mushrooms in a bowl and pour hot water over. Let sit for 30 minutes. After 30 minutes, drain the mushrooms and reserve about 1/2 the mushroom stock. Strain the stock through a paper towel to remove any dirt or particles and set aside.

❷ Meanwhile, heat the olive oil in a large sauté pan over medium-high heat. Add the wild mushrooms and sauté the mushrooms for 2 to 3 minutes or until slightly wilted. Add the green onions, tomatoes, shallot, garlic, and 1/2 teaspoon of salt. Continue to sauté for 5 minutes.

❸ Add the Marsala wine, vegetable stock, and remaining 1/2 teaspoon of salt. Bring to a boil. Reduce heat and simmer, uncovered, until liquid has nearly evaporated, about 10 minutes.

❹ Add the reserved porcini mushrooms to the pan. Whisk the tapioca flour into the reserved mushroom stock and add to the ragu. Allow ragu to continue to simmer until thickened, about 3 to 5 minutes. Stir in parsley, remove from heat, and serve warm over polenta, rice, or quinoa noodles.

Serves: 4. Preparation Time is 10 minutes. Inactive Preparation Time is 30 minutes. Cooking Time is 25 minutes.

"I knew a peanut allergy could cause an emergency situation, but until my son's diagnosis I did not know how it could affect ordinary decisions on a daily basis."

SCOTT WILLIAMS (FATHER TO MAC), POLICE OFFICER, ST. PAUL, MN

Chapter 6

Side Dishes

While generally afterthoughts, side dishes often perfect a meal by providing complementary and contrasting flavors and textures to an entrée. In seeking to help you maintain a balance in your life and minimize time spent preparing meals, I once again offer numerous recipes consisting solely of ingredients that you can purchase at your local grocery store. Many are easy to prepare and others are satisfying enough to serve as a main course. Best of all, the variety of these side dishes gives you many alternatives to those two common hypoallergenic standbys, rice and potatoes.

Baked Stuffed Yellow Peppers

Both versions of the following stuffed pepper recipes are excellent side dishes, especially during the summer. They are wonderful accompaniments to meats fresh off the grill or work beautifully as the main course for Vegetarian dinners.

❡◎❡

INGREDIENTS

4 medium yellow bell peppers

2 cups cooked long-grain rice

4 tablespoons chopped, jarred sun-dried tomatoes

2 tablespoons chopped fresh basil

1 tablespoon chopped fresh parsley

1/2 teaspoon ground coriander

1/2 teaspoon sea salt

4 tablespoons olive oil, plus more for drizzling

1 cup chopped red onion

2 cloves garlic, chopped

INSTRUCTIONS

Preheat oven to 375°F.

❶ Lightly oil a baking dish that will hold the peppers snugly. Using a sharp knife, carefully cut the tops off the peppers. Do not discard the tops. Remove the seeds and membrane from inside. Place the peppers upright in the baking dish and set aside.

❷ Combine the cooked rice, sun-dried tomatoes, basil, parsley, coriander, and sea salt in a bowl and set aside.

❸ Heat the olive oil in a large skillet over medium heat. Add the onion and garlic. Cook until the onion becomes transparent, about 5 minutes. Remove from heat and add the rice mixture to the pan. Stir until ingredients are evenly distributed.

❹ Fill each pepper with equal amounts of the rice mixture. Replace pepper tops and drizzle with oil.

❺ Cover the dish with aluminum foil. Bake for 45 minutes, or until the peppers become tender. Remove foil and bake for an additional 15 minutes. Serve warm or at room temperature.

RECIPE NOTES

The peppers can be stuffed up to one day ahead of time and stored in the fridge. Let the peppers sit on the counter for 30 minutes before baking to bring them back to room temperature.

Serves: 4. Preparation Time is 15 minutes. Cooking Time is 1 hour.

Baked Stuffed Orange Peppers

¶◎¶

INGREDIENTS

4 medium orange bell peppers

4 cups water

1 cup polenta or cornmeal

1 teaspoon salt

1/4 cup golden seedless raisins

1/4 cup dried currants

2 medium shallots, chopped

2 tablespoons chopped fresh cilantro

1 tablespoon ground cumin

1/2 teaspoon cinnamon

INSTRUCTIONS

Preheat oven to 375°F.

❶ Lightly oil a baking dish that will hold the peppers snugly. Using a sharp knife, carefully cut the tops off the peppers. Do not discard the tops. Remove the seeds and membrane from inside. Place the peppers upright in the baking dish and set aside.

❷ Bring water to a boil. Slowly pour polenta and salt into boiling water, whisking constantly until all polenta is incorporated and mixture begins to thicken. Switch to wooden spoon, remove from heat, and continue to stir until polenta mixture is thick as paste.

❸ Add raisins, currants, chopped shallots, and cilantro. Stir.

❹ Add cumin and cinnamon and give one or two quick stirs.

❺ While the polenta is still warm, fill each pepper with equal amount. Replace pepper tops, cover with foil, and bake for 25 minutes. Remove foil and continue baking for an additional 10 to 15 minutes.

RECIPE NOTES

🍲 Discard the tops and sprinkle 1/4 cup of bread crumbs over top of peppers and drizzle with olive oil.

Serves: 4. Preparation Time is 15 minutes. Cooking Time is 40 minutes.

Risotto

Risotto is a traditional Italian dish often made with Arborio rice. The rice is first cooked briefly in an oil until evenly coated and the rice starts to turn translucent. Then broth is added slowly, one ladle at a time. Traditional risotto recipes include "Risotto alla Milanese," made with chicken or beef stock and saffron, and "Risotto al Barolo," made with red wine. But literally thousands of variations exist, both with vegetables and meat, and other risottos are made with various wines, cheeses, and fruits.

I have created 5 fabulous hypoallergenic risotto recipes that you can use year-round, starting with the traditional Risotto Milanese. The others then pull in seasonal ingredients and flavors to provide you with a recipe for each season.

The key to these recipes is to use a coarse sea salt. Without the addition of cheese, salt becomes a vital ingredient. Using coarse rather than fine crystals will enhance the risottos with a punch of flavor throughout, rather than just resulting in a "salty" dish. Additionally, it is important to add the stock gradually and to stir the rice frequently. The end result should be a rice that is moist but firm. Consequently, you may not need all the stock, or you may use slightly more, since the smallest variation in temperature of the stock will affect the absorption process.

Risotto Milanese

¶⊙¶

INGREDIENTS

1/4 teaspoon crumbled saffron threads

1 cup white wine

8 cups chicken stock

2 tablespoons olive oil

1 medium white onion, chopped

2 cups arborio rice

1/4 cup fresh chopped parsley

1 teaspoon coarse sea salt

INSTRUCTIONS

❶ Stir saffron threads into white wine and set aside.

❷ Heat the stock to a simmer over low heat.

❸ Heat oil in a heavy saucepan over medium heat. Add chopped onion and sauté until softened, about 3 minutes.

❹ Add arborio rice and stir until well coated with oil.

❺ Add wine infused with saffron and stir until absorbed.

❻ Begin to add the stock in 1/2-cup increments. Cook until the rice has absorbed all the liquid, stirring constantly. Add another 1/2 cup of stock and repeat until all stock is used, or rice obtains desired consistency.

❼ Remove from heat; stir in chopped parsley and sea salt. Serve immediately.

RECIPE NOTES

Infusing the white wine with the saffron really enhances the flavor of this traditional risotto.

Serves: 4. Preparation Time is 5 minutes. Cooking Time is 40 minutes.

Wild Mushroom Risotto

†◎‡

INGREDIENTS

1 ounce dried porcini mushrooms

8 cups vegetable or mushroom stock

1/4 cup olive oil

2 medium shallots, minced

10 ounces assorted mushrooms, sliced (cremini, chanterelle, or portobello)

2 cups arborio rice

1 cup sherry

6 sprigs fresh thyme

1 teaspoon coarse sea salt

1/4 teaspoon pepper

INSTRUCTIONS

❶ Place dried porcinis and stock in a saucepan and bring stock to a boil. Reduce heat to low and simmer for 20 minutes.

❷ Heat oil in a heavy saucepan over medium heat. Add shallots and sauté until softened, about 3 minutes.

❸ Add sliced mushrooms to the pan and sauté until softened, about 5 minutes.

❹ Add arborio rice and stir until well coated with oil.

❺ Add sherry and stir until absorbed.

❻ Using a slotted spoon, remove porcini mushrooms from stock, rinse, chop, and add to sauté pan. If necessary, drain the stock through a paper towel to remove any particles. Return stock to saucepan and continue to simmer.

❼ Add the stock in 1/2-cup increments. Cook until the rice has absorbed all the liquid, stirring constantly. Add another 1/2 cup of stock and repeat until all stock is used, or rice obtains desired consistency.

❽ Remove from heat. Remove thyme leaves from sprigs and add to risotto along with sea salt and pepper. Serve immediately.

RECIPE NOTES

💡 Substitute beef stock for vegetable or mushroom stock.

🍲 Risotto Cakes: The consistency of the risotto for cakes should be less creamy than a traditional risotto, so reduce stock to 6 cups. After step 7, transfer risotto to a baking sheet to cool. To make the cakes, use a round mold (approximately 3 inches circumference). Fill molds with risotto and refrigerate until ready to bake. When ready, remove molds and bake in a 375°F oven for 12 to 15 minutes. Serve warm.

Serves: 4. Preparation Time is 30 minutes. Cooking Time is 40 minutes.

Asparagus Leek Risotto

⟨◎⟩

INGREDIENTS

7 cups chicken stock

1 pound asparagus, chopped into 1-inch pieces

1/4 cup olive oil

8 ounces leeks, coarsely chopped

2 cups arborio rice

1-1/2 cups champagne

1 tablespoon fresh lemon juice

2 teaspoons lemon zest

1 teaspoon coarse sea salt

INSTRUCTIONS

❶ Heat the stock to a simmer. Drop in chopped asparagus and blanch for about 3 minutes. Remove asparagus with a slotted spoon and set aside. Continue to simmer the stock over low heat.

❷ Heat oil in a heavy saucepan over medium heat. Add chopped leeks and sauté until the leeks begin to wilt, about 3 minutes.

❸ Add arborio rice and stir until well coated with oil.

❹ Add champagne and stir until absorbed.

❺ Begin to add the stock in 1/2-cup increments. Cook until the rice has absorbed all the liquid, stirring constantly. Add another 1/2 cup of stock and repeat until all stock is used, or rice obtains desired consistency.

❻ Remove from heat and stir in blanched asparagus, lemon juice, lemon zest, and sea salt. Serve immediately.

RECIPE NOTES

▢ Blanching the asparagus in the stock achieves two results. One, you can easily control the desired texture of the asparagus by limiting the cooking time. This recipe yields a consistency that is tender, but still firm. And two, nutritional values are maximized as the vitamins and nutrients released into the chicken stock will be absorbed into the rice.

💡 Substitute white wine for the champagne.

Serves: 6. Preparation Time is 10 minutes. Cooking Time is 40 minutes.

Summer Squash Risotto

This dish is a great way to utilize the abundant supply of summer squash that are so bright and delightful in the summertime. This dish's best attribute is that my kids gobble it up without realizing they are eating squash!

🍽️

INGREDIENTS

6 cups chicken stock

2 medium yellow squash

2 medium zucchini

4 tablespoons canola oil

1 medium white onion, chopped

2 cups arborio rice

1 cup white wine

1 tablespoon coarse sea salt

2 tablespoons fresh chopped parsley

INSTRUCTIONS

❶ Heat the stock to a very low simmer over low heat.

❷ Using a cheese grater, grate the squash and zucchini, yielding about 3 cups. Set aside.

❸ Heat oil in a heavy saucepan over medium heat. Add onions and sauté until translucent without browning, about 3 minutes.

❹ Add arborio rice and stir until well coated with oil.

❺ Add wine and stir until the wine is absorbed.

❻ Add grated squash, zucchini, and 1 cup of stock. Stir until all the liquid is absorbed.

❼ Continue to add the stock in 1/2-cup increments. Cook until the rice has absorbed all the liquid, stirring constantly. Add another 1/2 cup of stock and repeat until all stock is used, or rice obtains desired consistency.

❽ Remove from heat and stir in sea salt. Garnish with parsley and serve immediately.

Serves: 6. Preparation Time is 20 minutes. Cooking Time is 45 minutes.

Butternut Squash Risotto

Who doesn't love the warm flavor and bold color of butternut squash in the fall? Tradition-al complements to butternut squash are often sage and nutmeg. Quite frankly, I usually tire of sage by mid-October and anything with the word "nut" raises anxiety levels in our house. So I put an interesting spin on this risotto by adding orange zest and prosciutto and may I just say – Wow! The hint of orange gives the squash a fresh sweetness which works wonders with the salty crispiness of the prosciutto, while neither ingredient overpowers the soft flavors of the squash.

¶⊙¶

INGREDIENTS

3 pounds butternut squash
    (3 cups cooked and cubed)

6 cups chicken stock

3 tablespoons olive oil, divided

6 ounces prosciutto

1 medium yellow onion, chopped

2 cups arborio rice

1 tablespoon coarse sea salt

1 teaspoon orange zest

INSTRUCTIONS

Preheat oven to 375°F.

❶ Halve squash lengthwise and seed. Roast halves, skin side down, in a shallow baking pan in middle of oven until tender and golden, about 50 minutes. Remove from oven and set aside to cool. Remove skin and slice squash into 3/4-inch cubes. This step can be prepared a day or two in advance and stored in the refrigerator.

❷ Heat the stock to a low simmer over low heat.

❸ Heat 1 tablespoon of olive oil in a heavy saucepan over medium heat. Add prosciutto and sauté until prosciutto becomes dark brown and crispy. Remove prosciutto from pan and set aside.

❹ Add remaining olive oil and onion to the same pan. Sauté about 5 minutes. The onions will become brownish from the prosciutto.

❺ Turn heat to low, add arborio rice and stir until well coated with oil. Add 1 cup of stock. Stir until all the liquid is absorbed. Continue to add the stock in 1/2-cup increments. Cook until the rice has absorbed all the liquid, stirring constantly. Add another 1/2 cup of stock and repeat until all stock is used, or rice obtains desired consistency.

❻ Add the cooked cubed squash. Stir a few times to incorporate.

❼ Remove from heat and stir in orange zest and sea salt. Garnish with reserved prosciutto and serve.

RECIPE NOTES

💡 Substitute 3 cups of frozen and thawed butternut squash for fresh squash.

Serves: 6. Preparation Time is 50 minutes. Cooking Time is 40 minutes.

Rice Pilaf

This easy pilaf has simple ingredients yet a full flavor.

⫙◎⫙

INGREDIENTS

1/4 cup olive oil

1 small white onion, chopped

2 cups long-grain white basmati rice

1/4 cup dried currants

3-1/2 cups water

1 teaspoon salt

1/2 cup flax seeds

INSTRUCTIONS

❶ Heat the oil in a large saucepan over medium-high heat. Add the chopped onion and sauté until golden, about 6 to 8 minutes.

❷ Reduce heat to medium and add the rice, stirring until coated with oil and heated through, about 2 minutes. Be sure to continuously stir so the rice does not burn or stick to the pan.

❸ Add the currants and sauté while continuously stirring for 1 minute longer.

❹ Add the water and salt. Bring to a boil, stir, and reduce heat to low. Cover and simmer until the water is absorbed and the rice is tender, about 15 minutes. Remove from heat and let stand for another 5 minutes.

❺ Meanwhile, toast flax seeds in a small nonstick skillet over medium-low heat. Shake the pan often and toast until the shade deepens to a darker brown, about 3 minutes. Sprinkle over pilaf and serve.

RECIPE NOTES

Substitute currants with raisins, dried apricots, or cherries.

Freeze in airtight container or freezer bag up to 4 months.

Serves: 6. Preparation Time is 5 minutes. Cooking Time is 35 minutes.

Quinoa Pilaf

This is a fantastic pilaf when you are desperate for an alternative to rice. The cremini mushrooms, otherwise known as baby portabellas, not only complement the buttery flavor of the quinoa, but also add a meaty bite to the dish. It's hearty enough to be served as a vegetarian entrée.

INGREDIENTS

2 tablespoons olive oil

1 medium shallot, chopped

6 ounces cremini mushroom, sliced

1-1/2 cups quinoa

3-1/2 cups vegetable stock

1/4 cup shredded carrots

1/4 cup peas

2 tablespoons fresh chopped parsley

1 teaspoon salt

1/4 teaspoon pepper

INSTRUCTIONS

1. Heat olive oil in a medium saucepan over medium heat. Add the shallot and cook until translucent but not browned, about 3 minutes.
2. Add the mushrooms and sauté until cooked through, about 5 minutes.
3. Add the quinoa. Stir well to evenly coat and heat the quinoa without letting it burn. Cook for 2 minutes.
4. Add the vegetable stock, carrots, peas, parsley, salt, and pepper. Stir and bring to a boil. Reduce heat to low and simmer, covered, for about 15 minutes or until quinoa is partially cooked and most of the liquid is absorbed.
5. Remove from heat, quickly fluff the quinoa with a fork, cover, and allow to finish cooking for 10 minutes. Serve warm or chilled.

Serves: 4. Preparation Time is 5 minutes. Cooking Time is 35 minutes.

Pork Fried Rice

❡◎❦

INGREDIENTS

1/4 cup beef stock

1-1/2 tablespoons rice vinegar

1 tablespoon grapeseed oil

1/4 teaspoon sugar

3 tablespoons lard

16 ounces boneless pork loin chop, cut into 3/4-inch cubes

1-1/2 teaspoons salt, divided

1/2 cup frozen peas, thawed

4 ounces shiitake mushrooms

1/2 cup shredded carrots

1 head bok choy, halved and sliced into 1-inch strips

3 cups cooked brown rice, chilled

2 medium scallions, thinly sliced

INSTRUCTIONS

❶ In a small bowl, combine the beef stock with the vinegar, grapeseed oil, and sugar. Set aside.

❷ Heat the lard in a large skillet over high heat. Season the pork with 1/2 teaspoon of salt and add to the pan. Stir-fry for 3 minutes, or until outside of pork is no longer pink.

❸ Reduce the heat to medium and add the peas, mushrooms, carrots, and bok choy. Stir-fry until the vegetables are tender and the pork is cooked through, about 5 to 7 minutes.

❹ Stir in the cooked rice, scallions, beef stock mixture, and remaining 1 teaspoon of salt. Stir-fry until the rice is hot. Remove from the heat and serve warm. Top with pickled ginger, jarred lemon grass, or slices of avocado.

RECIPE NOTES

♀ If your diet will allow it, substitute sesame seed oil for the grapeseed oil. You may also substitute one of these oils for the lard. However, using lard really enhances and evenly distributes the pork flavor throughout.

Serves: 4. Preparation Time is 5 minutes. Cooking Time is 10 minutes.

Spanish Rice

¶◎⫯

INGREDIENTS

1/4 cup olive oil

1 cup long-grain white rice

1 medium yellow onion, chopped

1 medium green pepper, chopped

1 clove garlic, minced

2 cups chicken stock

1 14-ounce can chopped tomatoes, drained

1/2 teaspoon paprika

1/2 teaspoon chili powder

1/2 teaspoon salt

1/4 teaspoon pepper

INSTRUCTIONS

Preheat oven to 350°F.

❶ In a large ovenproof skillet heat olive oil over high heat. Add the rice and sauté for 2 minutes, stirring to ensure it is evenly coated.

❷ Reduce heat to medium and add onion, pepper, and garlic. Sauté until the onions and garlic are golden and softened and the rice is browned, about 5 minutes.

❸ Add remaining ingredients and bring to a boil. Stir once, cover, and bake in oven until liquid is absorbed and rice is tender, about 20 minutes. Remove cover and continue to bake for 10 to 15 minutes, or until the top of the rice is slightly crispy. Serve warm.

RECIPE NOTES

Toasting the rice brings about a fabulous smoky and almost nutty flavor that makes this dish as satisfying as a meal in itself.

Freeze in airtight container or freezer bag up to 4 months.

Serves: 4. Preparation Time is 5 minutes. Cooking Time is 45 minutes.

Garlic Smashed Potatoes

¶◎�ſ

INGREDIENTS

2 cloves garlic

1 teaspoon olive oil

2 pounds russet or Idaho potatoes, peeled and cut into chunks

2 teaspoons salt, divided

2 tablespoons lard

1 cup rice milk, divided

1 tablespoon canola oil

1/2 teaspoon pepper

INSTRUCTIONS

Preheat oven to 400°F.

❶ Cut and discard the top third of each head of garlic. Loosely wrap garlic in aluminum foil and drizzle olive oil on exposed garlic. Roast in oven for approximately 50 minutes, or until garlic is golden brown and caramelized. Remove from oven and set aside until cool enough to handle. Once cool, grasp the root end of each garlic head and gently squeeze to remove the caramelized cloves from the skin. Extract about 10 to 12 cloves and set aside.

❷ Meanwhile place peeled potatoes in a large pot and cover with cold water. Add 1 teaspoon of salt and bring to a boil. Reduce heat to a simmer and continue to simmer, uncovered, for 20 minutes or until potatoes are tender. Remove from heat and drain potatoes.

❸ Transfer potatoes to the bowl of an electric mixer, along with the reserved garlic and lard. Using the paddle attachment, mix on medium speed until the potatoes are smooth and the lard has melted.

❹ Switch to low speed and slowly add 1/4 cup rice milk, canola oil, remaining 1 teaspoon of salt, and pepper. Mix to combine. Continue to add rice milk in 1/4-cup increments until desired consistency is obtained. Depending on the type of potato, more or less milk may be needed.

❺ Switch to the whisk attachment of the electric mixer. Quickly whisk potatoes until light and fluffy, about 1 minute. Serve immediately.

RECIPE NOTES

♡ Substitute shortening for the lard.

🍲 Top with crumbled bacon or Caramelized Onions, recipe on page 204.

Serves: 4. Preparation Time is 5 minutes. Cooking Time is 50 minutes.

Twice-Baked Potatoes

†◎‡

INGREDIENTS

1 head garlic

1/2 teaspoon olive oil

4 large russet potatoes, about 2 pounds

4 ounces scallions

4 medium roma tomatoes, chopped

1-1/2 teaspoons salt

1/2 teaspoon pepper

1 cup rice milk

2 tablespoons fresh chopped chives

INSTRUCTIONS

Preheat oven to 400°F.

❶ Cut and discard the top third of the head of garlic. Loosely wrap garlic in aluminum foil and drizzle olive oil on exposed garlic. Roast in oven for approximately 50 minutes, or until garlic is golden brown and caramelized. Remove from oven and set aside until cool enough to handle. Once cool, grasp the root end of garlic head and gently squeeze to remove the caramelized cloves from the skin. Extract about 6 to 8 cloves and set aside.

❷ At the same time, rinse and scrub potatoes. Pat dry with paper towel and pierce each potato once with a fork. Bake potatoes in oven with garlic for 45 minutes. Remove from oven and allow to cool slightly before handling.

❸ Chop the scallions, using only the white onion section. Combine in a small bowl with tomatoes, salt, and pepper. Set aside.

❹ Slice each potato lengthwise. Scoop out the flesh and transfer to a large mixing bowl. Add the roasted cloves of garlic. Using an electric mixer, beat the potato mixture while slowly adding rice milk.

❺ Add scallion mixture to potatoes and stir a few times by hand.

❻ Fill each potato with equal amounts of stuffing and sprinkle chopped chives on top. Place stuffed potatoes on a large baking sheet and return to oven. Bake for 15 minutes, or until top of potatoes are browned. Serve warm.

Serves: 4. Preparation Time is 5 minutes. Cooking Time is 1 hour 5 minutes.

Mashed Sweet Potatoes with Bourbon and Apples

¡◎¡↑

INGREDIENTS

2 pounds sweet potatoes

1/3 cup rice milk

1/4 cup bourbon whiskey

1/4 cup packed brown sugar

2 tablespoons unsulfured molasses

1/2 teaspoon orange zest

1/4 teaspoon ground nutmeg

1 medium Granny Smith apple, peeled, cored, and coarsely chopped

INSTRUCTIONS

Preheat oven to 350°F.

❶ Prick sweet potatoes with fork and bake for 50 minutes, or until tender. Allow to cool and slice each potato lengthwise. Scoop out flesh and place in large mixing bowl. Discard skins.

❷ Add remaining ingredients, except apple, to the large mixing bowl. Using an electric mixer, beat at medium speed, scraping bowl often, until well mixed and no lumps remain.

❸ Stir in chopped apple by hand. Transfer to an 8-inch square baking dish and bake for 20 minutes or until heated through. Serve warm.

RECIPE NOTES

💡 Substitute 3/4 cup raisins for the chopped apple.

🍲 Reserve the potato skins, place on a cookie sheet, and fill the skins with equal amounts of the potato mixture. Bake the skins for 20 to 25 minutes. Serve warm.

Serves: 4. Preparation Time is 5 minutes. Cooking Time is 1 hour 10 minutes.

Sweet Potato Cakes

This recipe provides a wonderful side dish for Thanksgiving and a great way to get kids excited to eat a power ingredient: the sweet potato.

¡◎¡¡

INGREDIENTS

2 pounds sweet potatoes

1/2 medium red bell pepper, chopped

1/2 medium yellow bell pepper, chopped

1/2 medium yellow onion, chopped

2 tablespoons chopped fresh cilantro

1-1/2 teaspoons ground coriander

1-1/2 teaspoons ground cumin

1 teaspoon salt

1/2 teaspoon pepper

3 teaspoons sugar

2 tablespoons fresh lime juice

2 cups bread crumbs, divided

4 cups canola oil for frying

INSTRUCTIONS

Preheat oven to 400°F.

❶ Slice sweet potatoes in half and wrap in aluminum foil. Bake in oven until cooked and soft, about 45 minutes. Scoop out the flesh of potatoes and put in bowl. Discard skins. Mash the potatoes until they achieve a smooth consistency.

❷ Meanwhile, add bell peppers, onion, and cilantro to a food processor. Chop until vegetables are minced.

❸ Combine cooked sweet potatoes with chopped vegetables in large bowl. Add spices, salt, pepper, sugar, lime juice, and 1/2 cup of bread crumbs. Mix well and refrigerate for a minimum of 2 hours and up to 24 hours.

❹ Heat canola oil in a large sauté pan. The oil should measure about 2 inches deep; more or less oil may be needed.

❺ Remove sweet potato mixture from refrigerator. Form the potato mixture into small cakes and coat heavily with remaining bread crumbs.

❻ Working in batches, drop the potato cakes into hot oil and fry until the cakes are golden brown, about 2 to 3 minutes per side. Remove from oil, drain on a paper towel, and sprinkle with salt (optional). Serve immediately.

RECIPE NOTES

Freeze cakes prior to frying, after step 3. When ready, heat oil and fry frozen cakes for 5 to 7 minutes per side.

Serves: 6. Preparation Time is 15 minutes. Cooking Time is 50 minutes.

Blooming Onion

We rarely eat out as a family, with the exception of the occasional dinner at Outback Steakhouse. I was thrilled to learn about their gluten-free menu, cross-contamination knowledge, and stringent cooking practices. Although my daughter is allergic to many foods other than just gluten, she can safely eat a grilled steak (plain, no seasoning), baked potato, and steamed vegetables. The thrill of eating out outweighs her invariable menu options. However I always catch her eye drifting to the continuous traffic of "bloomin' onions" passing by our table. So I set out on a mission to figure out a way to make a blooming onion gluten-free and allergen-free. My version of the blooming onion became a fast favorite in our house. Now when we visit Outback Steakhouse and see their "bloomin' onion" pass by our table, my daughter exclaims satisfactorily, "Oh, we have those at home!" While I typically reserve the blooming onion for special occasions, the equally satisfying, easy-to-make onion rings have become a regular side dish in our house.

🍴◎🍴

INGREDIENTS

8 cups canola oil for frying

1 large Vidalia or other sweet onion

2 cups pancake mix

1 tablespoon paprika

1/2 teaspoon chili powder

1/2 teaspoon cayenne pepper

2 teaspoons salt

1/2 teaspoon pepper

1 cup sparkling water

INSTRUCTIONS

❶ Heat oil in a fryer or large Dutch oven. The oil should be high enough to completely submerge the onion; more or less oil may be needed. The temperature of oil should reach approximately 350°F.

❷ Meanwhile, slice 3/4" off the top of the onion, leaving the root end intact. Remove the papery skin. With a sharp chef's knife, make slices from the center of the onion outwards, cutting down to about 1/2" from the root end (do not cut all the way through). The cuts should look like the spokes of a wagon wheel. Depending on the size of the onion, you will want to make a total of 12 to 16 cuts, spaced evenly. Gently spread out the pieces of onions so that it resembles a flower in bloom.

❸ In a large bowl, whisk together the pancake mix, paprika, chili powder, cayenne pepper, salt, and pepper. Slowly add the sparking water. Add enough water to obtain a thick batter.

❹ Promptly dunk the onion in the batter. Be sure to spread the "petals" apart to get an even coating.

❺ Carefully place onion in fryer. Fry for about 2 to 3 minutes or until golden. Remove and carefully ensure that petals are separating, using a utensil to help spread them if necessary. Recoat onion with batter and return to oil for about another 3 to 5 minutes. Remove from oil and drain on paper towels. Serve hot.

Serves: 4. Preparation Time is 5 minutes. Cooking Time is 10 minutes.

Onion Rings

♚☺♟

INGREDIENTS

2 large white onions

4 cups canola oil for frying

4 cups pancake mix

2 cups sparkling water

1 tablespoon salt, for sprinkling

INSTRUCTIONS

❶ Trim the ends of onions and peel. Cut onions into 1-inch slices and separate into rings.

❷ Heat canola oil in a large sauté pan. The oil should measure about 1 inch deep; more or less oil may be needed.

❸ Slowly whisk together pancake mix and sparkling water in a large bowl. The batter consistency should mimic the consistency of really thick pancake batter.

❹ Working in batches, coat rings of onion in batter and promptly fry in hot oil for 3 to 4 minutes, until evenly golden brown. Turn onions over and cook for another 2 minutes.

❺ Transfer onion rings to paper towels to drain and season with salt while hot. Repeat with remaining onion slices.

RECIPE NOTES

These fried onion side dishes require a gluten-free/allergen-free, pre-made pancake mix. The search for an acceptable pancake mix is definitely worth any extra effort, as these onion rings are so tasty and can be made in a snap. Note that hypoallergenic pancake mixes vary in ingredient composition. Accordingly, you may need more or less sparkling water to reach the desired consistency of the batter. Be sure to add the water slowly so it does not fizz over the top of the bowl.

Serves: 8. Preparation Time is 10 minutes. Cooking Time is 15 minutes.

Hush Puppies

¶◎¶

INGREDIENTS

2 cups cornmeal

1-1/2 cups bread crumbs, divided

1-1/2 teaspoons salt

2 tablespoons lard

2-1/3 cups boiling water

2 cups canola oil for frying

INSTRUCTIONS

1. Combine cornmeal, 1/2 cup of the bread crumbs, salt, and lard in a bowl. Add boiling water and stir thoroughly.
2. While the cornmeal mixture is still warm, roll into small, elongated oval shapes. Gently coat with remaining bread crumbs.
3. Heat oil in a large skillet. The oil should measure about 1-1/2 inches deep; more or less oil may be needed.
4. Drop hush puppies into oil and cook until browned on bottom, about 2 to 3 minutes. Turn once and cook other side until browned.
5. Drain cooked hush puppies on a paper towel, sprinkle with additional salt (optional), and serve warm.

RECIPE NOTES

Freeze Hush Puppies prior to frying in an airtight container for up to 4 to 6 months. Thaw before frying.

Serves: 6. Preparation Time is 10 minutes. Cooking Time is 10 minutes.

Roasted Garlic, Sausage, and Sage Stuffing

This stuffing is so amazing that I can't wait to make it every year at Thanksgiving. Try it once and not only will you get rave reviews, your guests will be fighting for the leftovers. I guarantee this recipe will become a favorite in your house, too.

🍽️

INGREDIENTS

3 heads garlic

1 cup olive oil, plus 1 teaspoon

10 ounces shredded carrots

1 large white onion, diced

2 celery stalks, diced

2 large green peppers, diced

32 ounces plain croutons, about 16 cups

3 pounds Italian sausage

1 tablespoon ground sage

1 tablespoon coarse salt

8 cups chicken stock

INSTRUCTIONS

Preheat oven to 400°F.

❶ Cut and discard the top third of each head of garlic. Loosely wrap garlic in aluminum foil and drizzle 1 teaspoon of olive oil on exposed garlic. Roast in oven for 50 minutes, or until garlic is golden brown and caramelized. Remove from oven and set aside until cool enough to handle. Once cool, grasp the root end of garlic head and gently squeeze to remove the caramelized cloves from the skin. Set roasted cloves aside.

❷ Meanwhile, heat remaining 1 cup of olive oil in a large sauté pan over medium heat. Add carrots, onion, and celery, and cook until onion is translucent, about 8 minutes. Add green peppers and cook 2 more minutes.

❸ Remove vegetables from heat and transfer to a large roasting pan or casserole. Add croutons (or toasted bread cubes) and set aside.

❹ In same skillet, cook sausage over medium heat until cooked through. Add cooked sausage to vegetables and croutons, along with ground sage and sea salt.

❺ Begin to add the chicken stock 1 cup at a time to the crouton mixture. Mix with your hands to incorporate all the ingredients. Continue to add stock until the stuffing is well moistened. Depending on croutons used, more or less stock may be needed to reach desired consistency.

❻ Add reserved cloves of roasted garlic, and stir to incorporate. Reduce oven temperature to 375°F and bake, uncovered, until stuffing is heated through, about 45 to 60 minutes. Serve warm.

(continued)

RECIPE NOTES

If unable to locate an acceptable brand of gluten-free/allergen-free croutons, simply cube your favorite gluten-free/allergen-free bread, spread on a cookie sheet, drizzle with olive oil, and toast in the oven at 300°F for 15 to 20 minutes.

Freeze in airtight container up to 2 months.

Serves: 10. Preparation Time is 10 minutes. Cooking Time is 1 hour 45 minutes.

Tamales

⫯◎⫯

INGREDIENTS

10 large ears of corn

1 tablespoon corn oil

1 medium red bell pepper, diced

1-1/2 cups corn flour

3/4 teaspoon baking powder

1 teaspoon salt

1 teaspoon cumin

1/2 cup lard

1 cup water

INSTRUCTIONS

Preheat oven to 350°F.

❶ Remove husks from the corn. Reserve the large husks and discard the flimsy and small inside husks. Soak the large husks in a bowl of hot water.

❷ Remove the corn kernels from the cobs saving all the juices, yielding about 1-1/2 cups of corn.

❸ Heat the corn oil in a medium sauté pan over medium-high heat. Add the corn and red pepper. Stir constantly and cook until corn becomes golden brown, about 5 to 7 minutes.

❹ Meanwhile, combine the corn flour, baking powder, salt, and cumin together and set aside.

❺ In a large mixing bowl, begin to beat the lard to loosen it up. Add the corn and peppers. Gradually add the corn flour mixture and water, alternating corn flour then water. Continue beating until the filling becomes smooth and somewhat creamy, about 5 minutes.

❻ Drain the husks thoroughly in a colander and pat dry with paper towels. Place a husk on a flat surface. Spoon 2 to 3 tablespoons of corn filling in the center and spread it lightly lengthwise. Bring the top and bottom ends of the husk to the center, overlapping slightly. Wrap another husk around cross-wise to cover exposed filling. If necessary, use one more husk to cover any filling and seal and secure the shape. Using kitchen string, tie securely crosswise and make a knot. Repeat with remaining filling and husks.

❼ Individually wrap tamales in aluminum foil. Place about 1 tablespoon of water in each wrap and seal the foil closed. Make sure the seam is on top so the water does not drip out. Place in the oven and bake for 30 minutes. Serve warm.

(continued)

RECISE NOTES

This recipe calls for corn flour. Corn flour, or masa flour, is popular in the Southern and Southwestern U.S. and in Mexico. It is made from dried corn that has been soaked in lime water and ground into fine flour. It is similar to cornmeal except that it is ground to a finer consistency than cornmeal and should not be confused with cornstarch, which is known as "cornflour" in Great Britain. Although more difficult to locate, corn flour should be used for this recipe.

Substitute approximately 1 tablespoon of shredded pork for 1 tablespoon of corn filling.

Serves: 8. Preparation Time is 20 minutes. Cooking Time is 40 minutes.

Polenta Wedges

ⵑ◎ⵑ

INGREDIENTS

3 cups water

1-1/4 teaspoons salt, divided

1 cup cornmeal

1 tablespoon fresh chopped thyme

2 tablespoons olive oil

INSTRUCTIONS

❶ Bring the water to a boil in a medium saucepan. Reduce heat to low-medium. Add 1 teaspoon of salt, then gradually pour in the cornmeal, whisking constantly to prevent lumps, about 3 minutes. Change to a wooden spoon and continue to cook the polenta, stirring often, until it resembles the consistency of oatmeal, about 15 minutes. Stir in thyme.

❷ Pour polenta into a 9×13-inch baking dish. Cover and refrigerate polenta until cold and firm, about 2 hours (and up to 2 days in advance).

❸ Preheat broiler in oven. Cut the polenta into wedges (or rectangles), yielding about 8 pieces. Brush polenta with olive oil and sprinkle with remaining 1/4 teaspoon of salt. Broil in oven until the top becomes crisp and slightly charred, about 5 minutes. Serve alone as a side dish or top with your favorite topping such as mushroom ragu, tapenade, caponata, or sun-dried tomato pesto.

RECIPE NOTES

Wrap wedges individually in aluminum foil and freeze up to 2 months.

Serves: 4. Preparation Time is 5 minutes. Inactive Preparation Time is 2 hours. Cooking Time is 25 minutes.

Green Bean Casserole

¶◎⊩

INGREDIENTS

2 15-ounce cans green beans, drained

1-1/4 cups Cream of Mushroom Soup, recipe on page 85

1/2 cup bread crumbs

1 cup Caramelized Onions, recipe on page 204

INSTRUCTIONS

Preheat oven to 350°F.

❶ Combine the green beans and cream of mushroom soup in a 1-1/2-quart casserole or glass baking dish. Bake in oven, covered, for 20 minutes.

❷ Remove casserole from oven and top with bread crumbs and caramelized onions. Return to oven and continue baking, uncovered, for 5 to 10 minutes, or until bubbly. Serve warm.

RECIPE NOTES

This recipe requires a combination of the Cream of Mushroom Soup recipe and the Caramelized Onions, both of which can be prepared ahead of time and frozen.

Serves: 6. Preparation Time is 5 minutes. Cooking Time is 30 minutes.

Roasted Bell Pepper Medley

¡◎!¡

INGREDIENTS

2 medium yellow bell peppers

2 medium orange bell peppers

2 medium red bell peppers

1/4 cup olive oil

1 medium shallot, chopped

1 clove garlic, minced

3 tablespoons chopped fresh basil

4 tablespoons capers

1/2 teaspoon salt

1/4 teaspoon pepper

INSTRUCTIONS

Preheat the broiler.

❶ Place peppers on a nonstick baking sheet. Broil until the skins blister and begin to brown, about 15 minutes. Turn peppers 2 to 3 times during the broiling process to ensure all sides are roasted. Set peppers aside until cooled to room temperature. Peel the skins off the peppers. Seed peppers and slice into 1/2-inch strips.

❷ Toss peppers together with remaining ingredients. Serve immediately, or cover and refrigerate for up to 2 days.

RECIPE NOTES

If preparing this dish in advance, wait to add the capers and basil until just before serving. This will keep the dish vibrant and full of fresh flavors.

Serves: 6. Preparation Time is 10 minutes. Inactive Preparation Time is 20 minutes. Cooking Time is 15 minutes.

Roasted Balsamic-Glazed Vegetables

¡◎¦¡

INGREDIENTS

2 large carrots, chopped

2 tablespoons olive oil, divided

1/2 teaspoon salt

3 tablespoons honey

1/2 cup balsamic vinegar

1 large red onion, chopped

1 medium zucchini, chopped

1 medium yellow squash, chopped

INSTRUCTIONS

Preheat oven to 375°F.

❶ Toss the chopped carrots together with 1 tablespoon of olive oil and 1/2 teaspoon salt. Spread onto a rimmed baking pan and roast in preheated oven for 30 minutes.

❷ Meanwhile, combine the remaining tablespoon of olive oil with the honey and vinegar. Mix together and toss in a bowl with remaining chopped vegetables.

❸ After 30 minutes remove the carrots from oven. Toss carrots together with the remaining coated vegetables and spread all vegetables back on the rimmed baking sheet; you may need 2 baking sheets. Return to oven and roast for 25 minutes, turning once. Remove from oven and serve warm.

RECIPE NOTES

🍲 Try this balsamic glaze on chicken breasts or pork chops for quick and easy ways to create fantastic meals. Simply pour glaze over meat prior to baking to create instant perfection!

Serves: 4. Preparation Time is 5 minutes. Cooking Time is 55 minutes.

Corn and Black Bean Succotash

¶⊙¶

INGREDIENTS

1 15-ounce can black beans, drained and rinsed

1 15-ounce can corn, drained

1 medium red bell pepper, diced

1/3 cup balsamic vinegar

3 tablespoons olive oil

1/4 teaspoon pepper

1/2 teaspoon cumin

1/2 teaspoon chili powder

1/4 cup fresh chopped cilantro

INSTRUCTIONS

❶ Combine all ingredients in a medium glass bowl. Cover and refrigerate for 2 to 3 hours before serving.

RECIPE NOTES

Succotash can be made up to 2 days in advance; however, to maintain a fresh taste, wait to add the cilantro until just before serving.

Serves: 6. Preparation Time is 5 minutes. Inactive Preparation Time is 2 hours.

Pickled Corn Salad

This recipe provides a flavorful side dish for traditional Mexican entrées such as burritos and enchiladas, and is a nice alternative to rice.

🍴◎🍴

INGREDIENTS

1 medium red onion, diced

1 medium green bell pepper, diced

1/4 cup pimientos, drained and chopped

1/2 cup cider vinegar

1/2 cup water

1 teaspoon Dijon mustard

1/2 teaspoon celery salt

3/4 teaspoon salt

3 tablespoons sugar

2 15-ounce cans corn, drained

INSTRUCTIONS

❶ Combine all the ingredients except corn in a medium saucepan and bring to a boil. Lower heat, cover pan, and simmer for about 15 minutes.

❷ Remove pan from heat, add corn, cover, and allow to sit untouched for 10 minutes. Serve warm or chilled.

Serves: 6. Preparation Time is 5 minutes. Cooking Time is 25 minutes.

Fruited Acorn Squash Bake

TOIT

INGREDIENTS

2 medium acorn squash, halved and seeded

2 medium apples

2 medium pears

1/4 cup golden raisins

3 tablespoons brown sugar

1 tablespoon sugar

1/2 teaspoon cinnamon

1/8 teaspoon nutmeg

1 tablespoon grapeseed oil

1/4 cup apple cider

1 tablespoon honey

INSTRUCTIONS

Preheat oven to 350°F.

❶ Add about 1/4 cup of water to a glass baking dish and place squash cut side down in dish. Bake uncovered for 45 minutes.

❷ Meanwhile, peel and chop apples and pears. Combine in a bowl with raisins, brown sugar, sugar, cinnamon, and nutmeg.

❸ Heat oil in a large skillet over medium-high heat. Add fruit mixture and cook until fruit begins to brown, about 5 to 7 minutes.

❹ Add cider. Simmer the fruit for 8 to 10 minutes, or until fruit is tender but not mushy. Remove from heat.

❺ Remove squash from oven, pour out excess water, and dry the dish. Fill each squash half with equal amounts of the cooked fruit mixture. Return filled squash to dish, drizzle with honey, and bake for 15 minutes. Serve warm.

Serves: 4. Preparation Time is 10 minutes. Cooking Time is 1 hour.

Creamed Spinach

¶⊙¶

INGREDIENTS

2 tablespoons olive oil

1 medium shallot, minced

2 cloves garlic, minced

1 cup rice milk

1 tablespoon arrowroot starch

1/2 teaspoon salt

16 ounces frozen spinach, thawed and drained

INSTRUCTIONS

❶ Heat oil in a medium sauté pan over medium heat. Add shallot and garlic. Heat until softened but not browned, about 3 minutes.

❷ Meanwhile, whisk together rice milk, arrowroot starch, and salt. Add to pan, reduce heat to low, and stir until mixture thickens. Add spinach and stir until spinach is heated through. Remove from heat and serve immediately.

RECIPE NOTES

Arrowroot starch is a fantastic thickener and alternative to wheat flour, corn starch, or potato flour. It thickens at a much lower temperature so it is great for recipes in which you want to thicken a sauce without boiling.

Serves: 4. Preparation Time is 5 minutes. Cooking Time is 10 minutes.

Glazed Baby Carrots

¡◎¡¡

INGREDIENTS

1 teaspoon salt

1-1/2 pounds baby carrots

2 tablespoons honey

1 tablespoon brown sugar

1/2 medium orange, juiced (about 1/4 cup)

1 teaspoon orange zest

2 tablespoons fresh chopped dill, or 1 teaspoon of dried dill

INSTRUCTIONS

❶ Heat a pot of boiling water; add salt and carrots. Cook until carrots soften but are still firm in the center, about 6 to 8 minutes. Remove from heat and drain.

❷ Combine the honey, brown sugar, orange juice, and orange zest in a medium sauté pan. Heat over medium heat. Add cooked carrots and cook until carrots are glazed evenly, about 3 to 4 minutes. Remove from heat, stir in dill, and serve.

Serves: 4. Cooking Time is 15 minutes.

Caramelized Onions

¡◎¡¡

INGREDIENTS

1/4 cup olive oil

3 pounds Vidalia, or other sweet onions, thinly sliced

1/2 teaspoon salt

2 tablespoons sugar (optional)

INSTRUCTIONS

❶ Heat olive oil in a pan over low heat. Add sliced onions and sprinkle with salt. Cook over low heat, covered, for 1 hour.

❷ Stir onions and add sugar, if desired. Raise heat to medium-high. Continue to cook onions for another 20 minutes, uncovered, until golden brown. Stir occasionally to ensure they don't burn or stick to bottom of pan. Recipe yields about 2 cups.

RECIPE NOTES

Most traditional methods of cooking caramelized onions require sweating the onions over the lowest heat possible for at least 2 hours in order to draw the maximum sweetness out of the onions. However, most of these recipes also require butter, a lot of attention, and the addition of water to prevent burning. This hypoallergenic recipe maximizes the flavor and color of caramelized onions without requiring allergenic ingredients or exhausting cooking techniques.

By cooking the onions for 1 hour over low heat and covering the pan, the natural sugars of the onions will extract. Covering the pan ensures these liquids will not evaporate as the onions continue to cook in their natural, sweet juices. Accordingly, this hour of cooking needs little attention and no additional water, which could dilute the flavor.

By increasing the heat to medium-high after the first hour, the liquids will evaporate and the onions will begin to form a caramelized coating that brings forth its own unique flavors and delightful appearance. Increasing the heat may be frowned upon in conventional cooking practices, but without the addition of butter, it is difficult if not impossible to obtain a caramelized color at a low temperature setting.

Freeze in a resealable freezer bag up to 2 months. Thaw in refrigerator before using.

Serves: 6. Preparation Time is 5 minutes. Cooking Time is 1 hour 20 minutes.

Baked Beans

⏺◎⏺

INGREDIENTS

2 pounds white beans

2 tablespoons cider vinegar

10 ounces bacon, diced

1 large yellow onion, chopped

2/3 cup unsulfured molasses

1/2 cup brown sugar

1 teaspoon ground mustard

1 tablespoon salt

INSTRUCTIONS

❶ Cover the beans with water in a large pot. Allow to soak overnight. Drain, rinse, and return to pot.

❷ Add vinegar and enough water to cover the beans. Heat to boiling, reduce heat, and simmer, covered, for 15 minutes. Drain the beans, reserving about 2 cups of the liquid.

❸ Meanwhile, preheat oven to 350°F. Using a large, heavy-bottomed pot or Dutch oven, cook the bacon. Add the chopped onion and sauté for 2 minutes. Add the beans, 1 cup of reserved bean liquid, and the remaining ingredients. Bring to a boil. If mixture is too thick, add more bean liquid.

❹ Place pot in oven and bake, uncovered, for 2 hours, stirring occasionally. Serve warm. Store in refrigerator up to 5 days.

RECIPE NOTES

Serves: 8. Inactive Preparation Time is 12 hours. Cooking Time is 2 hours 20 minutes.

Refried Beans

❙◎❙❙

INGREDIENTS

2 slices bacon (optional)

2 tablespoons canola oil

1/2 medium white onion, chopped

2 cloves garlic, chopped

1 teaspoon chili powder

1 teaspoon ground coriander

1 teaspoon cumin

1 teaspoon salt

1/4 cup water

2 15-ounce cans pinto beans, drained and rinsed

1 tablespoon fresh chopped cilantro (optional)

INSTRUCTIONS

❶ Cook bacon in a medium sauté pan. Leaving the grease, remove cooked bacon, chop, and set aside (or reserve for another use).

❷ Add canola oil to pan (if using bacon, use only 1 tablespoon). Heat over medium heat. Add onion and garlic and cook until lightly browned, about 4 minutes.

❸ Add spices and salt and sauté until fragrant, about 2 minutes. Remove from heat and allow ingredients to cool before transferring to a food processor or blender. Pulse a few times to mince the ingredients.

❹ Working in batches, add about 1/3 of the beans and 1/3 of the water to the processor. Pulse a few times until desired consistency is reached. Remove pureed batch to a large bowl and finish with remaining beans and water. Combine all three batches to incorporate all ingredients. If desired, stir in the fresh cilantro, sprinkle with bacon bits, and serve. Store in refrigerator up to 3 days.

Serves: 4. Preparation Time is 10 minutes. Cooking Time is 10 minutes.

Cole Slaw

¡©¡

INGREDIENTS

2 tablespoons sugar

1/4 cup rice vinegar

2 tablespoons canola oil

1 tablespoon orange juice

2 tablespoons poppy seeds

16 ounces shredded cabbage

1 cup shredded carrots

1/2 teaspoon salt

INSTRUCTIONS

❶ Dissolve sugar in vinegar. Add canola oil, orange juice, and poppy seeds. Stir until well blended.

❷ Shred the cabbage into 1/2-inch pieces. Add the carrots, vinegar mixture, and salt. Let stand 15 minutes before serving.

Serves: 8. Preparation Time is 5 minutes. Inactive Preparation Time is 15 minutes.

Classic American Potato Salad

A traditional American picnic is not complete without an old-fashioned potato salad. By old-fashioned potato salad, I refer to chilled chunks of potato nestled within a creamy base of egg and mayonnaise. Although people suffering from food allergies may not be able to indulge in such ingredients, my version of this creamy American classic will allow everyone to indulge. And without eggs or mayonnaise, this version of classic American potato salad is very picnic-friendly. My favorite potato salad tastes complete with chopped celery, chopped onion, and scallions, but feel free to use the creamy potato base along with some of your favorite potato salad additions.

🍴◎🍴

INGREDIENTS

1/2 pound Yukon Gold potatoes rinsed, scrubbed, and peeled

2 pounds red boiling potatoes rinsed, scrubbed, and quartered

1 tablespoon white wine vinegar

2 tablespoons lemon juice

2 tablespoons rice milk

2 tablespoons Dijon mustard

1/4 cup olive oil

1/4 cup canola oil

1 teaspoon salt

1/2 teaspoon pepper

1/4 cup sweet pickle relish

2 celery stalks, diced

2 medium scallions, chopped

1/2 medium white onion, chopped

1/2 teaspoon paprika

INSTRUCTIONS

❶ Bring a large pot of salted water to a boil. Add the peeled Yukon potatoes and boil for 10 to 12 minutes.

❷ Add the quartered, skin-on red potatoes to the same pot and continue to boil until tender, about 10 minutes. Drain. Place Yukon potatoes in separate mixing bowl and set aside. Rinse red potatoes with cold water and transfer to a large bowl. Drizzle red potatoes with white wine vinegar and set aside.

❸ In a small food processor or blender, pulse together the lemon juice, rice milk, and Dijon mustard. With the motor running, slowly pour in a steady stream of olive oil. Repeat with the canola oil.

❹ Using a fork, mash the Yukon potatoes and add to food processor along with the salt and pepper. Puree until smooth and creamy. Pour the creamy potato base over the red potatoes.

❺ Toss potatoes together with the relish, celery, scallions, and onions. Cover and chill in the refrigerator for 2 hours before serving. Garnish with paprika.

RECIPE NOTES

To achieve a creaminess we all know and love without adding common allergens, I have devised a scrumptious and creamy base from Yukon Gold potatoes. Yukon Gold potatoes are great all-purpose potatoes known for their yellow flesh, creamy texture, and buttery flavor. Another excellent potato to use for this salad is the Yellow Finn potato, which has a slightly sweet flavor. The combination of the well-cooked yellow potato and rice milk provide the creamy texture while the oils and mustard act as emulsifiers to produce a wonderful, creamy consistency.

Serves: 6. Preparation Time is 10 minutes. Inactive Preparation Time is 2 hours. Cooking Time is 25 minutes.

Provençal Potato Salad

Ÿ◎Ħ

INGREDIENTS

2 teaspoons sea salt, divided

2 pounds Yukon Gold potatoes, or other yellow-fleshed potatoes

2 tablespoons dry white wine

2 tablespoons chicken stock

3 tablespoons champagne vinegar

1/2 teaspoon Dijon mustard

1/2 teaspoon pepper

1/2 cup olive oil

1/4 cup chives

2 tablespoons fresh chopped dill

2 tablespoons fresh chopped parsley

INSTRUCTIONS

❶ Bring a large pot of water to a boil. Add 1 teaspoon of sea salt.

❷ Meanwhile, chop the potatoes into generous, bite-size chunks. Drop the potatoes into the pot of boiling water and cook until they are cooked through and tender enough to be pierced with a fork, about 15 minutes. Drain in a colander.

❸ Place drained potatoes in a large mixing bowl and toss gently with the wine and chicken stock. Allow potato mixture to stand about 10 minutes or until all the liquid has been absorbed.

❹ Combine the vinegar, mustard, remaining 1 teaspoon of sea salt, and pepper in a small bowl. Slowly whisk in the olive oil. Continue to whisk the mixture until the oil has emulsified. Add the vinaigrette to the potatoes and toss until well coated. Add the chives, dill, and parsley and toss together. Serve chilled or at room temperature.

RECIPE NOTES

In contrast to the American classic salad, the yellow potatoes are the main ingredient and are not acting as a creamy base. Consequently, do not over-cook the yellow potatoes in this recipe or they may fall apart and you will end up with a unique, but very tasty, version of mashed potatoes. If you have overcooked them, refrigerate potatoes for 3 hours prior to tossing with vinaigrette to firm them up and minimize breakage.

Add 2 to 4 ounces of cooked, chopped bacon or prosciutto.

Serves: 4. Preparation Time is 10 minutes. Cooking Time is 15 minutes.

Chilled Broccoli Salad

⌡◎⌠

INGREDIENTS

8 ounces bacon

1 large head broccoli

1/4 cup sugar

1/4 cup white wine vinegar

1/4 cup orange juice

1 teaspoon yellow mustard

3/4 cup canola oil

1 pint cherry tomatoes, halved

1/2 large red onion, diced

1/2 cup currants

1/4 cup sunflower seeds (optional)

INSTRUCTIONS

❶ Cook bacon; transfer to a paper towel to drain. Once cool, crumble bacon into 1/4-inch pieces. Set aside.

❷ Prepare a large ice bath and set aside. Chop the head of broccoli into flowerettes and the stem into bite-size pieces.Bring a large pot of water to a boil and add chopped broccoli. Blanch broccoli for 3 minutes, remove, and promptly transfer to the ice bath to stop the cooking. When broccoli is cold, transfer to a large bowl.

❸ Meanwhile, combine the sugar, vinegar, orange juice, and mustard together in a small bowl. Whisk in the oil until well incorporated. Pour over broccoli.

❹ Add the tomatoes, onion, currants, and crumbled bacon. Toss well. Sprinkle with (optional) sunflower seeds just prior to serving. Store in refrigerator up to 1 day.

Serves: 8. Preparation Time is 10 minutes. Cooking Time is 15 minutes.

"When I talk with people about my allergies they are often surprised how severe the allergic reaction can be. I carry, and have had to use, an epi pen."

MARY PAT MCMANUS (PICTURED WITH CO-WORKERS AMBER SCHEIBEL AND SHELLY RUCKS),
PRESCHOOL TEACHER, ST. PAUL, MN

Chapter 7

Dressings, Sauces, and Condiments

I had been practicing hypoallergenic cooking for well over a year before I realized that we had stopped eating salads entirely. After much trial and a lot of error, I finally gave up trying to locate a safe bottled dressing. And so I gave up on salads, since I believed I couldn't possibly spend even more time in the kitchen making my own dressing. However I soon realized I could use all the time I spent reading the labels of ready-made dressings to make a delicious dressing from scratch. In fact, I could actually save time if I made my own. Suddenly, I starting concocting batch after batch of flavorful dressings. And by flavorful, I mean far superior in taste to any bottled dressing available. I was astonished how easily and quickly I could whip up a dressing. It only required a few minutes of otherwise idle time spent waiting for another dish to come out of the oven. Consequently, I have not checked the labels of bottled dressings in years.

I have since discovered similar benefits of making my own sauces and condiments as well. By making my own from scratch and hence alleviating the hassle of reading labels, I've also eliminated ingredients that are questionable for the food-sensitive individual, like preservatives, MSG, and food dyes.

Creamy Herb Dressing

This dressing is fabulous tossed with mesclun greens and served with your favorite salad toppings. I also love this dressing with a nice grilled steak salad. Simply drizzle the dressing over the steak for a vibrant presentation.

⊺◎⫟

INGREDIENTS

2 medium avocados

1 cup rice milk

2 tablespoons fresh tarragon, chopped

1 tablespoon fresh basil, chopped

1 tablespoon cilantro, chopped

1 tablespoon lime juice

2 tablespoons rice vinegar

1/2 teaspoon salt

INSTRUCTIONS

❶ Peel and pit the avocados. Using a food processor, puree the avocado with rice milk. Depending on size of avocados, you may have to adjust the quantity of rice milk to obtain desired consistency.

❷ Add the remaining ingredients and blend to desired consistency. Use dressing immediately or refrigerate for up to 2 days.

Serves: 8. Preparation Time is 10 minutes.

Sweet Vidalia Vinaigrette

The best place to find Vidalia onions is at a road stand in Georgia in the middle of May. However, local markets everywhere carry the onion seasonally. This vinaigrette is fabulous drizzled over sliced cucumbers in the summertime.

INGREDIENTS

1 large Vidalia or other sweet onion

3/4 cup rice vinegar

3/4 cup canola oil

3/4 cup sugar

1 tablespoon ground mustard

1/2 teaspoon salt

1/4 teaspoon pepper

INSTRUCTIONS

❶ Thinly slice the onion and combine all ingredients in medium saucepan. Mix well, heat over medium-high heat, and bring to a boil. Reduce heat and continue to simmer, uncovered, until liquid begins to thicken, about 5 minutes.

❷ Remove from heat and allow to cool slightly. Transfer the mixture to a food processor and pulse. Do not blend, but pulse until onions are approximately 1/4 inch in length. Use immediately or refrigerate for up to 3 days.

RECIPE NOTES

♀ This recipe works well with yellow, white, or even red onions. Simply increase the sugar content to 1 cup if substituting one of these onions for the Vidalia onions. Note that the color of the onion will affect the ultimate appearance of the vinaigrette. Red onions will yield a fresh, pinkish hue, which is the perfect accompaniment to a spinach salad with fresh raspberries.

Serves: 8. Preparation Time is 5 minutes. Cooking Time is 10 minutes.

Smoky Chipotle Dressing

I keep this dressing in a plastic squeeze bottle and drizzle it over any and everything. The unique color and spicy kick of the dressing are enhanced with a smooth, smoky undertone that really adds a flavorful punch to everything it touches. It can add a festive flair to the chopped Mexican salad while giving meats off the grill a fresh, slow-cooked, smoky flavor. Although this dressing does not last as long as the others, it can be made in a snap.

⊺◎⫯

INGREDIENTS
1 medium chipotle pepper in adobo sauce

1 medium avocado

1-1/2 cups rice milk

2 tablespoons lime juice

2 tablespoons paprika

2 tablespoons chopped fresh cilantro

1 teaspoon salt

INSTRUCTIONS
❶ Place all ingredients in a blender or food processor. Puree until smooth. Use immediately or refrigerate up to 2 days.

RECIPE NOTES

▫ Chipotle peppers in adobo sauce are available in small cans in the Mexican and Spanish food sections of most major grocery stores. The adobo sauce in which the peppers marinate harvests a great deal of heat. Accordingly, if you desire a super spicy dressing, add a few drops of the adobo sauce to the dressing. Proceed with caution; you can always add more.

▫ The acidity from the lime juice will help maintain the avocado's freshness and minimize oxidation. Fortunately the color of this dressing masks any browning of the avocado.

▫ Smoky Chipotle Dip: Reduce the rice milk and lime juice to 3/4 cup and 1 tablespoon, respectively. Serve alongside blooming onions, tortilla chips, French fries, or raw veggies.

Serves: 10. Preparation Time is 10 minutes.

Honey Mustard Dressing

This is my favorite dressing and is way too delicious to be reserved exclusively for salad greens. I love using it as a dip for chicken fingers and pretzels, or as a spread on chicken or turkey sandwiches.

¡◎¡¡

INGREDIENTS

1/4 cup honey

2 tablespoons white wine vinegar

2 tablespoons yellow mustard

1 tablespoon corn syrup

1/2 teaspoon salt

1/2 cup safflower oil

INSTRUCTIONS

❶ In a blender or small food processor, pulse together the honey, vinegar, mustard, corn syrup, and salt.

❷ With the motor running, slowly pour in the safflower oil in a steady stream. Transfer dressing to a glass cruet or storage container. Store in the refrigerator for up to 2 weeks. Bring dressing to room temperature and shake well before using.

RECIPE NOTES

Safflower oil is a flavorless, colorless oil expressed from the seeds of the safflower. This oil contains more polyunsaturates than any other oil, has a high smoke point so that it is ideal for deep frying, and works great with salad dressing containing ingredients that solidify when chilled, like honey or mustard.

Substitute canola oil for safflower oil.

Quick Chicken Curry Salad: Combine 1/2 cup dressing with 1/2 teaspoon curry powder. Toss together with diced, cooked chicken breast and golden raisins. Serve over salad greens or on toasted sandwich bread.

Serves: 8. Preparation Time is 5 minutes.

Balsamic Vinaigrette

¡◎¡¡

INGREDIENTS

1 small shallot, chopped

1 clove garlic, chopped

2 medium basil leaves (optional)

2 teaspoons coarse grain mustard

1/4 cup balsamic vinegar

1/2 teaspoon salt

1/4 teaspoon pepper

1 cup olive oil

INSTRUCTIONS

❶ Combine the shallot, garlic, and basil (optional) in a small food processor or blender. Pulse a few times until shallot and garlic are well minced. Add the mustard, vinegar, salt, and pepper and pulse a few more times.

❷ With the motor running, add the oil in a slow, steady stream. Use immediately or store in refrigerator up to 2 weeks (or 5 days if using fresh basil).

RECIPE NOTES

The American Dietetic Association (ADA) released the 6th edition of its Manual of Clinical Dietetics, which offers revised guidelines for the treatment of celiac disease. Among the ingredients listed on their safe list of foods for individuals avoiding gluten is distilled vinegar, no matter what its source. These guidelines mean that individuals avoiding gluten do not need to avoid foods containing unidentified vinegar. But what about vinegars with "grain" numbers on the label? A "grain" is a number used to specify a vinegar's acetic content, not to indicate that a grain is present. Many brands of distilled white vinegar are sourced from corn rather than glutinous grains, while wine vinegars and apple cider vinegars are generally sourced from grapes and apples, respectively. However, you should always check with a manufacturer to determine that your selected brand fits your dietary needs.

Serves: 8. Preparation Time is 5 minutes.

Raspberry Vinaigrette

¶◎¶

INGREDIENTS

1/3 cup honey

1/4 cup red wine vinegar

1/2 teaspoon salt

2/3 cup canola oil

1-1/2 cups raspberries, fresh or frozen and thawed

INSTRUCTIONS

❶ In a blender or small food processor, blend the honey, vinegar, and salt.

❷ With the motor running, slowly pour in the canola oil in a steady stream.

❸ Add the raspberries and pulse a few times to incorporate. Do not overblend. Transfer dressing to a glass cruet or storage container. Store in the refrigerator for up to 3 days. Bring to room temperature and shake before serving.

RECIPE NOTES

If using frozen raspberries, make sure they are room temperature. Otherwise, the honey will solidify.

Serves: 8. Preparation Time is 5 minutes.

Asian Vinaigrette

This is a fabulous dressing for the Asian chicken salad. Simply drizzle this vinaigrette over a mélange of sliced cucumber and onion, or substitute it for coleslaw dressing to create an amazing Asian coleslaw.

🍽️

INGREDIENTS

1 small shallot

2 tablespoons grated ginger root

1 tablespoon diced celery

1/4 cup rice vinegar

1 tablespoon water

1 tablespoon tomato paste

2 tablespoons sugar

1 teaspoon salt

1/2 cup canola oil

1/4 teaspoon red pepper flakes (optional)

INSTRUCTIONS

❶ Combine all ingredients, except oil and red pepper flakes, in a small food processor or blender. Pulse a few times to mince and combine. With the motor running, slowly add the canola oil. Remove from blender, add the red pepper flakes (optional), and shake. Serve immediately or store in refrigerator up to 2 weeks.

Serves: 8. Preparation Time is 5 minutes.

Creamy Italian Dressing

This dressing has so much zest and zing, you will find yourself wanting to use it on more than just salads. It serves as a wonderful marinade for chicken as well as a fabulous flavor enhancer for pasta salads.

¶⊙¶

INGREDIENTS

1 head garlic

1-1/2 teaspoons olive oil, for drizzling

2 medium shallots

2 tablespoons lemon juice

2 tablespoons white wine vinegar

2 teaspoons Dijon mustard

2 teaspoons fresh chopped thyme

1 teaspoon fresh chopped rosemary

1/2 teaspoon dried oregano

1/2 teaspoon dried marjoram

1/2 teaspoon red pepper flakes

1 teaspoon salt

1/2 teaspoon pepper

3/4 cup canola oil

INSTRUCTIONS

Preheat oven to 400°F.

❶ Slice off the top third of garlic head and wrap with aluminum foil. Drizzle olive oil over the top. Repeat with shallots. Roast in the oven for 50 minutes. Remove garlic and shallots from oven and allow to cool before handling. Once cool, squeeze the cloves from the papery peels and into a small food processor or blender.

❷ Add the lemon juice, vinegar, mustard, herbs, salt, and pepper. Puree mixture until smooth.

❸ With the machine running, slowly pour the oil though the feed tube while continuously blending ingredients. Use immediately or store in refrigerator up to 2 weeks.

RECIPE NOTES

The creaminess of this dressing is enhanced by combining two techniques. Roasting the shallots for nearly an hour enables them to act as a thickening agent, while adding the mustard acts as an emulsifier that stabilizes the texture. If the dressing is too thick, add up to another 1/2 cup of canola oil.

Serves: 6. Preparation Time is 5 minutes. Cooking Time is 50 minutes.

French Dressing

INGREDIENTS

1/2 cup ketchup

1/2 cup canola oil

1/4 cup white wine vinegar

1/4 cup sugar

1 teaspoon garlic powder

1 teaspoon salt

INSTRUCTIONS

❶ Whisk all ingredients together in a medium bowl. For best results, chill for 2 hours prior to serving. Serve immediately or store in refrigerator for up to 3 weeks.

Serves: 6. Preparation Time is 5 minutes.

Quick and Easy Greek Dressing

INGREDIENTS

1/2 cup extra virgin olive oil

3 tablespoons red wine vinegar

2 teaspoons dried oregano

1/2 teaspoon salt

1/4 teaspoon pepper

INSTRUCTIONS

❶ Combine all ingredients in a small container. Cover tightly and shake vigorously. Store in refrigerator for up to 2 weeks. Shake well before using.

Serves: 6. Preparation Time is 5 minutes.

Classic Greek Dressing

¶◎¶

INGREDIENTS

1 clove garlic, chopped

1/3 cup red wine vinegar

1 teaspoon Dijon mustard

1 teaspoon salt

1/2 teaspoon pepper

2/3 cup olive oil

1 teaspoon dried oregano

INSTRUCTIONS

❶ In a blender or small food processor, pulse together the garlic, vinegar, mustard, salt, and pepper.

❷ With the motor running, slowly pour in the olive oil in a steady stream. Transfer dressing to a glass cruet or storage container and add dried oregano. Stir or shake to combine. Store in the refrigerator for up to 2 weeks. Shake before using.

Serves: 6. Preparation Time is 10 minutes.

Derby Dressing

This particular recipe was inspired by the original Brown Derby dressing which traditionally includes Worcestershire sauce. I have substituted artichoke hearts and corn syrup to mimic the flavors of the original dressing, along with some of my own flavors that I feel best complement the ingredients of the Cobb salad.

¶◎¶

INGREDIENTS

1/4 cup red wine vinegar

2 teaspoons lemon juice

1 tablespoon corn syrup

1 tablespoon English mustard,
    or other hot mustard

2 medium-size canned artichoke hearts

1 teaspoon salt

1/2 teaspoon pepper

1/4 cup olive oil

3/4 cup canola oil

INSTRUCTIONS

❶ Combine vinegar, lemon juice, corn syrup, mustard, artichoke hearts, salt, and pepper in a blender. Pulse a few times to mix ingredients and mince artichoke hearts.

❷ Beginning with the olive oil, keep the motor running and slowly pour the oil though the feed tube while continuously blending ingredients. Repeat with canola oil. Use immediately or store in refrigerator up to 2 weeks.

Serves: 8. Preparation Time is 10 minutes.

Classic Tomato Sauce

⊺◎⊺

INGREDIENTS

1/4 cup olive oil

3 cloves garlic, chopped

1 medium white onion, chopped

1 medium carrot, shredded

3 pounds vine-ripe tomatoes, peeled, seeded, and coarsely chopped

2 tablespoons fresh chopped basil

1 teaspoon salt

1/2 teaspoon pepper

INSTRUCTIONS

❶ Heat olive oil in a large saucepan over medium-high heat. Add the garlic and onion and cook until they begin to brown, about 5 minutes. Reduce heat to medium. Add the carrot and cook until carrot softens, about 5 minutes.

❷ Add the tomatoes, crushing them between your fingers as you add them to the saucepan, ensuring all juice enters pan as well. Bring to a boil. Reduce heat to low, add basil, salt, and pepper, and simmer for 30 minutes, uncovered, until the sauce is thickened.

❸ Using a handheld immersion blender, puree sauce until it reaches your desired consistency. Store in refrigerator up to 1 week.

RECIPE NOTES

▢ Store in airtight containers up to 6 months.

▢ Substitute two 28-ounce cans of whole, peeled tomatoes with juice for the fresh tomatoes.

▢ Substitute 3/4 cup rehydrated sun-dried tomatoes for 3/4 pound of fresh tomatoes (or 14 ounces of canned tomatoes).

▢ Substitute fresh oregano, thyme, or parsley for the basil.

Serves: 4. Preparation Time is 10 minutes. Cooking Time is 40 minutes.

Bolognese Sauce

¡◎¡¡

INGREDIENTS

1/4 cup olive oil

1 medium white onion, diced

3 cloves garlic, minced

1 celery stalk, diced

1 medium carrot, diced

1 pound ground beef chuck

1 28-ounce can crushed tomatoes

2 tablespoons chopped flat leaf parsley

2 tablespoons chopped fresh basil

1 teaspoon salt

1/4 teaspoon pepper

INSTRUCTIONS

❶ In a medium soup pot, heat oil over medium heat. Add the onion and garlic and sauté until onions are soft and translucent, about 5 minutes.

❷ Add the celery and carrot and sauté until softened, about 5 minutes.

❸ Increase heat to medium-high and add ground beef. Cook until meat is cooked through, occasionally breaking up large clumps that may have formed.

❹ Add tomatoes, parsley, basil, salt, and pepper. Bring sauce to a boil, then reduce heat to low and continue to simmer, uncovered, until sauce thickens, about 30 minutes. Serve warm over pasta or spoon over polenta wedges.

RECIPE NOTES

🍲 For a thicker, less-chunky version, allow ingredients to cool slightly following step 2, then transfer to a blender or food processor to puree vegetables. Return to pan and continue with step 3.

❄ Freeze in airtight containers up to 3 months.

Serves: 4. Preparation Time is 5 minutes. Cooking Time is 50 minutes.

Puttanesca Sauce

¶◎↑↑

INGREDIENTS

2 pounds tomatoes

2 tablespoons olive oil

3 large shallots, minced

2 cloves garlic, minced

1/3 cup Sicilian (or other green) olives, pitted and chopped

1/3 cup Niçoise (or other black) olives, pitted and chopped

1/4 cup capers, drained

1/2 teaspoon dried basil

1/2 teaspoon dried oregano

1/2 teaspoon salt

1/2 teaspoon red pepper flakes

2 tablespoons tomato paste

INSTRUCTIONS

❶ Bring a large pot of water to a boil. Add tomatoes and blanch for 1 to 2 minutes. Immediately transfer tomatoes to an ice bath. When cool, peel skin from tomatoes; coarsely chop and seed them. Set aside. Alternatively, you could use two 28-ounce cans of whole peeled tomatoes, drained.

❷ Heat olive oil in a large sauté pan or soup pot over medium heat. Add shallots and garlic. Sauté until the shallots start to sweat and become translucent, about 5 minutes.

❸ Add the blanched tomatoes and the remaining ingredients. Bring to a boil, reduce heat, and continue to simmer until the sauce is thickened and slightly reduced, about 40 minutes. Serve warm on top of pasta, chicken, or polenta wedges.

RECIPE NOTES

Freeze in airtight containers up to 3 months.

Serves: 4. Preparation Time is 10 minutes. Cooking Time is 45 minutes.

Sun-Dried Tomato Pesto

Try this amazing version of pesto on top of toasted bread, tossed with pasta, or served as a sauce for chicken. My favorite way to eat this pesto is tossed with rice pasta and leftover chicken for a quick and delightful lunch.

¶◎¶¶

INGREDIENTS

7 ounces sun-dried tomatoes

2 cloves garlic, chopped

1 cup fresh basil leaves

1 teaspoon coarse sea salt

1/2 teaspoon white pepper

1 cup olive oil

INSTRUCTIONS

❶ Bring a pot of water to a boil. Add sun-dried tomatoes and boil for 10 minutes to soften the tomatoes. Drain tomatoes, place in a blender or food processor, and puree.

❷ Add the garlic, basil, salt, and pepper to the food processor. Blend until finely chopped.

❸ With the motor running, slowly add the olive oil until the mixture is smooth and creamy. Serve immediately or store in refrigerator up to 5 days.

RECIPE NOTES

Pesto Pasta: Cook 16 ounces of pasta. Reserve up to 1 cup of the pasta cooking water and drain pasta. Toss pesto with pasta and use add cooking water slowly to thin to desired consistency.

Serves: 4. Preparation Time is 5 minutes. Cooking Time is 10 minutes.

Enchilada/Taco Sauce

¶◎¶

INGREDIENTS

2 cups tomato sauce

1/2 cup water

1/2 teaspoon chili powder

2 teaspoons cumin

1/2 teaspoon onion powder

1 tablespoon white wine vinegar

1 teaspoon garlic powder

1 teaspoon garlic salt

1/2 teaspoon paprika

1/2 teaspoon cayenne pepper (optional)

INSTRUCTIONS

❶ Combine all ingredients in a medium saucepan over low-medium heat. When sauce begins to simmer, reduce heat to low and continue to simmer, covered, for 20 minutes. Allow to cool and, if necessary, transfer to a blender to puree if the tomato sauce is chunky. Use immediately or store in refrigerator up to 5 days.

RECIPE NOTES

Freeze in airtight containers up to 4 months.

Serves: 4. Preparation Time is 5 minutes. Cooking Time is 20 minutes.

Classic Barbecue Sauce

Coca Cola is one of the world's most recognizable and widely sold commercial brands. Its popular advertising slogan "I'd Like to Buy the World a Coke" has had a lasting connection with the viewing public. Actually, advertising surveys consistently identify it as one of the best commercials of all time. Whether you are familiar with the ad or not, I have no doubt you are all familiar with the soft drink which has established a common connection among people everywhere.

INGREDIENTS
1 12-ounce can Coca Cola Classic
1 cup ketchup
1 cup chopped white onion
1/4 cup white wine vinegar
1 teaspoon chili powder
1 teaspoon salt

INSTRUCTIONS
❶ Combine all ingredients in a medium saucepan over medium-high heat. Bring sauce to a boil. Reduce heat to low and simmer, covered, for approximately 40 minutes, stirring occasionally.

❷ Remove cover and simmer for 5 minutes. Remove from heat and allow sauce to cool slightly. Transfer to a blender and puree. Use immediately or store in refrigerator for up to 3 weeks.

RECIPE NOTES
This sauce is very easy to make. Using a can of Coca Cola Classic is a quick and convenient way to add a sweet, original flavor to your sauce, while the caramel color enhances the appearance. If you cannot have soda, try the more traditional sauce on the next page.

Serves: 6. Cooking Time is 45 minutes.

Home-Style Barbecue Sauce

No one should have to forego the wonderful sizzling sound of slathered meats hitting the hot grills. And now with this allergen-free recipe for barbecue sauce you don't have to. Not only is this recipe easy to make, it is very versatile and can spice up the simplest dish in minutes. Once you have mastered the base sauce, mix it up with some of the zesty variations that follow.

¶◎⫞

INGREDIENTS

4 pounds tomatoes, seeded and coarsely chopped

1/4 cup water

1-1/2 teaspoons salt

1/2 teaspoon pepper

2 teaspoons ground ginger

1/2 cup packed dark brown sugar

1/4 cup white wine vinegar

1/4 cup unsulfured molasses

INSTRUCTIONS

❶ Place tomatoes in a medium saucepan over low-medium heat. Simmer until the mixture liquefies, about 30 minutes. Allow mixture to cool slightly before transferring to a food mill to process and remove skins and residual seeds. (Food mills are very convenient, especially for preparing table foods for babies. Alternatively, press tomatoes through a fine sieve, reserving the juice while extracting the skins.)

❷ Return the tomato juice to the saucepan along with remaining ingredients. Bring to a boil over high heat. Reduce heat to low and continue to simmer, uncovered, for approximately 45 minutes.

❸ Remove sauce from heat and allow to cool slightly before transferring to a blender to puree. Use immediately or store in refrigerator up to 2 weeks.

RECIPE NOTES

🗒 Most recipes for barbecue sauce list ketchup as an ingredient. A lot of ketchup brands are conveniently free of all 8 common allergens and are gluten-free, but what a shame it would be to go without barbecue sauce because you cannot have bottled ketchup. Consequently, I cooked up this scrumptious sauce for those with sensitivities to bottled ketchup.

💡 Substitute 1 28-ounce can of crushed, peeled tomatoes for the fresh tomatoes. Skip step 1 and reduce salt to 3/4 teaspoon.

Serves: 6. Cooking Time is 1 hour 15 minutes.

Honey Barbecue Sauce

⛭

INGREDIENTS

1/2 cup barbecue sauce

2 tablespoons honey

INSTRUCTIONS

❶ Combine ingredients in a small, microwave-safe bowl. Microwave on high for 1 minute. Stir and enjoy.

Serves: 4. Preparation Time is 5 minutes.

Spicy Barbecue Sauce

⛭

INGREDIENTS

1/2 cup barbecue sauce

1/8 teaspoon Tabasco sauce

INSTRUCTIONS

❶ Combine ingredients and enjoy.

Serves: 4. Preparation Time is 5 minutes.

Sweet and Spicy Dipping Sauce

¶◎¶

INGREDIENTS

1 cup Tabasco sauce

3 tablespoons packed brown sugar

2 tablespoons ketchup

INSTRUCTIONS

❶ Combine all ingredients in a small bowl. Stir until sugar dissolves. Use immediately or store in refrigerator for up to 2 weeks.

Serves: 12. Preparation Time is 5 minutes.

Cranberry Relish

¶◎¶

INGREDIENTS

16 ounces cranberries, fresh or frozen and thawed

2 medium Granny Smith or other tart apples, chopped with skin on

2 large oranges, peeled and separated into segments

2 cups sugar

1 tablespoon orange zest

INSTRUCTIONS

❶ Using a food processor, combine cranberries, apples, and orange segments. Pulse a few times to incorporate ingredients.

❷ With motor running, slowly add the sugar and puree the mixture. Stir in orange zest, cover, and refrigerate for 4 hours before serving. Relish can be stored in refrigerator up to 2 days.

Serves: 8. Preparation Time is 5 minutes. Inactive Preparation Time is 4 hours.

Red Pepper and Eggplant Confit

¶◎⫪

INGREDIENTS

2 large red bell peppers

1 medium eggplant

4 cloves garlic, minced

1 28-ounce can whole tomatoes in juice, drained and coarsely chopped

1 cup olive oil

1/2 teaspoon salt

1/2 teaspoon red pepper flakes

1/4 teaspoon pepper

INSTRUCTIONS

Preheat the broiler.

❶ Place peppers on a nonstick baking sheet. Broil until the skins blister and begin to brown, about 15 minutes. Turn peppers 2 to 3 times during the broiling process to ensure all sides are roasted. Set peppers aside until cool enough to handle. Peel the skins off the peppers. Seed and chop peppers into 1-inch chunks.

❷ Reduce oven temperature to 350°F. Peel and cut the eggplant into 1-inch chunks. Toss eggplant and peppers together with remaining ingredients and spread mixture onto a large baking sheet with a rim. Cook in oven approximately 45 minutes, until vegetables are tender but not browned. You should stir the vegetables 2 to 3 times during the cooking process to ensure even cooking. Remove from oven and allow confit to cool before serving. Confit may be stored in the refrigerator, covered, up to 5 days.

Serves: 6. Preparation Time is 5 minutes. Cooking Time is 1 hour.

Cajun Seasoning

The following condiment recipes are fast and easy to create without having to worry about the generic "natural flavorings" or "spices" appearing on ingredient labels.

¶◎⫯

INGREDIENTS

1/4 cup paprika

3 tablespoons salt

2 tablespoons pepper

1 tablespoon dried oregano

1 tablespoon garlic powder

1 tablespoon ground mustard

1 tablespoon onion powder

1 tablespoon dried parsley

1 tablespoon cayenne pepper

1 tablespoon white pepper

1 tablespoon dried thyme

INSTRUCTIONS

❶ Combine all ingredients. Store in an airtight container in a cool, dark location for up to 6 months. Use to season chicken, steaks, or vegetables.

Serves: 24. Preparation Time is 5 minutes.

Creole Seasoning

Sprinkle a little of this on an everyday item and give it a little attitude. Use it in soup and potato salad or on french fries, baked potatoes, popcorn, corn on the cob, or in your Bloody Mary!

¶◎⫯

INGREDIENTS

2 tablespoons whole black peppercorns

1 tablespoon celery salt

6 whole bay leaves

1 teaspoon cardamom, whole

1 teaspoon mustard seed

3 whole cloves

1 teaspoon sweet paprika

1/4 teaspoon cinnamon

1/4 teaspoon ground ginger

1 teaspoon salt

INSTRUCTIONS

❶ Combine all ingredients in a spice grinder or small food processor. Grind well until mixture resembles a powder-like substance. Store in an airtight container in a cool, dark location for up to 6 months.

Serves: 24. Preparation Time is 5 minutes.

Southwest Spice Rub

This is a wonderful, easy spice mix that can be used wherever a Southwestern flair is desired. This recipe yields about 2 ¾ cups of spice. Since this recipe calls for a number of different spices, by making a large batch you can have this zesty concoction on hand at all times without having to maintain all these spices in your cabinet at the same time.

🍴

INGREDIENTS

2 tablespoons chili powder

2 tablespoons paprika

2 tablespoons ground cumin

2 tablespoons ground coriander

3/4 teaspoon cayenne pepper

1 tablespoon garlic powder

1-1/2 tablespoons dried parsley

2 tablespoons salt

1-1/2 teaspoons black pepper

INSTRUCTIONS

❶ Combine all ingredients. Store in an airtight container in a cool, dark location for up to 6 months.

Serves: 24. Preparation Time is 5 minutes.

"I am the owner and head chef of DinnerWhere – a personal chef service. I provide weekly, bi-weekly, and monthly meals for busy singles, couples, and families. I also do intimate dinner and cocktail parties. Very often I encounter clients that have food allergies and sensitivities that require my attention and creativity to ensure their health and overall satisfaction with my service."

THEO PETRON, PROFESSIONAL CHEF, DELLWOOD, MN

Chapter ❽

Sweets and Treats

In my family, the day is not complete without a little treat. Fortunately for most of us, food sensitivities to traditional sweet components are actually rare. I was thrilled to learn that it is unusual to have an allergy to chocolate, for example. And while sugar may send my daughter jumping through the roof, she is not allergic to it and I know that, despite her sugar-induced, erratic behavior, she will still be breathing after consuming it. Unfortunately, however, favorites such as chocolate pose risks to those with allergies, since many processed chocolate goods are either made with common allergens or they pose a high cross-contamination risk. Consequently, even if you don't have a chocolate allergy, many chocolate products are off-limits. But not if you make your own!

Early on I embarked on a frenzy of hypoallergenic baking and learned quite a bit. While not impossible, successful baking without gluten *and* eggs can be tricky. Egg-replacements can't always be substituted equally for eggs and often do not compensate for a lack of gluten in recipes. Consequently, baking treats without relying on the spongy elasticity properties of gluten and the rising capabilities of egg whites requires a bit of tinkering and thinking outside the box. In order to successfully accomplish hypoallergenic baking, you often need multiple flours and various starches just to make one recipe. Admittedly, this can be very inconvenient and a bit messy, and so you might ask why you should go to the trouble of mixing and measuring when there are many hypoallergenic, ready-made baking mixes already on the market. I've asked myself the same thing. Pre-diagnosis I turned to Betty Crocker for my baking needs. Post-diagnosis I often turn to pre-made hypoallergenic mixes. I'd rather have one box in my cupboard than maintain a pantry full of multiple flours necessary to bake just one cake.

But as we have all experienced, products we desire are not always available when we need them and convenience does come with a price tag, which can be hefty when it is allergen-free. And while mixes can be allergen-free, they frequently require the addition of a common allergen such as milk or eggs. When you substitute a safe ingredient for something else in a baking recipe – even when using mixes – it is extremely hard to maintain consistent results. Consequently, I have created some fabulous hypoallergenic baking recipes for traditional desserts, no substitutions required. Hopefully in the range of desserts will be one of your favorites. We all deserve to enjoy what we love.

As I've noted, one drawback of hypoallergenic baking is the multiple flours you need for just one recipe. Isn't it possible to just create one large batch of a multi-purpose flour to have on hand? I don't recommend creating a multi-purpose flour because hypoallergenic baking, like conventional baking, needs to be exact. While cooking encourages small deviations in the amount of certain ingredients, baking does not. A multi-purpose gluten-free/allergen-free flour mix will often consist of three to four different types of flours. Consequently, when you dip your measuring cup into the flour, the percentage combination of flours you obtain will differ each time. Accordingly, multi-purpose flours consisting of more than one type of flour will produce inconsistent results. While measuring for three different flours is time consuming, I believe it is worth the extra effort in order to assure your desserts turn out consistently. And trust me, your family will taste that extra love!

Cakes

Rumor has it that when General Mills and Pillsbury first introduced them in the late 1940s, boxed cake mixes were not readily accepted. Why? Because it was too easy. Simply adding water to a cake mix did not seem right; there was no sense of contribution. Baking a cake was an act of love and a cake mix that only needed water cheapened that love. It wasn't until General Mills altered the cake mix to require the addition of fresh eggs that cake mixes began to become more popular.

If General Mills could produce a cake without eggs in the late 1940s surely I could accomplish a similar task today. These cake recipes do not require any eggs, and friends and family will definitely taste a large amount of love with each scrumptious bite. With a hypoallergenic recipe for chocolate and vanilla cakes, the possibilities of creating variations of allergen-free cakes without gluten, eggs, or egg-replacement products is endless.

RECIPE NOTES

These cake recipes can be made with white sugar in lieu of evaporated cane juice, but the evaporated sugar results in a consistently better texture and cake shape. Evaporated cane juice is a finely granulated, easily soluble, general purpose sugar that will enhance any gluten-free baking application. It can be found at most specialty stores. The evaporated cane juice allows the other ingredients to maintain optimal elasticity, which will help the batter expand and rise properly. By absorbing and competing with the other starches for the liquid, evaporated cane juice creates a uniformly grained cake with a soft and smooth texture.

Other forms of evaporated cane juice include rapadura, turbinado, and sucanat. Sucanat is by far my favorite. These evaporated sugars can be used interchangeably with brown or white sugar. I prefer to use turbinado in place of brown sugar, while the sucanat works great in place of white sugar, particularly in chocolate recipes.

The combination of baking soda, vinegar, and variable oven temperatures work together to alleviate the need for eggs and egg-replacement products. When making these cakes, it is important to add the vinegar right before baking and promptly place the cake in the oven. Baking soda is a leavening agent that, when exposed to an acid (vinegar), releases carbon dioxide, which causes the batter to rise and become light and porous. If the batter sits for too long, the texture will become too airy.

The baking temperatures for the following two recipes vary. Since the cake begins rising right after the addition of vinegar, a higher oven temperature will allow it to bake faster and hold the shape. However, the oven temperature for the chocolate cake is slightly lower, as cocoa can burn on the edges before the cake's center is cooked. Accordingly, I have also adjusted the amount of baking soda to perfect the rising capabilities of each cake. The chocolate cake won't rise as high, but this recipe produces a rich, dense cake. And as a premier chocoholic, I find this is quite popular with my fellow addicts.

Vanilla Cake

¡◎¡¡

INGREDIENTS

1-1/3 cups evaporated cane juice

1/2 cup shortening

2 cups white rice flour

1/2 cup potato flour (starch)

1/2 cup tapioca flour

2 teaspoons baking soda

1/4 teaspoon salt

1/8 teaspoon xanthum gum

2 cups rice milk

1 tablespoon vanilla extract

2 tablespoons white distilled vinegar

INSTRUCTIONS

Preheat oven to 400°F.

❶ Lightly flour a 9×13-inch pan and line with parchment paper.

❷ Using an electric mixer or a hand-held mixer, cream together the evaporated cane juice and shortening until light and fluffy.

❸ Whisk together remaining dry ingredients. Begin to add dry ingredients to mixer slowly, alternating dry ingredients with rice milk. Continue to beat mixture well between each addition. When fully combined, add vanilla and mix until batter is smooth.

❹ When batter is smooth and mixed, add vinegar and stir quickly until evenly distributed. Promptly pour the batter into prepared pan and place in pre-heated oven.

❺ Bake at 400°F for 26 to 30 minutes or until an inserted toothpick comes out clean. Allow cake to cool before serving or frosting.

RECIPE NOTES

🍲 Marble Cake: Reserve 3/4 cup of the cake batter. Combine 1/3 cup evaporated cane juice, 1/4 cup shortening, and 1/4 cup cocoa powder with the reserved cake batter. Beat mixture for 1 minute and drop the chocolate batter by spoonfuls on top of the vanilla batter. Use a butter knife to make a swirl pattern. Bake immediately.

🍲 Orange Cake: Substitute 1 cup of orange juice for 1 cup of the rice milk. Additionally, add 1 tablespoon of orange zest.

🍲 Lemon Poppy Seed Cake: Add 1 tablespoon of lemon zest and 3 tablespoons of poppy seeds to the batter. Drizzle with lemon glaze.

Serves: 12. Preparation Time is 10 minutes. Cooking Time is 30 minutes.

Chocolate Cake

¶◎¶

INGREDIENTS

3/4 cup white rice flour

1/4 cup potato flour (starch)

1/4 cup tapioca flour

1/2 cup unsweetened cocoa powder

1 cup evaporated cane juice

1 teaspoon baking soda

1/8 teaspoon xanthum gum

1/2 teaspoon salt

1-1/4 cups cold water

1/2 cup safflower oil

2 teaspoons vanilla extract

2 tablespoons white distilled vinegar

INSTRUCTIONS

Preheat oven to 350°F.

❶ Lightly grease a 9-inch round (or 8 x 8-inch square) baking pan with a dab of canola oil and line with parchment paper.

❷ Whisk together dry ingredients in a mixing bowl and set aside.

❸ Mix water, oil, and vanilla extract together and whisk into dry ingredients. When batter is smooth and well mixed, add vinegar and stir quickly until it is evenly distributed. Promptly pour batter into prepared baking pan.

❹ Bake until an inserted toothpick comes out clean, about 26 to 30 minutes. Allow cake to cool before serving or frosting. Serve plain, dusted with powdered sugar, or topped with frosting or icing.

RECIPE NOTES

♀ Substitute canola oil for safflower oil.

🗇 Triple Chocolate Cupcakes: Add 1-1/4 cups of chocolate chips with the vinegar and drop into prepared cupcake tins. Bake for 20 to 22 minutes or until an inserted toothpick comes out clean. Top with Chocolate Frosting (page 242). Freeze in airtight container up to 1 month.

🗇 Hostess anyone?: Pour batter into prepared cupcake tins. Bake for 20 to 22 minutes or until an inserted toothpick comes out clean. Allow cupcakes to cool. With a sharp knife, cut a cone-shaped piece (about 1-inch in diameter and 3/4-inch thick) from the center of each cupcake. Fill centers with Marshmallow Filling (page 246). Top with Decadent Chocolate Glaze (page 245).

Serves: 8. Preparation Time is 10 minutes. Cooking Time is 20 minutes.

Vanilla Frosting

INGREDIENTS

2/3 cup shortening

1/4 cup rice milk

1-1/2 teaspoons vanilla extract

3 cups powdered sugar

INSTRUCTIONS

❶ In the bowl of an electric mixer fitted with the whisk attachment, whisk the shortening together with the rice milk and vanilla until light and fluffy.

❷ Working in batches, slowly beat in the powdered sugar. Continue to whip until the sugar is well incorporated and the frosting is thick and fluffy.

Serves: 12. Preparation Time is 10 minutes.

Chocolate Frosting

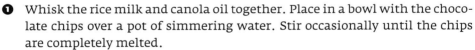

INGREDIENTS

1 cup rice milk

2 tablespoons canola oil

20 ounces chocolate chips

2 tablespoons light corn syrup

1/2 teaspoon vanilla extract

1 cup shortening

INSTRUCTIONS

❶ Whisk the rice milk and canola oil together. Place in a bowl with the chocolate chips over a pot of simmering water. Stir occasionally until the chips are completely melted.

❷ Remove from heat. Stir in the corn syrup and vanilla and allow chocolate mixture to cool to room temperature.

❸ In the bowl of an electric mixer fitted with the whisk attachment, whisk the chocolate mixture and shortening on medium speed for a few minutes until thick and fluffy.

Serves: 12. Preparation Time is 5 minutes. Inactive Preparation Time is 15 minutes. Cooking Time is 10 minutes.

Mocha Frosting

INGREDIENTS

1/2 cup rice milk

1/2 cup cold coffee (or espresso)

2 tablespoons canola oil

20 ounces chocolate chips

2 tablespoons light corn syrup

1/2 teaspoon vanilla extract

1 cup shortening

INSTRUCTIONS

❶ Whisk the rice milk, coffee, and canola oil together. Place in a bowl with the chocolate chips over a pot of simmering water. Stir occasionally until the chips are completely melted.

❷ Remove from heat. Stir in the corn syrup and vanilla and allow chocolate mixture to cool to room temperature.

❸ In the bowl of an electric mixer fitted with the whisk attachment, whisk the chocolate mixture and shortening on medium speed for a few minutes until thick and fluffy.

RECIPE NOTES

Substitute brown rice syrup for corn syrup.

Serves: 12. Preparation Time is 5 minutes. Inactive Preparation Time is 15 minutes. Cooking Time is 10 minutes.

Decadent Chocolate Icing

This icing adds a touch of heaven to the top of any baked good. It is very decadent, with a lusciously smooth texture, and is the perfect finishing touch to the chocolate cake.

🍽️

INGREDIENTS

2 tablespoons canola oil

1/2 teaspoon vanilla extract

1 cup sugar

1/3 cup cornstarch

4 tablespoons unsweetened cocoa powder

1/2 teaspoon salt

1 cup water

INSTRUCTIONS

❶ Mix canola oil and vanilla together in a small dish and set aside.

❷ Whisk together sugar, cornstarch, cocoa, and salt in a medium saucepan. Slowly whisk in water. Cook over medium heat until sauce begins to boil, stirring frequently. Boil for 1 to 2 minutes as sauce begins to thicken. Be careful not to boil for more than 2 minutes or the icing will become too thick and rubbery.

❸ Remove from heat and promptly stir in oil and vanilla. Allow icing to cool before using.

RECIPE NOTES

This icing freezes well but just be sure to ice the dessert first, then freeze the entire dessert. This recipe yields enough icing for one single-layer cake or 12 cupcakes. For a double-layer cake, double the recipe.

Serves: 12. Preparation Time is 5 minutes. Cooking Time is 10 minutes.

Decadent Chocolate Glaze

¶○¶↑

INGREDIENTS

1/2 cup powdered sugar

1-1/4 cup water, divided

2 tablespoons canola oil

1/2 teaspoon vanilla extract

1 cup sugar

1/3 cup cornstarch

4 tablespoons unsweetened cocoa powder

1/2 teaspoon salt

INSTRUCTIONS

❶ Whisk together powdered sugar, 1/4 cup water, canola oil, and vanilla in a small dish and set aside.

❷ Whisk together sugar, cornstarch, cocoa, and salt in a medium saucepan. Slowly whisk in remaining 1 cup of water. Cook over medium heat until sauce begins to boil, stirring frequently. Boil for 1 to 2 minutes as sauce begins to thicken. Be careful not to boil for more than 2 minutes or the icing will become too thick and rubbery.

❸ Remove from heat and promptly stir in powdered sugar mixture. Use promptly.

Serves: 12. Preparation Time is 5 minutes. Cooking Time is 10 minutes.

Espresso Glaze

♚◎♜

INGREDIENTS

4 teaspoons espresso powder

1/4 cup water

3 cups powdered sugar

1 tablespoon shortening, melted

1 teaspoon vanilla extract

INSTRUCTIONS

❶ Dissolve the espresso powder into the water. Whisk in the powdered sugar, shortening, and vanilla until smooth. Pour glaze over dessert and allow to set for a few minutes before serving, preferably in the refrigerator.

Serves: 12. Preparation Time is 5 minutes. Inactive Preparation Time is 10 minutes.

Marshmallow Filling

♚◎♜

INGREDIENTS

1 cup cold water, divided

2-1/2 teaspoons gelatin

2 cups sugar

1 teaspoon vanilla extract

INSTRUCTIONS

❶ In the bowl of an electric mixer, add 1/2 cup cold water. Lightly sprinkle the gelatin over the water. Allow the gelatin to soften, about 5 minutes.

❷ Meanwhile, combine the remaining 1/2 cup water with 2 cups of sugar over medium heat. Continue to stir until sugar is dissolved.

❸ Allow the sugar mixture to boil and reach a temperature of 238°F. Remove from heat and add the vanilla.

❹ Add sugar mixture to the softened gelatin. Using the whisk attachment, whip the mixture on a medium-high speed until soft peaks form, about 10 minutes. Use promptly.

Serves: 12. Preparation Time is 10 minutes. Inactive Preparation Time is 5 minutes. Cooking Time is 10 minutes.

Chocolate Roulade

¡◎!¡

INGREDIENTS

3/4 cup white rice flour

1/4 cup potato flour (starch)

1/4 cup tapioca flour

1/2 cup unsweetened cocoa powder

1 cup evaporated cane juice

1 teaspoon baking soda

1/2 teaspoon xanthum gum

1/2 teaspoon salt

1-1/4 cups cold water

1/2 cup safflower oil

2 teaspoons vanilla extract

2 tablespoons white distilled vinegar

1/2 cup powdered sugar, divided

1 batch of Marshmallow Filling,
    recipe on page 246

1 cup chocolate chips

INSTRUCTIONS

Preheat oven to 350°F.

❶ Lightly grease a 9×13-inch rimmed baking sheet (or a jelly roll pan) with a dab of canola oil and line with parchment paper.

❷ Whisk together dry ingredients in a mixing bowl and set aside.

❸ Mix water, oil, and vanilla extract together and whisk into dry ingredients. When batter is smooth and well mixed, add vinegar and stir quickly until it is evenly distributed. Promptly pour batter into prepared baking pan.

❹ Bake for 15 to 18 minutes, or until the center springs back when pressed lightly. Remove from the oven, place a sheet of parchment paper on top of the cake, then put a damp tea towel on top of the paper. Set aside to cool. Meanwhile, prepare the marshmallow filling.

❺ Dust a large piece of parchment with about half of the powdered sugar. Turn the cooled cake out onto it and peel off the original paper from the bottom. Spread with the marshmallow filling over the top and sprinkle with chocolate chips.

❻ Roll up the cake like a Swiss roll, starting with one of the short edges. Roll tightly to start with and use the paper to help. Sift the remaining powdered sugar over the top of roulade and serve.

RECIPE NOTES

Xanthum Gum is a fine, cream-colored powder that functions as a binder and stabilizer in gluten-free baked goods. To say that a little goes a long way is an overstatement, as a trace amount equal to approximately 1/8 of a teaspoon is more than enough to bind cakes and muffins together. So why does this recipe call for a whopping 1/2 teaspoon? Not only does xanthum gum bind baked goods, it makes them more flexible and provides a chewier texture. Adding more xanthum gum will gives this roulade the flexibility needed to ease the rolling process and minimize the chance of the cake sticking to the pan.

Serves: 8. Preparation Time is 10 minutes. Cooking Time is 20 minutes.

Old-Fashioned Jelly Roll

¡◯!¡

INGREDIENTS

1-1/3 cups evaporated cane juice

1/2 cup shortening

1-1/2 cups white rice flour

1 cup tapioca flour

1/2 cup potato flour

2 teaspoons baking soda

3/4 teaspoon xanthum gum

1/4 teaspoon salt

2 cups rice milk

1 tablespoon vanilla extract

2 tablespoons white vinegar

3/4 cup powdered sugar, divided

1 cup jelly, jam, or preserves

INSTRUCTIONS

Preheat oven to 375°F.

❶ Lightly flour a 9×13-inch pan and line with parchment paper.

❷ Using an electric mixer or a handheld mixer, cream together the evaporated cane juice and shortening until light and fluffy.

❸ In a separate bowl, whisk together remaining dry ingredients. Begin to add dry ingredients to shortening slowly, alternating dry ingredients with rice milk. Continue to beat mixture well between each addition. When fully combined, add vanilla and mix until batter is smooth.

❹ When batter is smooth and mixed, add vinegar and stir quickly until evenly distributed. Promptly pour the batter into prepared pan and place in pre-heated oven.

❺ Bake for 12 to 15 minutes or until the center springs back when pressed lightly. Remove from the oven, place a sheet of parchment paper on top of the cake, then put a damp tea towel on top of the paper. Set aside to cool.

❻ Dust a large piece of parchment with about 1/4 cup of the powdered sugar. Turn the cooled cake out onto it and peel off the original paper from the bottom. Spread an even coating of jelly over the top and dust with 1/4 cup of powdered sugar.

❼ Roll up the cake like a Swiss roll, starting with one of the short edges. Roll tightly to start with and use the paper to help. Sift the remaining 1/4 cup of powdered sugar over the top of roll and serve.

RECIPE NOTES

🗌 In addition to the xanthum gum, the tapioca flour has been proportionately increased in both this recipe and the recipe for chocolate roulade. This finely ground flour adds a chewy texture and springiness, as it lightens baked goods, making it a perfect ingredient to ensure a perfect roll every time.

🍲 Lemon Jelly Roll: Prepare the lemon filling from the Lemon Bars recipe (page 290). Spread evenly over the cake in lieu of the jelly. Allow the lemon filling to cool for 15 to 20 minutes before rolling the cake.

Serves: 12. Preparation Time is 15 minutes. Cooking Time is 15 minutes.

I Scream for Ice Dream

This recipe was not created to compete with Häagen-Dazs nor will it put Baskin-R
out of business anytime soon. However, this recipe is pure delight that will send s
of joy through households suffering from dual dairy and soy allergies, or those with s
peanut or tree nut allergies unable to find a safe brand of ice cream.

INGREDIENTS

1 medium vanilla bean (optional)

4 cups rice milk

1 cup sugar

1 teaspoon vanilla extract

2 tablespoons canola oil

3/4 teaspoon xanthum gum

2 tablespoons light corn syrup

INSTRUCTIONS

❶ Scrape the seeds from the vanilla bean (optional).

❷ Heat the rice milk, sugar, vanilla extract, and the optional vanilla seeds in a small saucepan only until the sugar is dissolved. Remove from heat, transfer to a bowl, and chill in the refrigerator for at least 3 hours.

❸ Whisk together the oil and xanthum gum. Pour the chilled rice milk mixture into a blender; add oil with xanthum gum and corn syrup. Blend until well mixed.

❹ Transfer the mixture to an ice cream maker and mix according to the manufacturer's directions. Serve immediately or spoon ice "dream" into a freezer container and freeze for a few hours before serving.

RECIPE NOTES

Rice milk is actually a grain milk, made from a combination of brown rice and water. It has a light, slightly sweet flavor that substitutes well for low-fat or fat-free cow's milk. Rice milk is considered an acceptable option suitable for those who are lactose-intolerant. Rice milk can also be used as a dairy substitute for coffee creamers and ice creams. Some brands are even fortified with essential vitamins. Due to the low fat content, it is generally not acceptable for infants as a replacement for milk or formula. However the low fat may be beneficial for those watching fat intake.

Chocolate: Add 1/4 cup of cocoa powder in step 2.

Mint Chocolate Chip: Add 1 tablespoon of crème de menthe in step 3. After blending, add 1 cup of chocolate chips before transferring to ice cream maker.

Peppermint Stick: Crush 3 to 4 candy canes and add just prior to transferring to ice cream maker.

Orange Sherbet: Substitute 2 cups of orange juice for 2 cups of rice milk.

Serves: 6. Preparation Time is 30 minutes. Inactive Preparation Time is 5 hours.

Chocolate Sauce

¡◎¡

INGREDIENTS

1/2 cup unsweetened cocoa powder

1 cup sugar

1/4 teaspoon salt

1 cup water

1 teaspoon vanilla extract

INSTRUCTIONS

❶ Combine cocoa powder, sugar, and salt in a medium saucepan. Add water and whisk together until smooth.

❷ Heat chocolate sauce over medium heat until it boils. Continue boiling for exactly one minute, being careful not to overboil. Remove from heat, stir in vanilla, and allow to cool. Serve warm or chilled. Store in refrigerator up to 3 weeks.

Serves: 4. Preparation Time is 5 minutes. Cooking Time is 5 minutes.

Hot Fudge Sauce

¡◎¡

INGREDIENTS

1/4 cup unsweetened cocoa powder

1/3 cup water

1 cup sugar

2 tablespoons light corn syrup

1 teaspoon vanilla extract

INSTRUCTIONS

❶ Combine the cocoa powder and water in a medium saucepan. Whisk together until smooth.

❷ Add the sugar and corn syrup and heat over medium heat. Bring chocolate mixture to a low boil, cover, and continue to boil without stirring for 3 minutes.

❸ Reduce heat to low, uncover, and continue to simmer for 2 more minutes, without stirring.

❹ Remove from heat, stir in vanilla, and serve warm. Store in refrigerator in an airtight glass jar for up to 2 weeks. Heat before serving.

Serves: 4. Preparation Time is 5 minutes. Cooking Time is 5 minutes.

Muffins

The following three muffin recipes contain the same proportions of white rice flour, potato flour (starch), and tapioca flour. A combination of these three flours is very common in gluten-free baking. As I have previously mentioned, I advise against making a large batch of an all-purpose flour that consists of multiple ingredients if you want to maintain consistent results. However, since I make these muffins all the time, it is convenient to have some ingredients pre-measured. Consequently, I prepare my own individual, ready-made muffin mixes by creating individual batches of dry ingredients and placing them in a large resealable bag. When I want to make muffins, I use one of my homemade "mixes" and have homemade muffins ready for my family with very little hassle.

- White rice flour is a finely ground flour that is very popular for gluten-free baking. The taste is so mild that it does not alter the flavor of the other ingredients, making it preferable to brown rice flour that has a slightly sweet and nutty taste. However, both rice flours have a somewhat gritty texture. Consequently, I generally add both potato and tapioca flour to create a suitable, gluten-free baking flour.

- Potato flour, otherwise known as potato starch or potato starch flour, is a very fine, gluten-free flour made from the starch of raw potatoes. It has a very bland taste and provides moisture retention as it helps bind baked goods.

- Tapioca flour is a smooth, white finely ground flour that imparts a chewier texture as it adds elasticity to baked goods.

Blueberry Muffins

🍴⊙🍴

INGREDIENTS

1-1/2 cups white rice flour

3/4 cup potato flour (starch)

3/4 cup tapioca flour

1 cup sugar

1 teaspoon baking powder, double-acting

1 teaspoon baking soda

1/2 teaspoon xanthum gum

1/2 teaspoon salt

1/2 cup shortening

1-1/4 cups rice milk

1 teaspoon vanilla extract

1 cup blueberries, fresh or frozen

1 teaspoon lemon zest

INSTRUCTIONS

Preheat oven to 350°F.

❶ Line a muffin pan with 12 baking cups.

❷ Whisk together the flours, sugar, baking powder, baking soda, xanthum gum, and salt in a bowl. Set aside.

❸ Melt the shortening on the stove top or in the microwave on high for one minute. Whisk the melted shortening together with rice milk and vanilla.

❹ Add the wet mixture to the dry ingredients and stir by hand. Gently fold in blueberries and lemon zest. Spoon batter into prepared muffin pan.

❺ Bake in oven for 22 to 25 minutes or until muffins are firm to the touch and tops are golden brown.

RECIPE NOTES

🍲 Just prior to baking, generously sprinkle the top of muffins with evaporated cane juice.

🍲 Glaze the top of cooled muffins with Lemon Glaze.

▭ Freeze muffins in a resealable freezer bag up to 4 months.

Serves: 12. Preparation Time is 10 minutes. Cooking Time is 25 minutes.

Cranberry Muffins

TOIT

INGREDIENTS

1-1/2 cups white rice flour

3/4 cup potato flour (starch)

3/4 cup tapioca flour

1 cup sugar

1 teaspoon baking powder, double-acting

1 teaspoon baking soda

1/2 teaspoon xanthum gum

1/2 teaspoon cinnamon

1/2 teaspoon salt

1/2 cup shortening

1-1/4 cups rice milk

1 teaspoon vanilla extract

1 cup cranberries, fresh or frozen

INSTRUCTIONS

Preheat oven to 350°F.

❶ Line a muffin pan with 12 baking cups.

❷ Whisk together the flours, sugar, baking powder, baking soda, xanthum gum, cinnamon, and salt together in a bowl. Set aside.

❸ Melt the shortening on the stove top or in the microwave on high for one minute. Whisk the melted shortening together with rice milk and vanilla.

❹ Add the wet mixture to the dry ingredients and stir by hand. Gently fold in cranberries. Spoon batter into prepared muffin pan.

❺ Bake in oven for 22 to 25 minutes or until muffins are firm to the touch and tops are golden brown.

RECIPE NOTES

Cranberry-Orange Muffins: Substitute 1/2 cup of orange juice for 3/4 cup of rice milk and add up to 1 tablespoon of orange zest.

Just prior to baking, sprinkle top of muffins with Streusel Topping.

Glaze the top of cooled muffins with Maple Glaze.

Freeze muffins in a resealable freezer bag up to 4 months.

Serves: 12. Preparation Time is 10 minutes. Cooking Time is 25 minutes.

Chocolate Chip Muffins

†◎�

INGREDIENTS

1-1/2 cups white rice flour

3/4 cup potato flour (starch)

3/4 cup tapioca flour

1 cup sugar

1 teaspoon baking powder, double-acting

1 teaspoon baking soda

1/2 teaspoon xanthum gum

1/2 teaspoon salt

1/2 cup shortening

1-1/4 cups rice milk

1 teaspoon vanilla extract

1-1/3 cup chocolate chips

INSTRUCTIONS

Preheat oven to 350°F.

❶ Line a muffin pan with 12 baking cups.

❷ Whisk together the flours, sugar, baking powder, baking soda, xanthum gum, and salt together in a bowl. Set aside.

❸ Melt the shortening on the stove top or in the microwave on high for one minute. Whisk the melted shortening together with rice milk and vanilla.

❹ Add the wet mixture to the dry ingredients and stir by hand. Fold in the chocolate chips. Spoon batter into prepared muffin pan.

❺ Bake in oven for 22 to 25 minutes or until muffins are firm to the touch and tops are golden brown.

RECIPE NOTES

🍴 Banana-Chip Muffins: Add 1 cup of mashed banana in step 3, reduce chocolate chips to 3/4 cup, and reduce sugar to 3/4 cup.

🍴 Chocolate-Chocolate Chip Muffins: Add 3 tablespoons of cocoa powder to dry ingredients. Add 2 tablespoons of rice milk to wet ingredients.

🍴 Glaze the top of muffins with Raspberry Glaze.

▭ Freeze muffins in a resealable freezer bag up to 4 months.

Serves: 12. Preparation Time is 10 minutes. Cooking Time is 25 minutes.

Banana Muffins

Quinoa flour is a wonderful complement to bananas, while sweet rice flour not only adds a sticky sweetness but also helps to bind the muffin batter together. The combination of this sweetness with the natural sugars from the bananas eliminates the need for cane sugar in this recipe, making it the perfect breakfast food or snack for those watching sugar intake.

🍽️

INGREDIENTS

1 cup sweet rice flour

1/2 cup quinoa flour

1/2 cup tapioca flour

2 teaspoons baking powder

1/2 teaspoon cinnamon

1/2 teaspoon salt

1/2 cup honey

1/3 cup safflower oil

1 teaspoon vanilla extract

2 tablespoons water

2 medium bananas, very ripe

INSTRUCTIONS

Preheat oven to 350°F.

❶ Combine the three flours, baking powder, cinnamon, and salt together in a large bowl.

❷ Combine the honey, oil, vanilla extract, and water together. Stir to incorporate and add to the bowl of flour mixture. Using a wooden spoon, mix ingredients together.

❸ Mash the ripe bananas with a fork and fold into the muffin batter. Spoon batter into prepared muffin tins and bake for 18 to 20 minutes, or until an inserted toothpick comes out clean. Allow to cool before serving.

RECIPE NOTES

Quinoa (pronounced keen-wa) is a natural whole "grain" grown in South America. It is referred to as a super grain because it contains more high-quality protein than any cereal grain, and is also a complete protein providing an almost ideal essential amino acid balance. Quinoa is actually not a grain at all, but botanically a "fruit" in the same family as beets, spinach, and chard. The National Academy of Science calls it "one of the best sources of protein in the vegetable kingdom." The highly nutritious quinoa flour is light and delicious with a delicate nutty flavor and is easy to digest.

Sweet rice flour is derived from a different type of short grain rice than white rice flour. It is stickier, but provides a smoother texture in baked goods than white rice. The sweet rice flour provides a wonderful balance to the quinoa flour that can result in a gritty texture.

Banana Bread: Place batter in a loaf pan and bake for 30 minutes.

Freeze muffins in a resealable freezer bag up to 4 months.

Serves: 12. Preparation Time is 10 minutes. Cooking Time is 20 minutes.

Lemon Glaze

¶◎¶

INGREDIENTS
2 cups powdered sugar

1/3 cup lemon juice

2 teaspoons lemon zest

INSTRUCTIONS
❶ Combine all ingredients together in a small bowl. Whisk the glaze until the sugar dissolves and all lumps are smoothed out. Drizzle the glaze over the top of the muffins or other dessert. Let the glaze set for a few minutes before serving.

RECIPE NOTES
To help smooth out lumps and ease the glazing process, place the glaze in the microwave on high for 30 seconds, stir, and promptly pour over desired dessert.

Serves: 12. Preparation Time is 5 minutes.

Raspberry Glaze

¶◎¶

INGREDIENTS
1/2 cup frozen raspberries, thawed and juices drained

1/2 tablespoon lemon juice

3 cups powdered sugar

INSTRUCTIONS
❶ Puree the raspberries with the lemon juice in a blender or small food processor until smooth.

❷ Combine the pureed berries with the powdered sugar in a bowl. Whisk until smooth. Spread over cooled muffins, cakes, or even sugar cookies. Allow the dessert to sit for a few minutes for the glaze to firm up before serving.

RECIPE NOTES
Substitute frozen and thawed strawberries, blueberries, or blackberries for the raspberries.

Serves: 12. Preparation Time is 5 minutes.

Maple Glaze

†◎‖

INGREDIENTS

1-1/2 cups powdered sugar

1 tablespoon maple sugar

1 teaspoon vanilla extract

1/3 cup maple syrup

INSTRUCTIONS

❶ Sift together dry ingredients. Pour in vanilla and maple syrup while constantly mixing. Spread or drizzle over dessert.

RECIPE NOTES

💡 Substitute 1 tablespoon of brown sugar for maple sugar.

Serves: 12. Preparation Time is 5 minutes.

Streusel Topping

†◎‖

INGREDIENTS

1/4 cup sorghum flour

1/2 cup packed brown sugar

1/2 teaspoon cinnamon

1/4 teaspoon nutmeg (optional)

2 tablespoons shortening

2 tablespoons flax seeds (optional)

INSTRUCTIONS

❶ Combine dry ingredients together. Using a pastry blender or butter knife, cut the shortening into the dry ingredients until the mixture resembles coarse bread crumbs. If desired, add flax seeds. Crumble topping over dessert.

Serves: 12. Preparation Time is 5 minutes.

Pumpkin Bread

This yummy bread is nutritious and delicious and is a wonderful substitute for a daily multi-vitamin. Enhanced with one of the top superfoods, amaranth, and charged with the high impact of vitamins from pumpkin, this snack is a surefire way to battle those first glimpses of the flu or common cold. The ingredient list may appear daunting, but the process is very easy and has little clean-up. This is one messy batter bowl you'll be thrilled to see your kids licking!

INGREDIENTS
1 cup amaranth flour
1/2 cup white rice flour
1/2 cup arrowroot starch
1 cup evaporated cane juice
2 teaspoons baking soda
1 teaspoon cream of tartar
1-1/2 teaspoons cinnamon
1/2 teaspoon ginger
1/4 teaspoon ground nutmeg
1/4 teaspoon ground cloves
1/2 cup chopped dates
1/4 cup dried currants
1-1/4 cups canned pumpkin
2 tablespoons fresh lemon juice
1/4 cup canola oil
1/3 cup water
1/3 cup honey

INSTRUCTIONS
Preheat oven to 375°F.

❶ Sift together flours, arrowroot starch, cane juice, baking soda, cream of tartar, and spices in a large bowl. Add dates and dried currants and set bowl aside.

❷ Mix together the pumpkin, lemon juice, oil, water, and honey in a small bowl.

❸ Add pumpkin mixture to dry ingredients, stir, and promptly pour batter into prepared loaf pan. Bake for 35 to 40 minutes.

RECISE NOTES

Other than quinoa, amaranth is the only grain that contains complete proteins. Additionally, amaranth provides a good source of dietary fiber and dietary minerals such as iron, magnesium, phosphorus, copper, and especially manganese. Magnesium is an especially important nutrient for those suffering from multiple food allergies, as other core sources of magnesium include peanuts, tree nuts, and fish.

This gluten-free grain has fiber content that is three times that of wheat, and its iron content is five times that of wheat. Amaranth also contains a high level of tocotrienols (a form of vitamin E) which have cholesterol-lowering capabilities in humans. Cooked amaranth is 90% digestible and because of this ease of digestion, it has traditionally been given to those recovering from an illness.

Despite all the nutritional benefits, amaranth has a stronger, slightly malt-like flavor than do other grains. Actually, Peruvians use fermented amaranth seed to make "chichi," or beer. Accordingly, when I cook or bake with amaranth, I generally mix it with other ingredients to mask or complement its strong flavor. For this recipe, the pumpkin and combination of spices allow the amaranth to give this bread a wonderful, earthy-like undertone. Other recipes that would be well suited to amaranth would be buckwheat pancakes or desserts sweetened with sugar. Amaranth has a stickier texture than do most grains, which assists in binding together ingredients. Just be careful not to overcook it, as it can become gummy.

To make pumpkin cupcakes, reduce baking time to 25 minutes.

Wrap bread in aluminum foil and freeze up to 2 months.

Serves: 12. Preparation Time is 10 minutes. Cooking Time is 40 minutes.

Poached Pears with Plum Sauce

¶◎¶

INGREDIENTS

1 medium vanilla bean

5 cups white grape juice

1/4 cup lemon juice

1 medium cinnamon stick

6 medium pears (Bosc of Anjou work well)

2 pounds plums, pitted and chopped

1/3 cup sugar

1/4 cup golden raisins

3 tablespoons fresh chopped mint leaves

INSTRUCTIONS

❶ Split the vanilla bean lengthwise and scrape out the inner seeds. Combine the seeds with the grape juice, lemon juice, and cinnamon stick in a large saucepan over high heat. Bring to a boil, then reduce heat to low and simmer.

❷ Peel the pears, but leave the stems intact. Slice off the bottom 1/8 inch of each pear to create a flat, stable base. As soon as the pears are peeled, place them in the pan of juices to prevent browning. Add the pears to the pan by laying each pear on its side so it is fully submerged in liquid. If necessary, add more grape juice or water to completely cover the pears. When all the pears are in the pan, cover the pan with a smaller-sized lid to keep pears submerged. This will ensure the pears are evenly coated.

❸ Simmer the pears for 25 to 30 minutes, turning the pears once or twice during the process. Remove pears with a slotted spoon and refrigerate until ready to serve.

❹ Remove cinnamon stick from the pan and add the plums and sugar. Stir until the sugar is dissolved. Increase heat to medium-high and boil liquid for approximately 30 minutes or until the liquid is reduced to about 1-1/2 cups and is slightly syrupy. Remove from heat, stir in raisins, and allow syrup to cool to room temperature naturally.

❺ To serve, stand pears upright in serving dish. Pour syrup over each chilled pear and decorate the outside with the plums and raisins. Garnish with fresh mint.

Serves: 6. Preparation Time is 15 minutes. Cooking Time is 1 hour 10 minutes.

Baked Apples

🍽

INGREDIENTS

1/2 cup raisins

3 tablespoons dried currants

1 teaspoon orange zest

3/4 cup packed brown sugar

3/4 cup water

1/4 teaspoon salt

1/2 teaspoon cinnamon

1/8 teaspoon ground cloves

6 large apples (any large baking apple will do)

INSTRUCTIONS

Preheat oven to 350°F.

❶ Combine raisins, currants, and orange zest together. Set aside.

❷ Combine the brown sugar, water, salt, cinnamon, and cloves together in a medium saucepan over medium heat. Stir to dissolve the sugar and heat to a boil. Reduce heat and simmer, uncovered, for 3 minutes.

❸ Meanwhile, scoop out the core from top of each apple, leaving a well. Do not cut all the way through. Place apples in an ungreased baking dish. Fill each apple with the raisin mixture and pour sugar mixture over the top. Bake, uncovered, for 30 to 35 minutes or until apples are tender. Let stand 15 minutes before serving.

Serves: 6. Preparation Time is 15 minutes. Cooking Time is 35 minutes.

Apple Crisp

¡○‼

INGREDIENTS

Filling

6 large apples (Granny Smith, Braeburn,
    or other tart apples work best)

1 tablespoon lemon juice

1/4 cup water

1 tablespoon tapioca flour

1/4 cup brown sugar, packed

1 teaspoon cinnamon

Topping

1 cup gluten-free oats

1/4 cup sorghum flour

1/2 cup brown sugar, packed

1/2 teaspoon salt

1/3 cup shortening, melted

INSTRUCTIONS

Preheat oven to 350°F.

❶ Peel and cut apples into 1-inch chunks and place in an 8×8-inch glass baking dish.

❷ Whisk together the lemon juice, water, and tapioca flour. Pour over apples. Sprinkle brown sugar and cinnamon on top and set aside.

❸ To make the topping, combine the dry ingredients together in a medium bowl. Add the melted shortening and mix together with hands until the ingredients are well combined but still crumbly. Sprinkle topping over the apples and bake for 40 minutes or until apples are tender and juices are bubbling. Serve warm.

RECIPE NOTES

♡ If sorghum flour is unavailable, substitute with an additional 1/3 cup of oats. Place the 1/3 cup of oats in a food processor and grind to a fine flour texture.

🍲 Apple-Berry Crisp: Substitute 2 cups of fresh or frozen berries of your choice for 2 apples.

🍲 Apple-Plum Crisp: Substitute 3 red plums (pitted and cut into chunks) for 2 apples. Substitute 1/4 cup white sugar for the brown sugar in the filling.

🍲 Pear-Cranberry Crisp: Substitute 4 pears (Bosc or Bartlett) and 2 cups fresh cranberries for the apples. Substitute 1/2 teaspoon ground ginger for 1/2 teaspoon of cinnamon.

Serves: 6. Preparation Time is 10 minutes. Cooking Time is 40 minutes.

Blueberry Peach Cobbler

¶⊚¶¶

INGREDIENTS

Filling

2 cups chopped peaches

3 cups blueberries

1/2 cup sugar

3 tablespoons pearl tapioca

2 tablespoons lemon juice

1 teaspoon lime zest

Topping

3/4 cup white rice flour

1/3 cup tapioca flour

1/4 cup potato flour (starch)

5 tablespoons sugar, divided

1-1/2 teaspoons baking powder,
   double-acting

1/2 teaspoon nutmeg

1/2 teaspoon salt

6 tablespoons shortening

1/3 cup rice milk

1 teaspoon vanilla extract

1 tablespoon safflower oil

INSTRUCTIONS

Preheat oven to 375°F.

❶ Combine the ingredients for the filling in a bowl and set aside for 15 to 30 minutes to allow the fruit juices to start softening the tapioca granules.

❷ Meanwhile, whisk together the white rice flour, tapioca flour, potato starch, 3 tablespoons of sugar, baking powder, nutmeg, and salt.

❸ Using a pastry blender or butter knife, cut the shortening into the dry ingredients until the mixture resembles coarse bread crumbs.

❹ Add the rice milk and vanilla. Mix with a wooden spoon or fork just until the dough comes together. Gently knead the dough a few times to press in any loose pieces.

❺ Place reserved fruit mixture in a lightly greased 9-inch pie pan or 8×8-inch baking dish. Using a little extra rice flour, gently roll out the topping and spread evenly over the baking dish. (Alternatively you could crumble the dough over the filling using your hands. Just be sure to cover the fruit entirely.) Brush the topping with oil and sprinkle the remaining 2 tablespoons of sugar on top. Bake in middle of oven for 45 minutes, or until top is golden brown and juices at the center are bubbling. Let cool for 15 minutes before serving.

(continued)

RECIPE NOTES

Tapioca is a wonderful, pure starch derived from the root of the cassava plant and can be found in many forms. Two popular forms are the small granules of pearl tapioca and the powdered form.

Tapioca-thickened fillings are crystal clear and retain a jelly-like consistency. Pearl tapioca, also known as instant or quick cooking tapioca, works particularly well as a thickener for a fruit filling. Since tapioca thickens juices faster than do other flours or cornstarch, it works famously in fruit fillings, especially berry, peach, or rhubarb, which throw a lot of juice when heated. As an added bonus, it also holds great throughout freezing and reheating. Be sure that the filling is completely covered with the topping or the moisture will evaporate from the filling and the granules won't dissolve.

Peach-Raspberry Cobbler: Substitute fresh or frozen and thawed raspberries or blackberries for the blueberries. Substitute lemon zest for the lime zest.

Cherry-Apricot Cobbler: Substitute 1 pound of fresh apricots for the peaches, 3 cups of fresh pitted cherries for the blueberries, and 2 tablespoons of arrowroot starch (or corn starch) for the pearl tapioca.

Serves: 8. Preparation Time is 30 minutes. Cooking Time is 45 minutes.

Inverted Strawberry Rhubarb Crostada

🍽️◎🍴

INGREDIENTS

Topping

1/2 cup potato flour (starch)

1/4 cup tapioca flour

3/4 cup sorghum flour

4 tablespoons sugar, divided

1/4 teaspoon xanthum gum

1/2 teaspoon salt

10 tablespoons shortening

3 tablespoons ice water

1 tablespoon safflower oil

Filling

1/2 cup sugar

4 stalks rhubarb, cut into 1-inch pieces

4 cups strawberries, halved

2 tablespoons lemon juice

3 tablespoons pearl tapioca

INSTRUCTIONS

Preheat oven to 375°F.

❶ Combine the flours, 2 tablespoons of sugar, xanthum gum, and salt in a food processor. Pulse once or twice to blend. Add the shortening and pulse until the mixture resembles a coarse meal. Add the ice water 1 tablespoon at a time and pulse until moist clumps form. Gather the dough into a ball then flatten into a disk. Wrap the dough in plastic and refrigerate until firm, about 1 hour.

❷ To make the filling, pour sugar over rhubarb and allow to sit for 10 minutes to allow some of the juices to extract. Add the strawberries, lemon juice, and pearl tapioca and allow to sit for another 15 to 20 minutes to soften the tapioca. Place fruit mixture in a 9-inch round baking dish.

❸ Using some extra flour, roll out the refrigerated crust to a 12-inch diameter circle. Place the crust over the berries in the baking dish, folding in any extra pieces so the fruit is completely covered. Brush crust with oil and sprinkle with remaining 2 tablespoons of sugar. Bake until the crust is golden and the filling is bubbling, about 40 minutes. Serve warm.

🍲 Inverted Very-Berry Crostada: Substitute 2 cups of raspberries and 2 cups of blackberries for the rhubarb and strawberries.

Serves: 8. Preparation Time is 30 minutes. Inactive Preparation Time is 1 hour.

Pineapple Upside-Down Cake

¡◎¡¡

INGREDIENTS

1/3 cup shortening

2/3 cup brown sugar

1 teaspoon vanilla extract

1/2 teaspoon cinnamon

1/2 teaspoon salt

8 slices canned pineapple

4 medium maraschino cherries, halved

1 vanilla cake mix, recipe on page 240

1/4 cup pineapple juice

INSTRUCTIONS

Preheat oven to 400°F.

❶ Combine the shortening, brown sugar, vanilla, cinnamon, and salt in a 9-inch round oven-proof skillet. Heat over medium heat until shortening melts and sugar dissolves.

❷ Remove from heat and arrange pineapple slices over the brown sugar mixture. Place a cherry half in the middle of each slice.

❸ Prepare vanilla cake recipe, substituting 1/4 cup of pineapple juice for 1/4 cup of rice milk or other liquid. Pour batter over skillet and bake in oven for 35 to 40 minutes or until a toothpick comes out clean.

❹ Invert the skillet onto a serving plate. Peel off any pineapple pieces that are stuck to the skillet and place on top. Allow to cool for 20 to 30 minutes before cutting or serving.

Serves: 8. Preparation Time is 20 minutes. Cooking Time is 40 minutes.

Funnel Cakes

These funnel cakes are very quick and easy to make, and more importantly, they are also fun to make. I have to admit that sometimes I dread when my kids request pancakes in the morning, but I always seem to have the energy to whip up a batch of these. Individualize the cakes by making different shapes with the batter. Give a little someone some extra love by making a funnel cake in the shape of the first letter of their name and you will have your kids requesting homemade funnel cakes.

¡◎¡¡

INGREDIENTS

2 cups pancake mix

1/4 cup brown sugar, packed

1 cup rice milk

2 tablespoons honey

2 tablespoons safflower oil

2 teaspoons baking powder, double-acting

1/2 teaspoon salt

2 cups canola oil for frying

1/2 cup powdered sugar

INSTRUCTIONS

❶ Combine pancake mix, brown sugar, rice milk, honey, safflower oil, baking powder, and salt. Mix well. The batter should be slightly thinner than pancake batter.

❷ In a large skillet or deep-fat fryer, heat approximately 2 cups of canola oil to 375°F. Cover the bottom of a funnel spout with your finger. Ladle 1/2 cup batter into funnel. Holding the funnel several inches above the skillet, release finger and move the funnel in a spiral motion until all of the batter is released. Fry for 2 minutes on each side or until golden brown. Drain on paper towels and sift powdered sugar over top. Repeat with remaining batter.

RECIPE NOTES

⊞ Due to variations in gluten-free/allergen-free pancake mix, you may need to add or reduce the amount of rice milk. If the batter becomes too runny, add more mix.

♡ Substitute canola oil for safflower oil.

♡ The batter can be poured using a liquid measuring cup or plastic bag with the corner snipped rather than with a funnel.

⌂ Substitute 1 cup sugar plus 2 teaspoons of cinnamon for the powdered sugar. Or substitute 1/2 cup of sugar plus 1/2 cup of cocoa powder for the powdered sugar.

⌂ Dip funnel cakes into Decadent Chocolate Glaze or drizzle with Cookie Icing.

Serves: 6. Preparation Time is 5 minutes. Cooking Time is 5 minutes.

Vanilla Pudding

¡◎!¡

INGREDIENTS

6 tablespoons arrowroot starch

2 tablespoons powdered sugar

4 cups rice milk, divided

1/2 cup maple syrup

2 tablespoons honey

2 teaspoons vanilla extract

1/2 teaspoon nutmeg (optional)

INSTRUCTIONS

❶ Whisk together the arrowroot starch, powdered sugar, and 1 cup of rice milk. Set aside.

❷ Combine remaining rice milk, maple syrup, and honey in a medium saucepan over medium heat. Bring to a boil and stir in arrowroot mixture. Stir until mixture thickens, about 2 minutes.

❸ Remove from heat and stir in vanilla and nutmeg. Pour into individual serving dishes and refrigerate for 2 hours before serving.

RECIPE NOTES

Nutmeg. *Nut*meg? Isn't this cookbook supposed to be nut-free? Indeed it is. And despite the frightening name, nutmeg is actually a seed from the tree species *Myristica fragrans*. The hard, brown seed has a warm, spicy, sweet flavor. According to the latest research produced by the Food Allergy & Anaphylaxis Network (FAAN) as of October 2007, nutmeg is not classified as a tree nut.

Similar studies from FAAN address common questions concerning coconuts and water chestnuts. The coconut is in the palm family and, according to the Food and Drug Administration as of October 2006, it is a tree nut. Conversely, the water chestnut is not a tree nut. Rather it is an edible portion of a plant root known as a "corm" and, according to FAAN, is safe for someone who is allergic to tree nuts. However, as with any ingredient, you should not consume any of these ingredients if you are allergic to them.

Serves: 4. Preparation Time is 5 minutes. Inactive Preparation Time is 2 hours. Cooking Time is 5 minutes.

Lemon Sorbet

⌁◎⌁

INGREDIENTS

1-1/2 cups sugar

2 tablespoons light corn syrup

1-1/2 cups water

2 tablespoons lemon zest

1-1/4 cup lemon juice

INSTRUCTIONS

❶ In a medium saucepan over medium heat, combine sugar, corn syrup, and water until sugar dissolves. Add lemon zest. Stir until mixture comes to a boil. Boil for 2 minutes. Add the lemon juice, stir well, and remove from heat. Strain lemon mixture through a fine sieve; transfer to an airtight container. Note: At this point you could chill the lemon mixture and use an ice cream maker to complete, or proceed to step 2.

❷ Cover and freeze the lemon mixture for 2 hours. When it is semi-solid, break the sorbet up with a fork and return to freezer for at least 2 hours. Once the sorbet is firm, transfer to a blender or food processor to process until smooth. Cover tightly and store in freezer until ready to use.

RECIPE NOTES

For a unique presentation, serve this tasty sorbet in lemon cups. To do so, cut off the top 1/3 of the lemon (not the stem end) and reserve the top. Cut off the bottom 1/8 of the lemon to allow lemon to stand upright. Using a paring knife or grapefruit knife, remove the flesh of the lemon. Freeze the lemon cups for at least one hour or overnight. Fill each cup with sorbet, replace the top, and freeze again until ready to serve.

Freeze sorbet in an airtight container up to two weeks.

Serves: 8. Preparation Time is 10 minutes. Inactive Preparation Time is 4 hours. Cooking Time is 5 minutes.

Watermelon Ice

Growing up, I loved to walk to the New Canaan Sweet Shop after school for an Italian ice. Although I loved the lemon flavor, I could not ignore the dazzling pink hues of the watermelon ice. This simple watermelon ice is the perfect refreshment for an after-school treat on a hot, humid day.

🍴◎🍴

INGREDIENTS

4 cups cubed, seedless watermelon chunks

1-1/2 cups ice cubes

3/4 cup sugar

1/4 cup lime juice

INSTRUCTIONS

❶ Place all ingredients in a blender and process until smooth. Place in an air-tight container in the freezer until slushy, about 1 hour. Serve in individual paper cups or snow-cone cups.

RECIPE NOTES

Serves: 6. Preparation Time is 5 minutes.

Popsicles

Popsicles are simple treats that can be easily made by freezing any juice. However, if you are in search of a refreshing concoction with more intriguing flavor, try one of these equally simple popsicle recipes.

¡◎¡†

INGREDIENTS
2 quarts cranberries, fresh or frozen and thawed
2 cups sugar
1/2 cup lime juice
1/2 cup water

INSTRUCTIONS
❶ Combine all ingredients in a food processor or blender. Puree until smooth. Pour into popsicle molds and freeze for 4 hours until firm.

RECIPE NOTES

♀ Substitute blueberries and lemon juice for the cranberries and lime juice.

🍶 Cocktail Popsicles: Substitute strawberries and tequila for the cranberries and water.

Serves: 16. Preparation Time is 10 minutes. Inactive Preparation Time is 4 hours.

Patriot Popsicles

¡◎¡†

INGREDIENTS
1 cup cranberry juice (or other red beverage such as cherry or raspberry juice)
1 cup white grape juice (or other clear beverage such as Gatorade or lemonade)
1 cup blue flavored Kool-Aid (or other blue beverage such as Gatorade)

INSTRUCTIONS
❶ Line up eight 3-ounce paper cups on a baking sheet, or use store-bought popsicle molds. Pour 2 tablespoons of cranberry juice into each cup. Freeze for 2 hours, or until firm, but still slushy.
❷ Remove cups from freezer and poke a popsicle stick into the center of each cup of juice. Pour 2 tablespoons of white grape juice in each cup and freeze for 2 hours.
❸ Remove cups from freezer and pour 2 tablespoons of blue Kool-Aid in each cup. Freeze until hard. Peel off paper cups to serve.

Serves: 8. Preparation Time is 5 minutes. Inactive Preparation Time is 6 hours.

Fudgsicles

¶◎¦

INGREDIENTS

3 cups rice milk

1/3 cup sugar

3 tablespoons unsweetened cocoa powder

6 tablespoons light corn syrup

3 tablespoons canola oil

2/3 cup chocolate chips

INSTRUCTIONS

❶ Whisk together the rice milk, sugar, cocoa powder, light corn syrup, and canola oil. Set aside.

❷ Melt the chocolate chips in a double boiler over hot water. Transfer melted chocolate to a bowl of an electric mixer.

❸ Working in batches, use the whisk attachment to slowly whisk the rice milk mixture into the melted chocolate. Continue to mix until smooth.

❹ Pour the chocolate mixture into popsicle molds and freeze until hard, about 6 hours.

RECIPE NOTES

If you do not have popsicle molds, pour chocolate mixture into small paper cups and freeze for 2 hours to firm up. Remove from freezer and place popsicle sticks in middle. Return to freezer for 4 more hours to harden. To serve, peel paper cup off of fudgsicle. Serve immediately or wrap individually in plastic wrap and store in freezer for up to 4 weeks.

Store in freezer in popsicle molds for up to 2 weeks. Or remove fudgsicles from mold, wrap individually in plastic wrap, and store in freezer up to 4 weeks.

Serves: 8. Preparation Time is 10 minutes. Inactive Preparation Time is 6 hours. Cooking Time is 5 minutes.

Chocolate Chip Cookies

For Andrea and Caeleb. It is every mother's right to make her child homemade, chocolate chip cookies.

¡◎¡¡

INGREDIENTS
1 cup sorghum flour
3/4 cup potato flour (starch)
1/2 cup tapioca flour
1 teaspoon baking soda
1 teaspoon baking powder
1/2 teaspoon xanthum gum
1-1/2 teaspoons salt, divided
1 cup shortening
2 tablespoons rice milk
3/4 cup brown sugar, packed
3/4 cup sugar
2 tablespoons canola oil
2 teaspoons vanilla extract
2 cups chocolate chips

INSTRUCTIONS
Preheat oven to 350°F.

❶ Sift together flours, baking soda, baking powder, xanthum gum, and 1 teaspoon salt. Set aside.

❷ Using an electric mixer, cream together the shortening with the rice milk and remaining 1/2 teaspoon salt. Add the brown sugar and granulated sugar and mix until well blended. Add canola oil and vanilla. Be sure to scrape the sides of the bowl to ensure everything is well incorporated.

❸ Working in batches, slowly beat in the flour mixture. Scrape down the side of the bowl between batches.

❹ Add chocolate chips and stir by hand.

❺ Drop by rounded tablespoonfuls onto a nonstick cookie sheet. Bake for 10 to 12 minutes. Allow to cool for 2 to 3 minutes before removing from cookie sheet. Yields 24 to 36 cookies.

RECIPE NOTES

🗒 Creaming the shortening with rice milk enables the shortening to achieve the creaminess of butter while the salt draws out the flavors of both. Adding 2 teaspoons of vanilla gives these cookies an extra punch of flavor to compensate for the lack of flavor in allergen-free shortenings.

🍲 This recipe yields flat cookies. For a thicker cookie, add an additional 1/4 cup of sorghum flour and 1 tablespoon of potato starch.

To create a different flavor base, try this flour alternative: measure out 1-1/2 cups of gluten-free oats, then grind in a food processor. To this add 1/4 cup sorghum flour, 1/4 cup potato flour, and 1/4 cup of tapioca flour.

Refrigerated Cookie Dough: Prepare recipe through step 5. Form dough into a log shape on a piece of parchment paper. Wrap paper around dough. Wrap the log with aluminum foil and freeze. When ready to use, thaw in fridge for 2 to 4 hours. Slice into individual cookies and bake, or use in any recipe calling for refrigerated cookie dough.

Serves: 36. Preparation Time is 15 minutes. Cooking Time is 12 minutes.

No-Bake Cookies I

One downside of preparing so many meals is that my oven is always on. This can make hot summer days even stickier. The following recipes provide two versions of no-bake cookies. Both are wonderful ways to keep kids involved in the kitchen.

¡◎¡¡

INGREDIENTS

2 cups sugar

1/2 cup rice milk

1 tablespoon safflower oil

1/2 cup shortening

4 cups oats

1/2 cup unsweetened cocoa powder

1/4 cup sorghum flour

1/2 cup mini marshmallows, quartered

INSTRUCTIONS

❶ Combine the sugar, rice milk, safflower oil, and shortening in a small saucepan. Heat over medium heat and stir until sugar dissolves.

❷ Continue to heat until boiling. Remove from heat and add in oats, cocoa powder, sorghum flour, and marshmallows. Stir until marshmallows are well coated.

❸ Drop by spoonfuls onto a greased cookie sheet. Allow cookies to set for 10 to 15 minutes before serving. Store in airtight containers in refrigerator for up to 1 week.

RECIPE NOTES

🔲 Safflower oil is rapidly becoming recognized as one of nature's most valuable vegetable oils and is sought after by health-conscious individuals. This oil is high in monounsaturated fatty acids and contains moderate levels of essential polyunsaturated fatty acids, thereby helping to reduce cholesterol and playing a critical role in the prevention of coronary artery disease. Although some claim this to be a flavorless oil, I believe it has a hint of buttery flavor and consequently, I love to bake with it.

💡 Substitute canola oil for safflower oil.

Serves: 12. Preparation Time is 15 minutes. Cooking Time is 5 minutes.

No-Bake Cookies II

🍴◎‼

INGREDIENTS

6 tablespoons rice milk

1-1/2 cups chocolate chips

4 cups mini marshmallows

1 teaspoon vanilla

2 cups crispy cereal

1 cup powdered sugar

INSTRUCTIONS

❶ Combine the rice milk and chocolate chips in a medium saucepan. Heat over low-medium heat until chocolate chips are melted, stirring continuously.

❷ Add in marshmallows and continue to heat and stir until marshmallows are melted.

❸ Remove from heat. Stir in vanilla and crispy cereal. Transfer the chocolate mixture to an 8-inch square pan and allow to cool on the counter for one hour.

❹ Using a melon ball scoop, form chocolate mixture into individual cookies. Using hands, roll cookies to firm up, then roll in powdered sugar. Serve cookies immediately or store in airtight containers in refridgerator for up to 1 week.

RECIPE NOTES

💡 Substitute canola oil for safflower oil.

Serves: 12. Preparation Time is 5 minutes. Inactive Preparation Time is 1 hour. Cooking time is 10 minutes.

Sugar Cookies

¶◎¶

INGREDIENTS

1 cup sorghum flour

3/4 cup potato flour (starch)

1/2 cup tapioca flour

1 teaspoon baking soda

1 teaspoon baking powder

1/2 teaspoon xanthum gum

1-1/2 teaspoons salt, divided

1 cup shortening

2 tablespoons rice milk

1-1/2 cups sugar

2 tablespoons canola oil

2 teaspoons vanilla extract

INSTRUCTIONS

Preheat oven to 350°F.

❶ Sift together flours, baking soda, baking powder, xanthum gum, and 1 teaspoon salt. Set aside.

❷ Using an electric mixer, cream together the shortening with the rice milk and remaining 1/2 teaspoon salt. Add the sugar and mix until well blended. Add canola oil and vanilla. Be sure to scrape the sides of the bowl to ensure everything is well incorporated.

❸ Working in batches, slowly beat in the flour mixture. Scrape down the side of the bowl between batches.

❹ Drop by rounded tablespoonfuls onto a nonstick cookie sheet. Bake for 10 to 12 minutes. Allow to cool for 2 to 3 minutes before removing from cookie sheet. Yields 24 to 36 cookies.

RECIPE NOTES

Sorghum flour is made from a slightly sweet grain that is an excellent substitute or alternative to white or brown rice flour. Actually, I prefer sorghum flour over rice flours when making cookies and bars. While rice flours work well in baked goods like cakes and muffins, these flours can leave a gritty texture in dough-based treats like cookies and bars.

Sorghum flour produces a much smoother texture as well as enhances moisture retention, which is particularly important when preparing egg-less recipes. Sorghum flour works particularly well with xanthum gum as a binder. As a general rule, I add about 1/2 teaspoon of xanthum gum per cup of sorghum flour.

Roll and Cut Sugar Cookies: Reduce both the rice milk and canola oil to 1 tablespoon each. Wrap dough in plastic wrap and refrigerate for 2 hours. Roll out dough using a little extra potato flour and cut with desired cookies cutters. Reduce baking time to 8 to 10 minutes.

Serves: 36. Preparation Time is 15 minutes. Cooking Time is 10 minutes.

Cookie Icing

This is a wonderful icing that is quite versatile. Use it for icing sugar cookies or for topping off your favorite muffin. The consistency is such that it allows you time to work with it, while the addition of the corn syrup gives the cookies a nice, hardened glaze.

¡◎¡¡

INGREDIENTS

2-1/2 cups powdered sugar

3 tablespoons rice milk

1 tablespoon light corn syrup

INSTRUCTIONS

❶ In a small bowl, stir together the powdered sugar and rice milk until smooth.

❷ Add the corn syrup. Mix well. If desired, divide into bowls and add food coloring.

Serves: 12. Preparation Time is 5 minutes.

Colored Sprinkling Sugar

A simple way to create safe, colored sugars for sprinkling on cookies or adding to cotton candy machines!

¡◎¡¡

INGREDIENTS

1/4 cup sugar

2 drops food coloring

INSTRUCTIONS

❶ Place sugar in a small resealable bag. Add food coloring and seal the bag. Using your fingers, move the sugar around to ensure an even coating and to break up any clumps. Continue to move the sugar until a uniform color results. To lighten the color, add more sugar, 1 tablespoon at a time. To darken the color, add more food coloring, one drop at a time.

❷ Open the bag and allow sugar to air dry for at least 4 hours.

Serves: 24. Preparation Time is 5 minutes. Inactive Preparation Time is 4 hours.

Whoopie Pies

A pie? A cake? A cookie? Whether you are familiar with whoopie pies or not, you and your family are sure to delight in this old-fashioned treat. Commonly found in New England, a whoopie pie is like a sandwich made of two soft chocolate cookies and a fluffy white filling. According to old Amish legend, the whoopie pie got its name when children would find these treats in their lunch bags and shout "Whoopeee!"

🍴◎🍴

INGREDIENTS

Cookies

1/4 cup unsweetened cocoa powder

3/4 cup white rice flour

3/4 cup tapioca flour

1/2 cup potato flour (starch)

1 teaspoon baking soda

1 teaspoon baking powder, double-acting

1 teaspoon salt

1/2 teaspoon xanthum gum

1/2 cup shortening

1 cup packed brown sugar

1 teaspoon vanilla

2 tablespoons canola oil

3/4 cup rice milk

Filling

1 tablespoon tapioca flour

1 cup rice milk

1 cup shortening

1-1/2 cups powdered sugar

2 teaspoons vanilla extract

INSTRUCTIONS

Preheat oven to 350°F.

❶ Lightly grease two baking sheets with shortening.

❷ Combine the cocoa, flours, baking soda, baking powder, salt, and xanthum gum in a bowl and set aside.

❸ In a large bowl of an electric mixer, cream together shortening, brown sugar, and vanilla.

❹ Whisk the canola oil into the rice milk.

❺ Working in batches, add the dry ingredients to the shortening, alternating dry ingredients with whisked rice milk. Beat until smooth.

❻ Using a large ice cream scooper or a 1/4-cup measuring cup, drop batter onto prepared baking sheets. With the back of a spoon spread batter into 4-inch circles, leaving approximately 2 inches between each cake. Bake 15 minutes or until they are firm to the touch. Remove from oven and let cool completely on a wire rack.

❼ Meanwhile, make the filling. In a small saucepan, whisk tapioca flour with rice milk until smooth. Heat over medium-high heat, stirring until thick, about 5 minutes. Remove from heat. Cover and refrigerate until completely cool.

❽ In a mixing bowl, cream together the shortening, powdered sugar, and vanilla. Add chilled rice milk mixture and beat for 5 minutes or until fluffy.

❾ Spread filling on half of the cakes and top with remaining cakes. Store in the refrigerator up to 5 days.

RECIPE NOTES

Use Marshmallow Filling for filling.

Wrap pies individually and freeze for up to 3 months.

Serves: 12. Preparation Time is 20 minutes. Inactive Preparation Time is 1 hour. Cooking Time is 15 minutes.

.rispy Bars

Rice Krispie treats are probably the most universally recognized, and frequently prepared, homemade treat in American households. Just about every American kid has eaten one. Although genuine Rice Krispies contain malt flavoring, there are now many brands of crispy rice cereal and marshmallows that are allergen-free and gluten-free, allowing those on hypoallergenic diets to once again consume an American classic.

¡◎!¡

INGREDIENTS

2 tablespoons shortening

10 ounces marshmallows (or 4 cups of mini marshmallows)

1/2 teaspoon vanilla extract

1/4 teaspoon salt

6 cups crispy rice cereal

INSTRUCTIONS

❶ Prepare a baking dish by greasing with a dab of shortening or covering with waxed paper.

❷ Melt shortening in large pot over low-medium heat. Add marshmallows, vanilla, and salt. Stir continuously until marshmallows are completely melted and smooth.

❸ Remove from heat. Add crispy rice cereal. Stir until well coated.

❹ Using a greased spatula or waxed paper, press mixture evenly into prepared baking dish. Allow to cool and cut into squares.

RECIPE NOTES

In lieu of butter, I have traditionally used shortening. However, since shortenings are often flavorless, I've discovered that the addition of salt and vanilla not only improve the taste but cut down on the sugary flavor from the marshmallows, which can be overpowering with some brands of gluten-free cereals.

Serves: 12. Preparation Time is 10 minutes. Cooking Time is 5 minutes.

Caramel Popcorn

¶⊙¶

INGREDIENTS

1 cup brown sugar, packed

1/2 cup light corn syrup

1/4 cup water

1 teaspoon salt

1/8 teaspoon cream of tartar

1 teaspoon vanilla extract

1/2 teaspoon baking soda

10 cups popcorn

INSTRUCTIONS

Preheat oven to 250°F.

❶ In a saucepan, combine the brown sugar, corn syrup, water, salt, and cream of tartar. Heat over medium heat, stirring frequently until the mixture begins to boil.

❷ Once the mixtures boils, stop stirring and reduce heat to low-medium. Allow caramel mixture to simmer for approximately 5 to 7 minutes or until the syrup reaches a temperature of 270°F.

❸ Remove the syrup from heat, stir in vanilla, and baking soda. Pour syrup over popcorn, stirring to coat.

❹ Spread coated popcorn onto a nonstick pan and bake for approximately 1 hour, stirring occasionally. Allow popcorn mixture to cool. Break apart and serve or store in airtight container for up to 3 weeks.

RECEIPE NOTES

Cream of tartar? Contrary to what you might assume, cream of tartar is not a by-product of dairy, but rather it is a crystalline acid that forms on the inside of barrels during winemaking. This sediment is purified and ground to a powder called cream of tartar. According to the Food Allergy & Anaphylaxis Network, as of October 2007, cream of tartar is not classified as a by-product of milk. However, you should not consume it if you are allergic to it. Cream of tartar is often combined with baking soda to make baking powder. By separating the two ingredients in this recipe rather than using baking powder, the inherent properties of each ingredient are utilized. The cream of tartar adds a creamier texture to the sugary syrup while also stabilizing and adding volume to this snack once the baking soda is added. If you have a corn allergy and are unable to locate a corn-free baking powder, try substituting 1/4 teaspoon baking soda plus 3/4 teaspoon cream of tartar for every 1 teaspoon of baking powder.

Step 4 may seem like overkill, but it really allows the popcorn to become evenly coated. If you simply don't have the time, try the microwave: After pouring the caramel over the popcorn, divide the caramel corn into brown paper lunch bags. Microwave each bag for 30 to 40 seconds, remove the bag from the microwave, and shake it. Repeat process four times for each bag. Open the bags carefully and spread out the corn to cool.

Serves: 6. Preparation Time is 10 minutes. Cooking Time is 1 hour.

Chocolate-Covered Popcorn

†◎††

INGREDIENTS

1-1/2 cups sugar

1/4 cup shortening

1/4 cup unsweetened cocoa powder

2 tablespoons light corn syrup

1 teaspoon salt

1 teaspoon vanilla extract

10 cups popcorn

INSTRUCTIONS

❶ Combine the sugar, shortening, cocoa, corn syrup, and salt in a medium saucepan. Heat over medium heat until chocolate mixture begins to boil. Reduce heat to low-medium and continue to simmer until mixture thickens slightly, about 5 minutes.

❷ Remove from heat and immediately stir in vanilla. Pour over popcorn, stirring to coat. Let stand for about 30 minutes before serving. Store in airtight containers in refrigerator up to 1 week.

RECIPE NOTES

Substitute 2 cups of mini marshmallows for 2 cups of popcorn.

Serves: 6. Inactive Preparation Time is 30 minutes. Cooking Time is 10 minutes.

Brittle Candy

A favorite treat of mine to have on hand during the holidays, this candy has such an amazing, rich, buttery taste that it is hard to believe butter is not present.

¶◎⁋

INGREDIENTS

1 cup sugar

1 cup dark corn syrup

1 teaspoon salt

1 tablespoon baking soda

INSTRUCTIONS

❶ Line a 9×13-inch baking dish or rimmed baking sheet with parchment paper.

❷ In a large, heavy saucepan combine sugar, corn syrup, and salt over medium heat. Stir constantly and bring mixture to a boil.

❸ Once mixture is boiling, continue to cook without stirring until it reaches hard-crack stage or 270°F on a candy thermometer. Note: As the syrup reaches this stage, the bubbles on top will become smaller, thicker, and closer together.

❹ Remove from heat and immediately stir in baking soda. Promptly spread mixture into the prepared pan. Allow to cool, break into pieces, and serve. Or store in an airtight container in the refrigerator for up to 1 month.

RECIPE NOTES

The best way to incorporate your favorite addition is to evenly spread the add-in over the prepared pan, then pour the candy mixture on top. Add-ins can include: 1/2 cup flax seeds, 1/2 cup chocolate chips, 1/2 cup crunchy cereal, 3/4 cup mini marshmallows, or simply dip the corners of candy into Decadent Chocolate Glaze.

Serves: 8. Inactive Preparation Time is 30 minutes. Cooking Time is 10 minutes.

Taffy

¡◎¡↑

INGREDIENTS

2 tablespoons canola oil

1-1/2 cups sugar

1-1/2 cups unsulfured molasses

2/3 cup water

1/4 cup shortening

1/2 teaspoon vanilla extract

1/4 teaspoon salt

1/8 teaspoon baking soda

INSTRUCTIONS

❶ Lightly grease a pan and a sharp knife with canola oil.

❷ Combine sugar, molasses, and water together in a deep saucepan. Heat over medium heat, stirring occasionally, until it reaches a temperature of 260°F.

❸ Remove from heat and promptly stir in the shortening, vanilla, salt, and baking soda. Transfer mixture to the prepared pan and allow to cool until cool enough to handle, but still a little warm, about 10 minutes.

❹ Grease your hands with remaining oil and begin pulling the taffy. Gather into a ball and pull. Repeat this process of continuous pulling for about 5 minutes, or until taffy becomes slightly opaque and develops a satin-like finish.

❺ Pull taffy into ropes, approximately 1/2-inch wide. Set on counter and, using the greased knife, slice the ropes into 1-inch pieces. Individually wrap taffy pieces in wax paper. Enjoy immediately or store in an airtight container for up to 1 month.

Serves: 24. Preparation Time is 10 minutes. Inactive Preparation Time is 10 minutes. Cooking Time is 10 minutes.

Marshmallow Eggs

These are an easy and fun way to personalize marshmallows or add a unique touch to any holiday.

¶◎¶

INGREDIENTS

1 cup powdered sugar

2/3 cup cold water

1 tablespoon gelatin, plus 2 teaspoons

1/2 cup water

2 cups sugar

1 cup colored sprinkling sugar (or choice of store-bought sprinkles)

INSTRUCTIONS

❶ Line a baking sheet with parchment paper. Lightly sprinkle powdered sugar over pan.

❷ In the bowl of an electric mixer, add 2/3 cup cold water. Lightly sprinkle the gelatin over the water. Allow the gelatin to soften, about 5 minutes.

❸ Meanwhile, combine the 1/2 cup water with 2 cups of sugar over medium heat. Continue to stir until sugar is dissolved.

❹ Allow the sugar mixture to boil and reach a temperature of 238°F. Remove from heat and add to the gelatin. Using the mixer's whisk attachment, whip the mixture on a medium-high speed until soft peaks form, about 10 minutes.

❺ Immediately transfer whipped marshmallow into a piping bag or prepared large plastic bag with the corner snipped off. Gently squeeze the bag and pipe out an oval egg (or other desired shape) onto the prepared pan. Immediately sprinkle with colored sanding sugar before piping the next egg. Allow the eggs to set before moving, about 10 to 15 minutes.

RECIPE NOTES

🍲 Marshmallows: Prepare a 9×13-inch baking dish by lining with parchment paper. Sprinkle powdered sugar on top. Instead of piping, pour entire batch or whipped marshmallow into the dish and spread. Sprinkle additional powdered sugar on top and allow marshmallow to set. Cut into squares.

🍲 Pipe the whipped marshmallow directly onto a cupcake in lieu of frosting. Sprinkle with colored sugar or stick under the broiler of your oven for 2 minutes for a toasty marshmallow treat.

🍲 Pipe the whipped marshmallow directly onto a birthday cake to spell out recipient's name or best wishes!

Serves: 12. Preparation Time is 10 minutes. Inactive Preparation Time is 30 minutes. Cooking Time is 10 minutes.

Indoor S'mores

Indoor s'mores and berry brûleé are perfect, creative treats for adults and children alike. Making these together provides a great way to get kids involved in the kitchen. My son loves watching me blowtorch his dessert while my daughter artistically decorates the crust with slices of her favorite fruit.

🍽️

INGREDIENTS

6 slices bread
1 tablespoon canola oil
1 tablespoon cinnamon (optional)
1 cup Decadent Chocolate Icing, recipe on page 244
2 cups miniature marshmallows

INSTRUCTIONS

❶ Toast slices of bread. If using sandwich bread, slice each piece in half. Spread a few drops of canola oil (or other flavorless oil) on each slice. Dust with cinnamon (optional).

❷ Spread 1 tablespoon of chocolate icing on each slice and top with mini marshmallows.

❸ For best results use a small hand-held kitchen torch to toast the marshmallows. Ignite the torch and with a slow, sweeping motion, guide the flame directly on the surface of the marshmallows. The nozzle should be 2 to 3 inches from the surface, with the tip of the flame licking the marshmallows, until lightly browned. If you do not own a kitchen torch use the broiler of your oven and broil for approximately 2 minutes, or until the marshmallows are toasty brown.

RECIPE NOTES

🍲 Instead of chocolate, spread honey and a sprinkle of cinnamon over each slice of bread.

🍲 For a healthier yet equally enticing version, substitute 1 cup of sliced strawberries, 2 bananas, 1 cup of sugar, and 2 teaspoons of cinnamon for the chocolate and marshmallows. Alternate slices of strawberry and banana on top of each piece of toast. Mix the sugar and cinnamon together. Sprinkle approximately 1 tablespoon over each piece of toast and torch. Serve for breakfast!

Serves: 8. Preparation Time is 5 minutes. Cooking Time is 5 minutes.

Berry Brûlée

†◎ǁ

INGREDIENTS

1 package pizza dough mix

1 tablespoon safflower oil

1/2 cup sugar

1 teaspoon cinnamon

1 medium vanilla bean (optional)

3 cups berries, any combination, fresh or frozen and thawed

1 teaspoon lemon zest

INSTRUCTIONS

Preheat oven to 350°F.

❶ Prepare pizza dough according to instructions. Roll dough out onto a non-stick baking sheet (or one lined with parchment paper). Dough should be about 1/4-inch thick. Using a pizza slicer, cut off the edges to create a pie-shaped circle. Using your fingertips, gently press around the circumference of the crust to create a decorative edge. Brush the top of the crust and edges with oil. Bake until the crust is cooked through but not browned, about 8 to 10 minutes. Remove from oven and allow to cool slightly.

❷ Combine the sugar and cinnamon in a small bowl. If desired, cut the vanilla bean in half, lengthwise. Using the back of a butter knife, scrape along the inside of the bean, collecting the small seeds. Add the seeds to the cinnamon sugar and set aside.

❸ Decoratively arrange berries on crust. Garnish with lemon zest and sprinkle cinnamon sugar on top.

❹ For best results, use a small hand-held kitchen torch to melt sugar. Ignite the torch and with a slow, sweeping motion, guide the flame directly on the surface of the fruit. The nozzle should be 2 to 3 inches from the surface, with the tip of the flame licking the sugar. The sugar will melt slowly at first and then caramelize. If you do not own a kitchen torch, use the broiler of your oven and broil for approximately 2 minutes, or until the sugar caramelizes.

RECIPE NOTES

For a sweeter crust, substitute rice milk for the liquid required in your pizza crust mix.

Serves: 8. Preparation Time is 10 minutes. Cooking Time is 10 minutes.

Lemon Bars

⦿⦿⦿

INGREDIENTS

Crust

1/2 cup shortening

1/2 cup honey

1/3 cup brown sugar, packed

1/2 teaspoon salt

1-1/2 cups quinoa flakes

1-1/2 cups sorghum flour

Lemon Filling

2 tablespoons potato flour (starch)

2 tablespoons tapioca flour

1 teaspoon baking powder, double-acting

1/4 teaspoon xanthum gum

6 tablespoons water

1 cup sugar

1/4 cup corn starch

1/4 teaspoon salt

1 cup water

2 large lemons, juiced (about 1/2 cup)

1 tablespoon canola oil

2 drops yellow food coloring (optional)

1/4 cup powdered sugar

INSTRUCTIONS

Preheat oven to 350°F.

❶ Prepare the crust. Melt shortening in microwave or in a saucepan over low heat until liquefied. Combine melted shortening with honey, brown sugar, and salt.

❷ Add the quinoa flakes and sorghum flour. Mix together using your hands. Press mixture into a nonstick 9×13-inch baking pan and bake for 8 to 10 minutes, taking it out before crust begins to brown. The crust should remain slightly flaky as the lemon filling will seep into any gaps and hold it together.

❸ Prepare the filling. In a small bowl, combine the potato flour, tapioca flour, baking powder, and xanthum gum. (Alternatively, you could use about 1/4 cup of an egg replacement product.) Using an electric mixer, slowly whip in 6 tablespoons of water. Continue to beat until the base becomes smooth and fluffy, about 5 minutes.

❹ Combine the sugar, corn starch, and salt in a medium saucepan. Whisk in 1 cup of water and lemon juice. Heat over medium-high heat until sugar dissolves.

❺ Add the whipped base to the saucepan and stir continuously. Continue to cook and stir until mixture becomes smooth and thickens. It will continue to thicken rapidly. It is done when the lemon filling begins to pull away from the sides of the saucepan. Remove from heat and stir in the oil and optional food coloring.

6 Spread lemon filling over the prepared crust and allow to cool for 30 minutes. Sift powdered sugar on top before serving. Store in airtight containers in refrigerator up to 3 days.

RECIPE NOTES

Freeze in airtight containers up to 3 months.

Serves: 8. Preparation Time is 20 minutes. Cooking Time is 20 minutes.

Cranberry Bars

�◎ǁ

INGREDIENTS

1/2 cup sugar

2 cups frozen cranberries

4 tablespoons tapioca flour, divided

1 cup gluten-free oats

3/4 cup brown sugar, packed

1/2 cup sorghum flour

1/4 cup potato flour (starch)

1 teaspoon salt

6 tablespoons shortening

INSTRUCTIONS

Preheat oven to 350°.

❶ Sprinkle the sugar over cranberries and allow cranberries to come to room temperature. Transfer cranberries to a blender, add tapioca flour, and puree until smooth. Set aside.

❷ Combine remaining dry ingredients in a large bowl. Using a pastry blender or butter knife, cut the shortening into the dry ingredients until the mixture resembles coarse bread crumbs. Using your hands, mix the ingredients together until the mixture is crumbly, but holds together when pressed.

❸ Spread half the mixture into the bottom of a greased or nonstick 8x8-inch baking dish and lightly press together. Cover with prepared cranberries. Crumble remaining flour mixture on top. Bake in the bottom third of preheated oven for 45 to 50 minutes, or until the cranberries are bubbling and the topping is well browned. Allow to cool for 20 minutes, cut, and serve.

RECIPE NOTES

🍲 Substitute frozen blueberries for cranberries.

Serves: 6. Preparation Time is 5 minutes. Cooking Time is 50 minutes.

Granola Bars

With the addition of quinoa (pronounced keen-wa), these bars should more appropriately be called power bars. Quinoa is often referred to as a super grain because it contains more high quality protein than any cereal grain and provides an almost ideal essential amino acid balance. While no single ingredient can by itself furnish all the essential nutrients we need, quinoa comes as close to being complete as possible. This highly nutritious ingredient is light, delicious, and easy to digest, making it an ideal treat for young ones.

INGREDIENTS

3/4 cup shortening
3/4 cup honey
3/4 cup brown sugar, packed
1/2 teaspoon cinnamon
3/4 teaspoon salt
1-1/2 cups quinoa flakes
1-1/2 cups sorghum flour
1/3 cup cranberries, finely chopped
1/3 cup raisins, finely chopped

INSTRUCTIONS

Preheat oven to 350°F.

❶ Heat shortening in microwave or in saucepan over low heat until liquefied. Stir melted shortening together with honey, brown sugar, cinnamon, and salt.

❷ Add in the quinoa flakes, sorghum flour, cranberries, and raisins. Mix together until all ingredients are incorporated.

❸ Spread the mixture into a nonstick 8×8-inch baking dish and bake for 10 to 12 minutes, taking it out before the bars begin to brown. Remove from oven, cool and cut into rectangles.

RECIPE NOTES

In lieu of the cranberries and raisins, try these other tasty combinations: 1/3 cup each dried apples and cranberries; 1/3 cup each dried blueberries and cherries; or, 1/4 cup flax seeds, 1/3 cup chocolate chips, and 1/4 cup mini marshmallows, quartered.

Freeze in resealable freezer bags up to 4 months.

Serves: 8. Preparation Time is 10 minutes. Cooking Time is 10 minutes.

Eight Layer Bars!

The unassuming star of this recipe is the crystallized ginger. It offers the perfect balance of spicy and sweet and has the exceptional ability to complement other flavors without dominating them. The refreshing aroma and peppery tang are sure to make these bars a household favorite.

INGREDIENTS

Crust
3/4 cup shortening
1-1/2 cups sorghum flour
1 cup quinoa flakes
1/3 cup brown sugar, packed
1/2 teaspoon salt

Caramel Filling
1/2 cup shortening
1/2 cup maple sugar
1 tablespoon maple syrup
1/3 cup crystallized ginger, minced
1/4 cup light corn syrup
2 tablespoons rice milk
1/2 teaspoon salt

Topping
1-1/2 cups miniature marshmallows
1/2 cup crispy rice cereal
1/2 cup raisins
1 cup chocolate chips
1/3 cup flax seeds

INSTRUCTIONS
Preheat oven to 350°F.

❶ Prepare the crust. Melt shortening in microwave or in a saucepan over low heat until liquefied. Combine melted shortening with sorghum flour, quinoa flakes, brown sugar, and salt. Press mixture into the bottom of a greased 9×13-inch baking dish.

❷ Prepare caramel filling. Melt the shortening in a small saucepan over low-medium heat. Add maple sugar, maple syrup, crystallized ginger, corn syrup, rice milk, and salt. Stir continuously until sugar is dissolved. Remove from heat and pour 1/2 caramel mixture over crust.

❸ Promptly layer on the mini marshmallows, crispy rice cereal, and raisins. Pour the remaining 1/2 of the caramel mixture on top followed by the chocolate chips and flax seeds. Bake in oven for 8 to 10 minutes. Remove from oven and allow to cool completely before cutting.

RECIPE NOTES

💡 Substitute brown sugar for the maple sugar and increase maple syrup to 2 tablespoons.

Serves: 8. Preparation Time is 20 minutes. Cooking Time is 20 minutes.

Glossary

The following glossary includes the packaged hypoallergenic products used in creating the recipes for this cookbook. The purpose of this glossary is to assist the user in obtaining desired products. These products did not contain any of the eight common allergens, and were gluten-free and dairy-free, at the time of the author's use. However, due to cross-contamination risks and changes in ingredients and manufacturing processes, please contact the manufacturer to ensure the listed product meets your dietary needs before consuming.

Product	Source	Manufacturer Information		Phone Number	Website
Amaranth Flour	Nu-World Foods Amaranth Flour	Nu-World Foods		(630) 369-6819	www.nuworldfoods.com
Arrowroot Starch	Miss Roben's Arrowroot Starch	Allergy Grocer	91 Western Maryland Parkway, Unit #7 Hagerstown, MD 21740 USA	(800) 891-0083	www.allergygrocer.com
Bread	Tapioca Loaf	Ener-G Foods, Inc.	5960 First Avenue South, PO Box 84487 Seattle, WA 98124-5787	(800) 331-5222	www.ener-g.com
Bread Crumbs	Ener-G Bread Crumbs	Ener-G Foods, Inc.	5960 First Avenue South, PO Box 84487 Seattle, WA 98124-5787	(800) 331-5222	www.ener-g.com
Chocolate Chips	Dairy- & Soy-Free Semi-Sweet Chocolate Chips	Enjoy Life Foods	3810 River Road Schiller Park, IL 60176	(847) 260-0300	www.enjoylifefoods.com
Crispy Cereal	Perky's Nutty Flax	Enjoy Life Foods	3810 River Road Schiller Park, IL 60176	(847) 260-0300	www.perkysnaturalfoods.com
Croutons	Plain Croutons	Ener-G Foods, Inc.	5960 First Avenue South, PO Box 84487 Seattle, WA 98124-5787	(800) 331-5222	www.ener-g.com

Product	Source	Manufacturer Information		Phone Number	Website
Hot Dog and Hamburger Buns	Tapioca Hamburger and Hot Dog Buns	Ener-G Foods, Inc.	5960 First Avenue South, PO Box 84487 Seattle, WA 98124-5787	(800) 331-5222	www.ener-g.com
Marshmallows	Jet-Puffed Marshmallows	Kraft Foods Global, Inc.	Northfield, IL 60093-2753		www.kraftfoods.com
Oats	Lara's Rolled Oats	Cream Hill Estates		(866) 727-3628	www.creamhillestates.com
Pancake Mix (Blooming Onion, Onion Rings, Burrito Bake)	Namaste Waffle & Pancake Mix	Namaste Foods			
Pancake Mix (Funnel Cakes)	Miss Roben's Pancake and Waffle Mix	Allergy Grocer	91 Western Maryland Parkway, Unit #7 Hagerstown, MD 21740 USA	(800) 891-0083	www.allergygrocer.com
Pasta:					
Alphabet Rice Noodles	Mrs. Leeper's Rice Alphabets	Distributed by American Italian Pasta Company			
Fusilli	Brown Rice Pasta Fusilli	Tinkiyáda Rice Pasta	120 Melford Drive, Unit 8, Scarborough, Ontario, Canada M1B 2X5	(888) 323-2388	www.tinkiyada.com
Penne	Brown Rice Pasta Penne	Tinkiyáda Rice Pasta	120 Melford Drive, Unit 8, Scarborough, Ontario, Canada M1B 2X5	(888) 323-2388	www.tinkiyada.com
Quinoa and Corn	Ancient Harvest	Quinoa Corporation	PO Box 279, Gardena, CA 90248	(310) 217-8125	www.quinoa.net
Rotini	Orgran Buckwheat Pasta	Orgran Natural Foods	47-53 Aster Avenue Carrum Downs Victoria 3201 Australia	(03) 9776 9044	www.orgran.com
Spaghetti	Brown Rice Pasta Spaghetti Style	Tinkiyáda Rice Pasta	120 Melford Drive, Unit 8, Scarborough, Ontario, Canada M1B 2X5	(888) 323-2388	www.tinkiyada.com
Tri-Color Sprial Noodles (Pasta Salad)	Mrs. Leeper's Rice Vegetable Twists	Distributed by American Italian Pasta Company			

Product	Source	Manufacturer Information		Phone Number	Website
Pizza Dough Mix	Miss Roben's Corn-Free Pizza Crust Mix	Allergy Grocer	91 Western Maryland Parkway, Unit #7 Hagerstown, MD 21740 USA	(800) 891-0083	www.allergygrocer.com
Potato Flour (Starch)	Miss Roben's Potato Flour	Allergy Grocer	91 Western Maryland Parkway, Unit #7 Hagerstown, MD 21740 USA	(800) 891-0083	www.allergygrocer.com
Quinoa Flakes	Ancient Harvest Quinoa Flakes	Quinoa Corporation	PO Box 279, Gardena, CA 90248	(310) 217-8125	www.quinoa.net
Quinoa Flour	Ancient Harvest Quinoa Flour	Quinoa Corporation	PO Box 279, Gardena, CA 90248	(310) 217-8125	www.quinoa.net
Rice Milk	Pacific Low Fat Rice Plain and Vanilla	Pacific Natural Foods	19480 sw 97th Avenue Tualatin, OR 97062	(503) 692-9666	www.pacificfoods.com
Shortening	All Vegetable Shortening	Spectrum Naturals	Spectrum Organic Products, Inc. Petaluma, CA 94954		www.spectrumorganics.com
Sorghum Flour	Miss Roben's Sweet Sorghum Flour	Allergy Grocer	91 Western Maryland Parkway, Unit #7 Hagerstown, MD 21740 USA	(800) 891-0083	www.allergygrocer.com
Sweet Rice Flour	Miss Roben's Sweet Rice Flour	Allergy Grocer	91 Western Maryland Parkway, Unit #7 Hagerstown, MD 21740 USA	(800) 891-0083	www.allergygrocer.com
Tapioca Flour	Miss Roben's Tapioca Starch Flour	Allergy Grocer	91 Western Maryland Parkway, Unit #7 Hagerstown, MD 21740 USA	(800) 891-0083	www.allergygrocer.com
Unsweetened Cocoa Powder	Miss Roben's Cocoa Powder	Allergy Grocer	91 Western Maryland Parkway, Unit #7 Hagerstown, MD 21740 USA	(800) 891-0083	www.allergygrocer.com
White Rice Flour	Miss Roben's White Rice Flour	Allergy Grocer	91 Western Maryland Parkway, Unit #7 Hagerstown, MD 21740 USA	(800) 891-0083	www.allergygrocer.com
White Rice Flour	Miss Roben's White Rice Flour	Allergy Grocer	91 Western Maryland Parkway, Unit #7 Hagerstown, MD 21740 USA	(800) 891-0083	www.allergygrocer.com
Xanthum Gum	Miss Roben's Xanthum Gum	Allergy Grocer	91 Western Maryland Parkway, Unit #7 Hagerstown, MD 21740 USA	(800) 891-0083	www.allergygrocer.com

"I am not bound to win, but I am bound to be true. I am not bound to succeed, but I am bound to live by the light that I have."

ABRAHAM LINCOLN

Index

EIGHT DEGREES OF INGREDIENTS